Praise for
The BOYS *of* WINTER

"A wonderfully detailed enrichment of the greatest sports moment of the twentieth century. Wayne Coffey's fresh perspective artfully takes a twenty-five-year-old story and advances it to the present with an enhanced appreciation of that stunning, breathtaking, still too-amazing-to-believe accomplishment."
—Al Michaels

"The great stories can always be retold, but when they are retold with the emotion, the muscular prose, the freshness that Coffey brings to the Miracle on Ice, they seem new."
—Robert Lipsyte, author of *The Contender*

"First came the Hollywood version of the Miracle on Ice. Now comes the real story, rich in context and texture, as only a journalist and author like Wayne Coffey can report it and tell it."
—Harvey Araton, *New York Times*

"Brings 'Miracle' back to life."
—*USA Today*

"Sensational."
—*Baltimore Sun*

"Marvelous."
—*Minneapolis Star-Tribune*

"The 1980 U.S. hockey team has been mythologized in print and on screen for almost twenty-five years. Wayne Coffey's *The Boys of Winter* goes much deeper than that and, for the first time, gives us a clear picture of who these remarkable boys—and men—were . . . and are. It is a very fine book."
—John Feinstein, bestselling author of *A Civil War*, *The Last Amateurs,* and *Caddy for Life*

"No matter how many times I hear the story of the U.S. Olympic hockey team's heroics in Lake Placid in 1980, I want to hear it again. It is allegory, fable, wonderful drama. Now Wayne Coffey comes to the campfire to tell the tale again, raising the requisite lumps in the requisite throats, adding new details to the familiar pictures. Very nice work. Very nice, indeed."

—Leigh Montville, author of the *New York Times*
bestseller *Ted Williams* and *At the Altar of Speed*

"Stirring . . . riveting stuff."

—*Boston Globe*

"Meticulously researched, entertaining, and enlightening as an example of sportswriting and social history, Wayne Coffey has re-created the event that would eventually put the Cold War on ice. The *Boys of Winter* is the definitive book on a defining moment in American culture."

—Jay Atkinson, author of *Ice Time* and
Legends of Winter Hill

"There is so much in here that has never been told. This book brings the whole U.S. team, and the miracle of Lake Placid, to life. Ken Dryden's book *The Game* is widely considered to be the quintessential hockey book. Wayne Coffey has written the American version."

—John Dellapina, New York *Daily News*

"Wayne Coffey re-creates the excitement of the unlikely run the U.S. men's hockey team made through the 1980 Olympics, and gives the reader a clear sense of the context of that team's remarkable performance . . . an adventure that seems even more unlikely now than it felt twenty-five years ago."

—Bill Littlefield, host of NPR's *Only a Game*
and author of *Fall Classics*

The BOYS of WINTER

The BOYS of WINTER

The Untold Story of a Coach, a Dream, and the 1980 U.S. Olympic Hockey Team

Wayne Coffey

FOREWORD BY JIM CRAIG
AFTERWORD BY KEN MORROW

B\D\W\Y
Broadway Books
New York

Published in the United States by Broadway Books,
an imprint of the Crown Publishing Group,
a division of Random House LLC,
a Penguin Random House Company, New York.
www.crownpublishing.com

Broadway Books and its logo, B \ D \ W \ Y, are
trademarks of Random House LLC.

Originally published in slightly different form in
hardcover in the United States by Crown Publishers, an
imprint of the Crown Publishing Group, a division of
Random House LLC, New York, in 2005.

Grateful acknowledgment is made to Dan Brooks for
permission to reprint a note written by his father to the
members of the 1980 U.S. Olympic hockey team.
Reprinted by permission of Dan Brooks.

Library of Congress Cataloging-in-Publication Data
Coffey, Wayne R.
The boys of winter : the untold story of a coach,
a dream, and the 1980 U.S. Olympic hockey team /
Wayne Coffey.—1st ed.
1. Hockey—United States—History—20th century.
2. Winter Olympic Games (13th : 1980 : Lake Placid, N.Y.)
I. Title.
GV848.4.U6C65 2004   2004014163

ISBN 978-1-4000-4766-6
eISBN 978-0-307-23731-6

Printed in the United States of America

Design by Karen Minster

26 25

First Paperback Edition

For my bride, Denise Willi,
and our children,
Alexandra, Sean, and Samantha

CONTENTS

1980 U.S. OLYMPIC HOCKEY TEAM

NO.	PLAYER	HT	WT	BIRTH	HOMETOWN
GOALTENDERS					
30	Jim Craig	6–1	190	5/31/57	North Easton MA
1	Steve Janaszak	5–8	160	1/7/57	White Bear Lake MN
DEFENSEMEN					
6	Bill Baker	6–1	195	11/29/56	Grand Rapids MN
3	Ken Morrow	6–4	210	10/17/56	Davison MI
17	Jack O'Callahan	6–1	185	7/24/57	Charlestown MA
5	Mike Ramsey	6–3	190	12/3/60	Minneapolis MN
20	Bob Suter	5–9	178	5/16/57	Madison WI
FORWARDS					
9	Neal Broten	5–9	155	11/29/59	Roseau MN
23	Dave Christian	5–11	170	5/12/59	Warroad MN
11	Steve Christoff	6–1	180	1/23/58	Richfield MN
21	Mike Eruzione	5–10	185	10/25/54	Winthrop MA
28	John Harrington	5–10	180	5/24/57	Virginia MN
10	Mark Johnson	5–9	160	9/22/57	Madison WI
24	Rob McClanahan	5–10	180	1/9/58	St. Paul MN
16	Mark Pavelich	5–7	160	2/28/58	Eveleth MN
25	William Schneider	5–11	180	9/14/54	Babbitt MN
8	Dave Silk	5–11	190	1/1/58	Scituate MA
19	Eric Strobel	5–10	175	6/5/58	Rochester MN
27	Phil Verchota	6–2	195	12/28/56	Duluth MN
15	Mark Wells	5–9	175	9/18/57	St. Clair Shores MI

General Manager: Ken Johannson/Ralph Jasinski
Head Coach: Herb Brooks
Ass't. Coach: Craig Patrick
Goalkeeping Coach: Warren Strelow

COLLEGE	PREVIOUS TEAM
Boston University	Boston University
Univ. of Minnesota	Univ. of Minnesota
Univ. of Minnesota	Univ. of Minnesota
Bowling Green	Bowling Green
Boston University	Boston University
Univ. of Minnesota	Univ. of Minnesota
Univ. of Wisconsin	Univ. of Wisconsin
Univ. of Minnesota	Univ. of Minnesota
Univ. of North Dakota	Univ. of North Dakota
Univ. of Minnesota	Univ. of Minnesota
Boston University	Toledo (IHL)
Univ. of MN–Duluth	Univ. of MN–Duluth
Univ. of Wisconsin	Univ. of Wisconsin
Univ. of Minnesota	Univ. of Minnesota
Univ. of MN–Duluth	Univ. of MN–Duluth
Univ. of Minnesota	Milwaukee (IHL)
Boston University	Boston University
Univ. of Minnesota	Univ. of Minnesota
Univ. of Minnesota	Univ. of Minnesota
Bowling Green	Bowling Green

Skating Coach: Dick Vraa
Physician: Dr. V. George Nagobads
Trainer: Gary Smith
Equipment Manager: Bud Kessel

1980 U.S.S.R. OLYMPIC HOCKEY TEAM

NO.	PLAYER	POSITION
1	Vladimir Myshkin	G
20	Vladislav Tretiak	G
2	Viacheslav Fetisov	D
5	Vasily Pervukhin	D
7	Alexei Kasatonov	D
12	Sergei Starikov	D
14	Zinetula Bilyaletdinov	D
9	Vladimir Krutov	F
10	Alexander Maltsev	F
11	Yuri Lebedev	F
13	Boris Mikhailov	F
16	Vladimir Petrov	F
17	Valery Kharlamov	F
19	Helmut Balderis	F
22	Viktor Zhluktov	F
23	Alexander Golikov	F
24	Sergei Makarov	F
25	Vladimir Golikov	F
26	Alexander Skvortsov	F

Head Coach: Viktor Tikhonov
Ass't. Coach: Vladimir Yurzinov

FOREWORD

By Jim Craig

Years before I ever heard of Lake Placid or the Olympics, before I knew the name of a single Russian hockey player, I was a kid in Massachusetts who wanted to be the next Bobby Orr. I grew up skating on Holmes's Pond, which took its name from our next-door neighbor, Mrs. Holmes, who owned it. A man named Phil Thompson, our postman, was the person who told me I should try organized hockey in the Easton Junior Hockey League. He had already been working on it with my mother. He was a fine postman and an even better salesman.

The game we played against the Russians in Lake Placid twenty-five years ago has been acclaimed and saluted in every way possible, but for me, it has always felt like a passage on ice, the attainment of a dream that started on Mrs. Holmes's pond. It's impossible for me to separate the miracle that we achieved as a team with the memories and gratitude I have for all the people who helped me get there, from my mother and father, my sisters and brothers, to ten years' worth of coaches and friends and teammates. You don't make a journey like that alone. You make it with a lot of love and sacrifice. That's probably why I was searching the stands for my father after we won the gold medal against Finland. It was a moment that was begging to be shared.

I don't believe those Winter Games in Lake Placid will ever be duplicated. I don't say that because we beat maybe the greatest Soviet hockey team ever assembled, or even because Eric Heiden won five gold medals, a performance that I honestly think dwarfs what we did. I say it because there weren't doping scandals or judging scandals or an Olympic Village that was overrun with millionaires and professionals in Lake Placid. Herb Brooks, God rest his soul, wasn't coaching a Dream Team. He was coaching a team full of dreamers. There is a big difference. In Lake Placid, it didn't feel as if the Games were being run by corporations. It felt as if at the heart of them was a brotherhood of athletes, the best in the world, deep in the Adirondack Mountains.

I've visited quite a few places that have hosted the Olympics in the past, and you almost can't tell that the Games were ever there. You aren't in Lake Placid for more than a minute before you are flooded with Olympic memories, whether it's from seeing the Olympic Arena at the top of the hill, or the oval next door where Heiden skated into immortality. Whenever I'm in town, I like to go out at night when it's dark and quiet and the shops are closed, and stand in the middle of Main Street. I close my eyes and in an instant it takes me back to that magical Friday night of February 22, 1980, to the memory of walking down that same Main Street with Mike Eruzione and our fathers and other family members, and ABC's Jim Lampley interviewing us as we went. Snow was falling, and everywhere you looked people were waving flags and chanting, "U-S-A, U-S-A." We were in our primes, athletically and physically. We were surrounded by people we loved, getting loved some more by people we didn't even know. We had just done the impossible, and we were happy to be alive and thrilled to be Americans and thrilled to think that Herb was right: maybe we were meant to be here. It's a feeling you wish everybody could have at one point in their lives.

Being in that goal on that Friday night was the pinnacle of my athletic life, the greatest joy I have ever known as a hockey player. It was the culmination of a journey, and then other journeys followed, for all of us; that is what this book is really all about—the journeys that brought us to that semifinal game against the Soviet Union, and those we've taken since. Sometimes people ask me if I wish I could go back and do it again, if some part of me is sad that I will never experience that pinnacle again. You can't look back. You can't dial up euphoria on demand, or try to re-create what happened a quarter century ago. You move forward and you live your life and try to be a better person every day than you were the day before. You take each day as a new journey, even as you are grateful for the ones you have already had.

Jim Craig
North Easton, Massachusetts

The BOYS of WINTER

THE LAST
REUNION

Morning broke hot in St. Paul, Minnesota, on August 16, 2003. The sky was gray, the air as thick as porridge. Beneath the gilded dome of the Cathedral of Saint Paul, 307 feet over the east bank of the Mississippi River, men in dark suits and women in dark dresses fanned themselves to fend off the heat. It didn't work. It was a Saturday in Herb Brooks's hometown. There were an estimated 2,500 people in the cathedral, the fourth largest in the United States. Many of the people arrived a full ninety minutes early. On a day when you could melt a puck on the sidewalk, it was a little surreal to be memorializing a man who spent most of his life around the rink.

In the center of the cathedral, nineteen middle-aged men filed solemnly down the center aisle, behind the casket. They sat behind the family of Herb Brooks, who used to coach them. Most of them had thickened bodies and thinning hair, and sturdy athletic bearing, even in their suits, even a couple of decades past their primes. Their faces were heavy and sad.

The men were famous once. Some of them still are. They were the 1980 U.S. Olympic hockey team and Brooks had brought them together, twenty-four summers before. He had picked them and provoked them and pushed them, sometimes irritating them and often infuriating them, by his hardness and his aloofness, his scathing rebukes and his unrelenting mind games. Other than fast skaters and constant motion, Herb Brooks liked few things more than mind games, keeping people guessing, cultivating uncertainty as if it were a crop, because it was a productive feeling for a player to have; it would make him more motivated, work harder.

Now Herb Brooks had brought the 1980 Olympic team together again, five days after he became the first among them to die, in a one-car accident on Interstate 35 in Forest Lake, Minnesota. Brooks was returning home from the town of Biwabik, in the Iron Range area of northeast Minnesota, where he had attended a golf tournament and fund-raiser for the U.S. Hockey Hall of Fame. It was mid-afternoon and the pavement was dry. Brooks was less than a half-hour from his suburban St. Paul home when his Toyota Sienna minivan swerved out of control and rolled over, ejecting his body. Brooks was as principled and unyielding as any man alive; getting him to move off something he believed in was as easy as moving an iceberg. One of the things Herb Brooks did not believe in was seat belts.

This was only the second time the entire team had been together since February 25, 1980, the morning they left the Adirondack village of Lake Placid for the White House, red, white, and blue heroes at an average age of 21 years old. "It's the one reunion that nobody wanted to go to," said Buzz Schneider, who had been the oldest member of the team at 25.

But they all came. The only player missing from the funeral was the reclusive Mark Pavelich, who had paid his respects at the wake the night before.

In the pulpit, Mike Eruzione delivered a eulogy. He was the captain in 1980, and he remains the captain, the team's most recognizable name and face. His teammates call him Rizzie and tease him about his unabashed opportunism, how he has parlayed a weekend and a goal a quarter-century ago into a lifetime on the rubber-chicken circuit, talking about dreaming big and working hard and staying together, at upwards of $15,000 a pop, in a voice that leans a bit toward squeakiness. Brooks joined in the teasing, too. "Mike Eruzione believes in free speech," Brooks used to say. "He's just never given one." He gave one at the funeral, guided by his heart and the sentiments of his teammates, but without a formal text. Eruzione likened Brooks to a father whom you love deeply but don't always like because he pushes you so hard. "I firmly believe he loved our hockey team, but we didn't know it," Eruzione said.

———

Herb Brooks spent the afternoon of February 28, 1960, watching a hockey game in the house he grew up in. It was a Sunday on the east side of St. Paul, the last day of the 1960 Olympic Games. Brooks was 22, and he was sitting in the living room next to his father, Herb Sr., an insurance man and former coach of his son's junior hockey team. In the semifinals the night before, the U.S. hockey team had shocked the defending champions from the Soviet Union, 4–3. Now both Herbs were taking in the gold-medal game between the United States and Czechoslovakia, the images grainy and black and white, the sting as clear and cold as ice itself. How could the younger Brooks not feel stung when, on the cusp of an Olympic dream, he was tapped on the shoulder and told to go home? Days before the 1960 Olympics began, coach Jack Riley replaced Brooks on the roster. After months of recruitment, Riley had finally convinced 1956 Olympic standout Bill Cleary to rejoin the team. Bill Cleary's one condition was that his brother be able to play with him. Bob Cleary's head was pasted over Herb Brooks's body in the team picture. The United States scored five third-period goals and won the gold medal, 9–4. The Cleary brothers were a major reason why.

"Well, I guess the coach cut the right guy," Herb Sr. told his son.

Herb Brooks would go on to play for the 1964 and 1968 Olympic teams, and would recycle his father's line often in his life, unflinching in the face of its hardness. It was the greatest motivational tool he could ever ask for, and it would come to embody Brooks's own modus operandi as a coach: toughness on the brink of cruelty, passionate pursuit of perfection at the expense of feelings. Even in his photo in the 1980 team media guide, he already had his game face on, thin lips taut, face set, eyes deep and intense, roiling with ideas and insecurities and innovation. The photo fairly shouts, "Don't mess with me."

Brooks applied for the 1980 Olympic coaching job in the fall of 1978. He wasn't the coach selection committee's first choice—that was Bill Cleary, who'd gone on to coach at Harvard. But Cleary declined, so Brooks requested a meeting with Walter Bush, the general manager of the 1964 Olympic team Brooks played on and the head of the committee. Bush knew all about Brooks's impressive coaching résumé, how he'd taken over a last-place University of Minnesota Golden Gophers team in 1972 and captured three national titles in the next seven years. He was somewhat wary of him nonetheless. "Herb could be a one-man band," Bush said. "He wanted to be coach, general manager, everything. He had a way of irritating people at times." Yet Bush agreed to let Brooks interview for the job. Brooks and the other candidates—Boston University coach Jack Parker and Michigan Tech coach John MacInnes—met with the committee at the O'Hare Hilton. Armed with binders stuffed with details about everything but what brand of tape the players would wrap their sticks with, Brooks presented a plan regarding player selection, staffing, conditioning, pre-Olympic scheduling—all the variables that could help the United States compete for a medal against the Russians, Czechs, Swedes, and Canadians. But by far the most stunning part of the package was his proposed style of play.

Brooks wanted to abandon the traditional, linear, dump-and-chase style of hockey that had held sway in North America forever. He wanted to attack the vaunted Russians with their own game, skating with them and weaving with them, stride for high-flying stride. He wanted to play physical, unyielding hockey, to be sure, but he also wanted fast, skilled players who would flourish on the Olympic ice sheet (which is fifteen feet wider than NHL rinks) and be able to move and keep possession of the puck and be in such phenomenal condition that they would be the fresher team at the end. A hybrid style, Brooks called it. Brooks had played against the Russians through most of the 1960s and been fascinated by them ever since. Whenever he saw Anatoly Tarasov, the legendary Soviet coach, he would pump him with questions and take note of his methods. Before the 1979 world championships in Moscow, he snuck into Russian practices, and he cornered Igor N. Tuzik, coach of the Russian "B" team, at a Lake Placid tournament two months before the Olympics. "He wanted to know all the details," said Tuzik, now the vice president of the Russian Ice Hockey Federation. " 'Why? Why? Why? Why do passes go this way? When do you go off the boards? Why is the key the speed of the wing?' He wanted to know everything."

In the two decades that had passed since the U.S. team had upset them in Squaw Valley, California, the Russians not only had won every Olympic gold medal but had beaten the Americans by an aggregate score of 28–7. The Soviet team in Lake Placid would be perhaps their strongest ever. In Brooks's mind, the logic behind changing strategy was as clear as vodka on the rocks: *Why give up possession of the puck to the best stickhandling team in the world? Why play a reactive, checking game when it allows them to dictate tempo? How many times do we have to get hit with the same hammer and sickle before we learn?* Brooks's teams had largely played dump-and-chase hockey at Minnesota. He was calling for a switch no less radical than it would be for a grind-it-out football team to start flinging the ball downfield.

Bush and his committee were blown away by Brooks and the depth of his presentation. He got the job.

———

Inside the vast cathedral doors, someone had put up a large poster of the 1980 U.S. Olympic hockey team. If anyone thought this sacrilegious, the complaint was not aired. Nearby Salvation Army volunteers offered cups of cold water to mourners, who clutched service programs that showed Brooks on the ice in his 1980 USA warm-up suit, wearing hockey gloves and a whistle and a smile, looking uncharacteristically at ease. Beneath the picture it said:

HERBIE
1937–2003

On a table were keepsake bookmarks featuring a photo of Brooks as a Team USA player, ice shavings spraying in front of him. It was the same photo that had been displayed inside his casket and at the wake the night before. By the hundreds, people came to express condolences to Brooks's family, some waiting in line for two hours, many kneeling in prayer in front of the coffin. Alongside Brooks's body were a single rose and a little rolled-up American flag, an assortment of cards from his children and grandchildren. A drawing of a flower, colored by one of his grandchildren, peeked from the chest pocket of his suit.

Presiding over the service was Rev. John Malone of Assumption Catholic Church in St. Paul. "Most miracles are dreams made manifest," he said. "Herbie had a dream. The players had a dream. If we could all dream . . . and do our best, we could make this a better world. It's within our reach; it's within God's reach."

————

Brooks went looking for twenty-six players at the National Sports Festival in Colorado Springs in the summer of 1979. He had a good idea who his leading candidates would be. Brooks wasn't necessarily eyeing the most talented players or most prolific scorers—all-star teams don't win games, he kept telling his players—but for those most willing to rewire their games to embrace his system, skate hard and fast, and fit together as a whole. Hockey is the quirkiest and most capricious of sports, a game played at a dizzying pace, on a slippery surface, players coming on, players going off, championships decided by a bad bounce, a well-positioned blade, by whether a speeding disc hits the inside of the post or the outside. There are a million things a coach can't control. Brooks, an obsessive planner, was going to make sure he was on top of what he *could* control.

For two weeks sixty-eight of the country's top amateurs showed their stuff to Brooks and his nine-man advisory panel. Brooks punished them in drills on the ice and gave them a 300-question test to assess their psychological makeup off it. He was relentless. If they couldn't take this small sampling of life under Brooks, they wouldn't last through one Olympic practice shift. Most of the players were in a Colorado Springs biker bar named The Finish Line when they heard that the roster had been finalized. Even the surest bets—Mark Johnson, Ken Morrow, Jim Craig, and Neal Broten—felt relieved when they heard team general manager Ken Johannson call their names. It was a squad long on speed and skill, the better to shed the United States' dump-and-chase ancestry. Buzz Schneider was the only holdover from the 1976 Olympic team.

Brooks would have to pare six more players from the squad before the Olympics, but his more immediate challenge was finding a way to surmount the entrenched regionalism the players carried within them. Hockey wasn't played in many places then, but the places where it *was* played—Minnesota, Wisconsin, Michigan, and New England—were profoundly parochial pockets with fierce regional pride. The Easterners tended to be edgy and emotional and tart-tongued, seeming to pack skepticism in their equipment bags. The Minnesotans were more reserved and less cynical, more trusting and less vocal, guys who believed in hard work and selflessness and hunting and fishing, clinging to an unstated faith that things would work out, you betcha. Twelve Olympic team members were from Minnesota, and nine of them played for Brooks at the University of Minnesota in the Twin Cities (the U, as it is known throughout the state). Four were from Boston University, and two apiece were from Wisconsin and Michigan. Five of the guys on the team were on opposite sides of one of the nastiest college hockey brawls anyone could remember—the 1976 NCAA semifinal bloodbath between Minnesota and Boston University. The puck dropped, a minute later so did the gloves, and it was an hour before they played any more hockey. It was so bad that even Gopher trainer Gary Smith got into it, punching a BU player who had spit on him. Time had done little to heal the hostilities; bloodbath II broke out at the National Sports Festival in Colorado.

"Don't get regional," Brooks implored his players. His strategy for uniting the team was set from the start. He would make himself the enemy. A shared disdain for his ceaselessly demanding and Machiavellian ways would be the rallying cry, the reason guys would want to go out on the ice and bust their tails, just to show him. With distance and inscrutability, he kept nearly everyone anxious about their prospects for making the team, almost to the end.

"I'm not here to be your friend," Brooks told the players. "I'm here to be your coach." He would later call it his loneliest year in hockey.

The players traded horror stories, commiserated with one

another. "Eastern guys thought Brooks was singling them out for abuse, but the Minnesota guys told them he treated them that way, too," said Dave Silk, a rugged winger from Boston University who for a long time was convinced his coach loathed him. When the team exchanged gag gifts at Christmas before the Olympics, the gift for Brooks was a whip.

———

Two paunchy, middle-aged men in hockey sweaters walked slowly into the cathedral, toward the alcove where Herb Brooks's body lay. They were graduates of Brooks's alma mater, Johnson High School, and lifelong residents of the east side of St. Paul. They didn't know Brooks personally, but when you've grown up playing hockey around St. Paul, it's impossible not to feel a connection to him. The men had the halting body language of people who felt unentitled to be there. They sat near the end of a row in the back of the church and listened to the eulogies from Mike Eruzione and Bill Butters, a former player of Brooks's at the U. Butters, a wild college kid turned devout Christian, talked about how Brooks had "made a man of character out of a character like me," and about Brooks's beautiful skating technique, fleet and fluid, blades never even seeming to cut the ice. The men heard Butters read from the book of Proverbs and say, "As iron sharpens iron, so does one man sharpen another." No matter what Brooks achieved, especially after Lake Placid, he was disinclined to trade on his fame and was wary of people who wanted a piece of him or had a proposition for him. He seemed most at ease with his Minnesota homeboys, at Schwietz's Saloon on Payne Avenue, or Vogel's, another east-side watering hole, or drinking his Coors Light with old pals at his annual Fourth of July barbecue. The men said that Brooks never seemed to change even when he became a celebrity coach, and allowed that maybe that was what they liked about him best.

———

Brooks didn't just put up a wall between himself and the team; he threw in a moat and alligators, too. It was a way to make sure that his own regional bias, and his personal feelings, didn't get in the way of personnel decisions. "One of the first things Herb said when he hired me was, 'I'm going to be tough on them, and you are going to have to be the one who keeps everyone together,'" assistant coach Craig Patrick said. Patrick, a former All-American and a teammate of Brooks's on the 1967 U.S. national team, was an amiable, soft-spoken fellow who was impossible not to like. He was not only a man with nine years of pro experience but a scion of America's First Family of Pucks, his grandfather (Lester Patrick), father (Lynn Patrick), and uncle (Muzz Patrick) all having played and coached for the New York Rangers, dating to the early twentieth century (Lynn also was general manager of the Boston Bruins and St. Louis Blues). Patrick slid easily into the role of part-time sounding board and ombudsman, and full-time nurturer. It was an elaborate and flawlessly constructed game of good cop/bad cop.

The twenty-six-man roster had an August training camp in Lake Placid, then flew off to Europe for three weeks in September, a trip that was timed to keep the players out of sight as NHL training camps opened. The last thing Brooks needed was the pros poaching on his roster and fouling up his plans. It was the beginning of a five-month, sixty-one-game whirl against teams ranging from Reipas of Finland to the

Cincinnati Stingers of the Central Hockey League. Team officials worked out an arrangement with the CHL commissioner for games against the Olympic team to count in league standings, thereby ensuring a demanding schedule against motivated opponents. There was even a series of exhibitions against NHL clubs, a first for a U.S. Olympic team. Game after game, week after week, Brooks was consumed with reprogramming his team to play his new system, keeping his distance, punishing his players' bodies and working over their psyches, and letting Craig Patrick heal all the wounds.

———

In his eulogy Eruzione joked about how, even at age 48, he would be afraid that he'd done something wrong when Brooks would call the house, and how the conversations were so one-sided that he could go make a sandwich and come back and Herb would still be talking. He was sure that Brooks, an inveterate tinkerer, was already weighing in on celestial matters in his brutally candid, Brooksian way.

"Right now, he is saying to God, 'I don't like the style of your team. We should change it,' " Eruzione said. In the pews, a few thousand people laughed.

The wall that Brooks erected between himself and his players never really came down completely. At times it did, with some players more than others. But on the whole, he remained somewhat apart, the moat too deep and wide to cross, even after a couple of decades.

Lefty Curran, a longtime friend of Brooks and the star goaltender on the 1972 Olympic team that won the silver medal in Sapporo, Japan, was on the golf course with Brooks hours before his death.

"Herb had a hard time reaching over and coming to them," Curran said. "It would've been great if he could've embraced each and every one of them and say, 'I love you guys.' But Herb wasn't going to do that."

———

The Olympics broke Herb Brooks's heart in 1960 and made him the most celebrated American hockey coach in history two decades later. They were the emotional bookends of his competitive life, and what filled the shelf between them was a restless chase of the perfect game of hockey. He sought it desperately and wasn't happy when he didn't get it. There were high points along the road to Lake Placid, such as the holiday victory over Tuzik's Russian junior varsity, successive triumphs over Sweden and Czechoslovakia and Canada. But there were low points, too: a 9–1 thumping by the St. Louis Blues, a 1–0 loss to the AHL's Adirondack Red Wings, and most maddening of all to the coach, a 3–3 tie in Norway in mid-September. The low points stayed with Brooks much longer than the high points did.

Norway was a team the Americans should've trounced, and Brooks was disgusted with what he saw as an alarming lack of effort. "If you don't want to skate during the game, then you'll skate after it," he told the players. And so they did, lining up on the end line, ordered to skate Brooks's dreaded Herbies—the name they'd given to his sprints: end line to blue line and back, end line to red line and back, end line to opposite blue line and back, end line to end line and back. The crowd filed out and the Americans skated. The custodians turned out the lights and the Americans skated. The usually mild-mannered Mark Johnson whacked his stick on the boards and the Americans skated. George Nagobads, team physician for Brooks at the U and the Olympics, urged Brooks to stop. But he kept skating them, for close to an hour. The next night, the teams played again. The United States won, 9–0.

When the team did *not* respond so positively, there was no mistaking his angst. After the team lost four straight games to Canada around Thanksgiving of 1979, Lou Nanne, general manager of the Minnesota North Stars and an old friend of Brooks's, got a four a.m. phone call. There was only one person who called him at four a.m.

"I'm done with coaching," Brooks said. "That's it. This is going nowhere." He was ready to go back to Minnesota and tend to his plants and shrubs—perhaps Brooks's foremost interest outside hockey. He knew everything about them, including their formal Latin names. *Buxus sempervirens* wasn't a Finnish winger; it was a species of boxwood.

Nanne told him what he always told him. "Go to bed, Herb. I'll talk to you tomorrow."

Warren Strelow, the Olympic goalie coach who had grown up with Brooks on the east side of St. Paul, knew that Brooks could no more walk away from hockey than stop breathing. A dozen years before Lake Placid, he listened to Brooks struggling to find his way. Brooks had just retired from playing. He was selling insurance. His voice sounded hollow. He didn't care about annuities or the relative merits of whole life and term. "I don't know why I'm doing this," he said. Herb Brooks told his friend that all he wanted to do was be a hockey coach.

———

In the gauzy morning air, Jim Craig stood near the bottom of the cathedral steps and squinted into the haze. Three vintage airplanes had just flown over the church, the missing-man formation. Craig never much worried about being one of the guys when he was the Olympic goaltender, and he still doesn't. He wasn't thinking about the night 8,576 days before, when he backstopped history. Craig was looking around at all the hockey people, hundreds of them, and the non-hockey people, too, not just from 1980 but from places and connections that went back more than fifty years in Herb Brooks's life. There were fellow coaches and scouts, players and teammates, owners and trainers and rivals, from all over the country and all levels, mite to NHL. Not far from Jim Craig was John Mayasich, a Minnesota legend whom many regard as the greatest U.S. player never to play in the NHL. To the left was Tim Taylor, who had just started at Yale in 1979 when Brooks called and asked if he would be interested in being his Olympic assistant. Taylor turned Brooks down, not wanting to alienate his new athletic director. "It was the dumbest decision I ever made," Taylor said. Brooks teased him about it for years afterward. A few steps from the hearse was Joe Micheletti, who played on Brooks's first national championship team at the U and once was the biggest thing to come out of Hibbing, Minnesota, since Bob Dylan and Kevin McHale. "It's a cult in the richest, most positive sense of the word," Craig said.

Hockey is a club that holds its members tightly, the bond forged by shared hardship and mutual passion, by every trip to the pond, where your feet hurt and your face is cold and you might get a stick in the ribs or a puck in the mouth, and you still can't wait to get back out there because you are smitten with the sound of blades scraping against ice and pucks clacking off sticks, and with the game's speed and ever-changing geometry. It has a way of becoming the center of your life even when you're not on the ice. Brooks met his wife Patti in the emergency room of a Twin Cities hospital. She was a nurse. He had just fractured his hand skating into a goalpost.

———

After Lake Placid Brooks would make ten more stops in a nomadic coaching career, in places ranging from Davos, Switzerland, to St. Cloud, Minnesota, to New York, New York. He did superb work at most of those places, his teams skating fast and playing creatively. Brooks would look at an open sheet of ice and all he would see would be possibilities, new ways to break out and beat traps and exploit weaknesses. And the possibilities would never be greater than on a Friday night in upstate New York, February 22, 1980, so close to the Canadian border that you could hear French on the radio. It would turn out to be the pinnacle of his life in coaching, the three defining periods of nearly six decades spent around rinks, the reason, ultimately, why his death would be mourned as if he were a head of state, not another guy with a whistle around his neck.

For years people have been telling the players they remember exactly where they were the night the Americans played the Russians in Lake Placid. Such recall seems to come naturally in the wake of tragic events—President Kennedy's assassination, the *Challenger* disaster, September 11—but not so with good things. So that said something right there. People were desperate for something to feel positive about. There were hostages in captivity in Iran, seized by Iranian militants three months before the Games. The Soviets had just invaded Afghanistan, restoking old images of the Red Menace. Inflation was galloping along at 18 percent and interest rates were not far behind, and gloom was spreading faster than the lines at the gas pumps. For the first time in American history, when pollsters asked citizens about what life would be like in five years, a majority said they thought it would be worse, not better. Six months before the Olympics, President Carter gave a speech telling of "a crisis of the American spirit." The nation felt rudderless, less like a superpower than like a neighborhood weakling. And then came the Olympic semifinal against the Soviet Union, a Cold War on blue-white ice, specially tinted for television. The Soviets had their old red sweaters and steel-reinforced bodies and their swirling, high-speed game. They were grown men, seasoned pros. In the last four Olympiads, their record was 27–1–1, their goal differential 175–44. They were the Enemy, and they were tremendous. "It's David against Goliath, and I hope we remember to bring our slingshots," Brooks said.

They indeed brought their slingshots that Friday night, along with a wonderful confluence of good karma and dogged effort and fierce togetherness. There was no crisis of spirit around Herb Brooks's hockey team. They played with skill and heart and never got discouraged. If people wanted to make them out to be puck-toting patriots, saviors in skates, well, that was okay. When they themselves looked in the mirror, they saw hockey players. It was one more reason to fall for them. The most enduring heroes are people who don't try to be.

Brooks had a second tour of duty coaching the U.S. Olympic hockey team, in Salt Lake City in 2002. Most everyone hailed the work he did in taking the team to the silver medal, but nobody tried to pretend it was the same world that he had coached in at Lake Placid. The concept of amateurism in the Olympics is as obsolete as eight-track cassettes. The expression *Dream Team* has become part of the five-ring lexicon. The United States doesn't send anonymous college kids to the Games anymore. It sends NHL All-Stars. Glamour is way up at the Games, romance is way down, and the upshot is that there may never be another generation of kids like Eric Strobel and John Harrington and Mark Wells, going from utter anonymity to the cover of *Sports Illustrated*. The world seemed simpler in 1980, if not purer. You knew who your friends were, and who your enemies were. Eight years after the massacre in Munich, terrorism was by no means an unknown evil, but it wasn't the stuff of daily, deadly dispatches, either. There was no such thing as the Department of Homeland Security. There wasn't a $1.5 billion budget for security, as there was in Athens in the Summer Games of 2004. For most Americans, the bad guys were the Russians, and wouldn't it be great if we could somehow beat them in a hockey game?

"With the way the world has changed and the way the Olympics have changed, what we did will never happen again," goalie Steve Janaszak said.

———

In the moments before Herb Brooks's funeral began, the players from the 1980 Olympic team and thirty-three honorary pallbearers crowded in the basement of the Cathedral of Saint Paul, going over the final game plan for the salute to their coach. Then they went upstairs and executed it. A gospel singer named Tom Tipton sang "Battle Hymn of the Republic," and after 103 minutes of memoriam the casket that contained Herb Brooks's body and the miniature flag and the rose and sweet notes from his grandchildren was carried down the steps, beneath a curved canopy of hockey sticks raised up by the honorary pallbearers, a traditional salute in an untraditional place. Many of those holding sticks were fighting tears, and losing the fight. A lone bagpiper played. As the hearse left for the cemetery, the heat thickened and the players began saying goodbye again, their last reunion complete.

Even in their mourning, life was moving on, just as it had since 1980. Twelve of them went on to play in the NHL, and most of them have built lives and careers that fit somewhere between comfortable and prosperous. They are stock traders and coaches, oral surgeons and pilots, businessmen and horsemen. Many of them have kids in college or high school and do what guys in their forties do, joking about their shortage of hair, their excess of weight, and the twinges of pain and stiffness that didn't used to be there. They've known the joys of watching their sons and daughters grow; of taking in the wooded stillness of a lake house; and of finding their way after the miracle. They've known hardship, too, death and alcoholism and bleakness so deep that suicide seemed the only option. They deal with their residue of fame in ways as different as their personalities. A few of them embrace it and are actually engaged in it. Some feel defined by it and wish they weren't. Others wouldn't mind if they never had to field another 1980 question, and several don't want to talk about anything unless there is money in the discussion. The regionalism still surfaces from time to time; there have been some differences over money and the mechanics of various marketing deals. More than a few of the Midwestern guys feel there has been an Eastern bias to how their achievement has been represented over the years. "Even though everyone doesn't agree on everything, I think most of the guys know what's really important," Jim Craig said.

The players are, on the whole, generous with their reflections and feelings and time, recognizing the enduring power of their message, realizing that they made people feel better when there wasn't much to feel good about, reaffirming that Americans do have greatness and courage and unbreakable spirit within them. If Herb Brooks's passing reminded us that human beings have a shelf life, it also reminded us that miracles do not.

As game time neared on February 22, 1980, a quarter-century ago, some people looked at the first Olympic semifinal as a referendum with sideboards, Our Way vs. Their Way. Others did not. Either way, there was no denying that it was a game of striking contrasts. The Russians were pros, state-reared and state-supported, men who had largely been together for a decade. The Americans were mostly college kids who had their stipends and their majors and their dream and had become a team six months before. It was experience vs. youth, men vs. boys, champions vs. upstarts, communism vs. capitalism, on a sheet of ice in the Adirondack Mountains. What could one hockey game mean? What could it possibly change?

The twenty members of the 1980 Olympic hockey team did something extraordinary once. This is the story of a Friday night in Lake Placid, New York, and the men who lived it.

THE
FIRST PERIOD

Chapter One

WEEDING
THE GARDEN

Vladimir Petrov was skating in loose figure eights near center ice, his pace slow, his stick still and horizontal, a predator in wait. He edged in for the opening face-off. His two famous wings, Boris Mikhailov and Valery Kharlamov, were on his flanks. Petrov, No. 16, was perhaps the strongest player on the Soviet national team, with blacksmith arms and a bulging neck, a 200-pound slab of muscle who was possessed of the rarest of Russian weapons: a nasty slap shot. Historically, not many Russian players had one because for years not very many practiced slap shots, sticks being both in short supply and of inferior quality. If you wound up and cranked a slap shot, you stood a good chance of getting a splinter and having no stick to play with. "So we never slap puck," defenseman Sergei Starikov said. "We make good wrist shot instead." Petrov was 32, a two-time Olympic gold medalist and nine-time world champion. He didn't know much of anything about Mark Johnson, the U.S. center whom he was about to face off against, except that he wore No. 10 and he looked small and ridiculously young.

It was 5:06 p.m. in Lake Placid, and 1:06 a.m. in Moscow. Bill Cleary, star of the 1960 gold-medal team that had been the last U.S. team to beat the Soviets, had just finished a brief talk in the locker room. "There's no doubt in my mind—nor in the minds of all the guys on the '60 team—that you are going to win this game. You are a better team than we were," Cleary said. Herb Brooks followed him, standing at one end of Locker Room 5 in the new Olympic Field House, wearing a camel-hair sports coat and plaid pants that would've looked at home on the dance floor of *Saturday Night Fever.* The room was a cramped, unadorned rectangle with a rubber-mat floor and a steeply pitched ceiling, situated directly beneath the stands. You could hear stomping and chanting and feel the anticipatory buzz that was all over the Adirondacks. There was a small chalkboard to Brooks's right and a tiny shower area behind him, the players on the wood benches rimming the room all around him. On the ride to the arena, Brooks sat with assistant Craig Patrick and they talked about what Brooks was going to say to the team. Brooks loved intrigue, the element of surprise. His whole style of play was constructed on it, moving players around, changing breakout patterns, keeping people guessing about everything. Just when his players were sure he was completely inhumane, he'd throw a tennis ball on the ice for a diversion, or have guys play opposite-handed or in different positions, lifting morale and breaking the routine. "You're going to like it," Brooks said to Patrick of his talk. The locker room was intense and quiet. Defenseman Bill Baker caught the eye of backup goaltender Steve Janaszak, his former teammate at the University of Minnesota. "What do we do now?" Baker mouthed.

"Pray," Janaszak mouthed back.

Herb Brooks stood before his twenty players. The quiet got deeper. The coach pulled out a yellow scrap of paper and said, "You were born to be a player. You were meant to be here. This moment is yours."

Neal Broten, 20-year-old center, second youngest player on the youngest Olympic hockey team the United States had ever fielded, looked down at his skates. "I didn't know what he was talking about," Broten said. Broten was nervous, very nervous. He knew he could handle the skating, playing the game. The Russians' strength he wasn't so sure about. *Don't make any glaring mistakes,* he told himself.

Led by goaltender Jim Craig, the players charged out of the locker room, turned right and then right again. At the threshold of the ice, Craig paused and looked up for a second. The building was shaking from the cheers. He took it in, and it felt great. Ten days before, the players hadn't been much less anonymous than the Lake Placid goal judges. Now that they'd gone undefeated in five games and come from behind in four of them, they were Olympic darlings. Somebody rang a cowbell, a tinny touch of the Alps in the Adirondacks. "C'mon, Magic!" winger John "Bah" Harrington shouted to Mark Johnson from the end of the American bench. Magic was Johnson's nickname. If you ever saw him play you know why.

———

The last time the U.S. players had seen Petrov and his teammates was thirteen days earlier, in Madison Square Garden, where the Americans didn't lose so much as get annihilated.

That day began with the crowd jeering the Soviet national anthem and cheering every solid American check, and it ended with the fans in numbed silence, even before Soviet winger Alexander Maltsev put a red-coated exclamation point on things. Maltsev was 30 years old and would become the Soviet Union's all-time leading goal scorer in international competition. Speeding across the U.S. blue line in the third period, defenseman Dave Christian in front of him, Maltsev cruised left by the top of the circle and then began to spin, 360 degrees in a blur, the puck on his stick as if it were glued. When he was done spinning he started snapping, a backhand, inside the far post. In the U.S. goal, Steve Janaszak looked at Christian in disbelief and then laughed inside his mask.

"They were gods," Janaszak said. On the U.S. bench, trainer Gary Smith walked over to Brooks. "We don't have a chance against these guys," Smith said.

"No shit," the coach replied.

Brooks had spent months trying to debunk the aura surrounding the Soviets. He would talk about how Mikhailov, the fabled captain, looked like Stan Laurel, with his long face and jutting chin. He would tell his players that the team was getting old, that the Russians' time was past. It was a hard sell on a wintry Saturday in New York City, the U.S. players taking the ice with a bit of trepidation and a lot of awe. "It was hard to even warm up," Harrington said. "We looked down at the other end of the ice and there they were: Kharlamov, Petrov, Mikhailov. And I'm thinking, 'Holy smokes, there are the guys I saw beating the NHL All-Stars on TV.' We weren't just playing when the game started. We were watching them play, and by the time we felt like we belonged on the ice with them, it was 8–0."

The final score was 10–3 and merely confirmed what the hockey world already knew: there were the Russians, and then there was everybody else. Virtually everyone expected a similar result in the Olympics. As Harrington knew, the Russians had drubbed the best of the NHL, 6–0, on the same Garden ice the year before, and with their backup goaltender, a guy named Myshkin, no less. "What can change in two weeks?" asked Sergei Makarov, the young Russian star who would go on to a long NHL career. "You can't get whole new team." Even Mark Johnson said, "If you asked anyone on our team and they told you we could beat the Russians, they would've been lying."

Publicly, Brooks did nothing to discourage such thinking, saying the United States should forget the Russians and worry about sneaking away with a silver or bronze medal. Privately, he was not so convinced. In the Olympic format you didn't have to beat a team best-of-seven, or even best-of-five. You had to beat a team only once. The Americans were in superb shape and had a sturdy emotional makeup, honed from months of fending off their coach's verbal floggings. They could skate completely unburdened by expectation, just as their coach had scripted it. Before the game in Madison Square Garden, Brooks told the players to go out and have fun. He had never said anything close to that in the previous sixty pre-Olympic games. *Have fun?* Brooks had followed Warren Strelow's suggestion to let goaltenders Craig and Janaszak share time in the Garden goal, limiting the Soviet preview of Craig and sparing the No. 1 goalie any unnecessary angst. For the first half of that game, especially, the Americans weren't skating, attacking. Part of it was awe, but part of it was Brooks playing at least a little bit of possum.

Even Viktor Tikhonov, the Soviet Olympic coach, said that the U.S. team seemed to be holding something back. Brooks himself later described the Garden game as "a ploy." What could possibly be gained by playing the Russians tough, waking them up? Brooks was beginning to believe that if everything fell together, the United States could take the Russians into the third period in a tight game. That's all you could ask for. You get into that position, and you take your chances.

Six weeks after the death of Herb Brooks, Viktor Tikhonov stood in a barren room inside the arena that is home to the Central Sports Club of the Soviet Army (CSKA). He was 73 years old and surrounded by drab white walls. He had a gray tweed jacket and a flat face, and the vaguely beleaguered aura of a man who is the most decorated international coach in hockey history but may be most remembered for a game his team did not win.

"No matter what we tried we could not get that 10–3 game out of the players' minds," Tikhonov said. "The players told me it would be no problem. It turned out to be a very big problem."

———

Across the ice from the American amateurs was not simply a staggering assemblage of hockey talent but the end product of one of the most astonishing sporting dynasties ever developed. The Soviets did not look like much, at first glance, in their well-worn red sweaters and matching red helmets, their chunky skates that looked like Sputnik-era hand-me-downs. They would march into the arena in their long fur coats and fur hats, with strong Slavic faces and impassive expressions, the thick-bodied KGB guy never far away. Then it was into the locker room, into their gear, like a bunch of Clark Kents going into the phone booth, and soon they would be on the ice doing their supernatural tricks, passing from stick to stick to stick, a clacking, high-speed symphony performed by athletes with light feet and hard bodies.

"You'd get in the corner with one of those guys and they'd stick their ass out toward you, it was like pushing against cement," Neal Broten said.

The Soviets staged a *chuda* (miracle) of their own once, twenty-six years before Lake Placid. It came in 1954 in Stockholm during their first appearance in the world championships. It was led by Vsevelod Bobrov, the Bolshevik Bo Jackson, star not only of the Soviet hockey team but also of the national soccer team, a man known for both his prolific scoring and his disregard for rigorous training.

The Soviets were still new kids on the world-sport block at the time, as deep a mystery to the Western world as Siberia in January. They had excluded themselves ever since they came to power during the revolution of 1917, pronouncing their distaste for Western-style sports organizations and the Olympics, which Communist party leaders saw as the ultimate bourgeois institution, a certain road to imperialist ruin. The attitude changed, swiftly and markedly, after World War II. The Soviet Union had lost 28 million people in the war and was facing the most massive reconstruction project the world had ever seen. Sports began to be seen as a welcome and pleasant diversion, as Robert Edelman notes in his history of spectator sports in the U.S.S.R., *Serious Fun*, but it was not enough to merely play. Against a backdrop of heightening Cold War tensions and a recognition by party officials that sporting success could be a valuable propaganda tool, the goal, increasingly, was to win, for the motherland and to show the world that Karl Marx had it right. Or as the publication *Sovietskii sport* argued floridly, "We have created our own Soviet style in sport, the superiority of which has been demonstrated by our football, basketball and water polo players, gymnasts, boxers and wrestlers in the biggest international competitions. Our goal is to create in this new sport for us, Canadian hockey, our advanced Soviet style, in order that our hockey players, in a short time, will become the strongest in the world."

Nikolai Romanov, the postwar chairman of the government's Committee on Physical Culture and Sports, was among the first to feel the heat of the winning imperative. When the Soviet speed skaters were upset in the European championships in 1948, Romanov was removed from his job. He somehow got it back in 1952 but had learned his lesson well. Scheduled to compete in the 1953 world championships in Switzerland, the Soviet hockey team pulled out after Bobrov fell ill. "In order to gain permission to go into international competition, I had to send a note to Stalin guaranteeing victory," Romanov would write years later in his memoirs.

With Bobrov healthy if not a model of temperance, the Soviets surged into the 1954 semifinals against Canada, the most dominant hockey nation on earth. For years the Canadian custom was to send its senior-league champion to the world championships, men who had regular jobs by day and played their hockey by night. That year's Canadian representative was the East York Lyndhursts. It wasn't regarded as one of Canada's stronger entries, but what difference would that make? The Soviet Union did not have a single indoor hockey arena in the entire country. Though they had played a game called bandy—essentially field hockey on ice—for decades, the Soviets had formally begun to compete in ice hockey only after World War II.

Few people inside or outside the ancient brick walls of the Kremlin could fathom it when the Soviets scored a 7–2 triumph. Two years later, the Soviets captured their first Olympic gold medal, in Cortina, Italy, shutting out Canada's Kitchener Dutchmen. In a sport Canadians all but considered their birthright to rule, they found a new heavyweight in town. It was coached by Anatoly Tarasov and his co-coach Arkady Chernyshev, and it eschewed the rough play and dump-and-muck verticality that were the hallmarks of Canadian hockey, in favor of a system built on speed and criss-crossing movement. The Canadians couldn't have been more jarred if the Russians had spray-painted Marxist slogans in the Montreal Forum. A major shift in the ice-borne world—strategic, philosophical, and political—was on. Any lingering doubts about it were dispelled in the Summit Series of 1972, a historic eight-game competition between premier Canadian players from the NHL and the reigning world and Olympic champions from the U.S.S.R. The Soviets were still more than fifteen years away from playing in the NHL, and this was the first time they had ever competed against the world's top pro players. Most observers predicted a Canadian rout. "I wouldn't mind playing the Russians with the players we *won't* dress," said coach Harry Sinden, whose roster included Ken Dryden, Phil Esposito, and Brad Park. Sinden was somewhat less swaggering after the Russians took Game 1, 7–3, rolling over the Canadians like tanks on the tundra. Ultimately, Canada would take the series, 4–3–1, but rarely has victory been so chilling. "We would never feel the same about ourselves and our game again," Dryden would say much later in a symposium on Canadian hockey.

The emergent Soviet style was creative and free-flowing, full of drop passes and overlapping movements, an intricate offensive tapestry. Tarasov published his ideas about it voluminously, spreading his hockey gospel. He enjoyed American culture and loved to visit the United States, drinking vodka with his hosts and observing the differences in the two nations. Tarasov developed a fondness for mayonnaise on his trips and would sometimes walk down the condiment aisle of the supermarket, mesmerized by the assortment of jars and brands. He was likewise impressed by skyscrapers and the dolphins he witnessed on an outing to Sea World.

"Your people can build the world's tallest buildings," Tarasov once told his friend Lou Vairo, a USA Hockey executive who was a scout on the 1980 team and the Olympic coach in 1984. "You can make forty-nine different kinds of mayonnaise. You can teach dolphins to do the most complex tasks. Why can't you teach your hockey players to pass the puck more than two meters?"

The Soviets' ascendance into the top amateur team in the world came despite an array of obstacles. Dynamo Stadium, the principal venue for hockey in Moscow, was nothing but an outdoor rink set up inside a running track. It didn't even have rounded corners. Teams often played through blizzards, biting wind, and wicked cold. The lighting was dim and spotty, and according to Edelman, it would get darker yet between periods, when stadium workers, bowing to the austere economic conditions of the postwar era, would save electricity by turning the lights out altogether. Sticks were scarce and players wore bicycle helmets, and the inventory wasn't much more impressive in 1980. Their equipment man and trainer were always looking to trade sticks, scoop up supplies, benefit from the bounty of capitalism. "The trainer would ask if he could have a few Band-Aids, and he'd reach in and take the whole box," U.S. trainer Gary Smith said. "Here they were the greatest team in the world, a superpower, and they didn't have anything. It was actually kind of sad."

The Soviets were hard to play and even harder to know. Even as their methods became more familiar to the West, they remained a team cloaked in mystery, and fur, anonymous hockey assassins, robotic in their approach and unfaltering in their skating. The front of the uniforms featured the white block letters CCCP—Cyrillic shorthand for Union of Soviet Socialist Republics—and in their files were bogus occupations that labeled them as soldiers, engineers, or students, titular fictions that began in the 1940s to safeguard their amateur status and eligibility for the Olympics.

While they did not draw Western-sized paychecks, the Soviet players were, by any measure, professionals, training together nearly year-round—whether with their Russian club team or the national team as a whole—and accorded perks and privileges that were as alien to their fellow workers as a stock portfolio. Cars, nice apartments, vacation places on the Black Sea were common; it wasn't abnormal for the apartments to get nicer still after a major triumph. Adulation and international travel were part of the lifestyle, too. Of course the travel was made in the company of KGB agents, but the Russians grew up being watched. "You knew they were going to be with you, even if you didn't know who they were," said Vladimir Lutchenko, a longtime defensive stalwart and winner of two Olympic golds (1972 and '76) who would go on to serve as general manager of CSKA in Moscow. The most storied of all Russian hockey teams, CSKA was the feeder club for most of the stars on the national team.

Lutchenko grew up in the Moscow suburb of Remenskoe and was typical of how Soviet players of his era were developed. He started playing hockey at 6, showed promise, and by 12 was deemed gifted enough by Soviet sports officials to be placed in the CSKA school, where he would get rigorous training under skilled coaches. By 15 he was on the junior national team, and several years after that was wearing No. 3 and stationed on the blue line for Tarasov.

A rotund, jowly man with wayward white hair, Tarasov was a towering figure in hockey by the late 1960s. Lou Vairo, on one of his first visits to the Soviet Union, asked Tarasov for five drills to work on transitioning from defense to offense. Tarasov pushed his glasses back on his bulbous red nose and told Vairo to meet him at six a.m. the next morning and to have 100 drills ready for discussion. Vairo stayed up all night preparing. "There are two people in the hockey world you did not say no to. One was Herb Brooks, and the other was Anatoly Tarasov," he said. Tarasov reviewed Vairo's homework, then presented him with the five exercises he wanted. "My eyes were as wide as pucks," Vairo said. "There was nobody like Tarasov. Without question, he's the finest coach in ice hockey who ever was. He could motivate like nobody I've ever seen. I've seen him work with Swedish kids and Finnish kids. He didn't even speak their language and he could motivate them. He didn't just coach. He made players better."

And he didn't mind trying to help make American players better, maybe because they posed so little threat. Tarasov gave a talk at Northeastern University in Boston not long before Lake Placid, and 1960 hero Bill Cleary went to see him. Tarasov greeted Cleary with a bear hug and said, "Billy, you almost sent me to Siberia." Cleary invited Tarasov and his interpreter over to his house. Tarasov arrived with a bottle of vodka and the following greeting: "Ice, ice, ice." They reminisced and talked hockey and looked out over the Charles River, and when the vodka was gone, Tarasov grabbed the empty bottle, went outside, and tossed it into the shrubs. "Leave it there until the next time America wins the Olympic gold medal in hockey," he said, laughing. Cleary still has the bottle.

———

Brooks knew he'd need everything to break right for his team to get a shot at the Russians, and the Lake Placid schedule makers—a committee consisting of Hal Trumble, executive director of the Amateur Hockey Association of the United States (AHAUS); Robert Fleming, chair of AHAUS's international committee; William Croft, a technical adviser retained by the Lake Placid Olympic Organizing Committee; and Ken Johannson, the U.S. general manager—did all they could to cooperate. There were two six-team divisions in the Olympic hockey tournament, determined by seedings and sorted out by the International Ice Hockey Federation, the sport's worldwide governing body. The U.S. team was seeded seventh overall and was placed in the Blue Division, with Czechoslovakia, Sweden, West Germany, Norway, and Romania. The Red Division consisted of the Soviet Union,

Canada, Finland, Poland, Holland, and Japan. After the world championships in the spring of 1979, the committee met in the National Hotel in Moscow. A slap shot away from Red Square, the men drew up the entire twelve-team Olympic hockey schedule—dates, times, locations, and order of all games—and it wasn't a coincidence that the particulars fell the United States' way. Brooks didn't attend the meeting, but he had full input into the schedule gerrymandering. The home team always has an advantage in sports, and in the committee's mind, this was just a way of enhancing it a bit, like the fleet-footed baseball team that keeps its grass long to help its runners. The United States received another perk, too, setting up in the most spacious of the locker rooms. The Soviets, as world champions, were supposed to get first choice but were instead sent down the hall.

Sweden was selected to be the first U.S. opponent, the thinking being that the youthful Americans would be hyped up to play and would bring lots of energy against a strong team. The Czechs were second, because they were a very skilled and physical bunch, a team that could beat you up and that you didn't necessarily want to play two days before the medal round. Then came what figured to be the easiest games, against Norway and Romania, and finally, the last divisional game against West Germany, historically a nation that played the United States well. In 1976, a loss to the West Germans had knocked the United States out of medal contention. The committee took equal care in scheduling the Red Division games. The three top teams in the division—the Soviet Union, Canada, and Finland—had easy games in the beginning and the toughest games, against each other, at the end.

Play commenced on February 12, a day before Opening

Ceremonies, the extra day of competition necessary to ac-commodate the largest Olympic field in history. The Soviets opened against Japan and Holland (they won by a combined score of 33–4). The U.S. start wasn't nearly so auspicious, the decision to meet Sweden first very nearly backfiring. Pelle Lindbergh, future Philadelphia Flyer, was superb in goal for Sweden, and the United States was still down 2–1 with a minute to play when Brooks ordered Craig to vacate the goal and sent out six skaters. With 27 seconds remaining, defenseman Bill Baker scored on a slap shot, and a loss turned into a tie.

All ties are not equal. This was a phenomenal tie, and it carried over into Game 2, against the Czechs. A day after the U.S. athletes marched in opening ceremonies in cowboy hats, sheepskin coats, and blue jeans, the team played a game straight out of the frontier of its imagination, a Valentine's Day massacre over the second-best team in the world. The final score was 7–3, the most explosive offensive effort by a U.S. team since the gold-medal game in 1960 in Squaw Val-ley, also against the Czechs. This time the United States scored five times over 26 minutes in the second and third periods, playing creative, aggressive, and dazzlingly artful hockey. "It was the best game we played in the tournament," defenseman Ken Morrow said. Even the Russians were stunned at the result. Buzz Schneider, who had become friendly with renowned Soviet goaltender Vladislav Tretiak during previous international competitions, ran into him after the game in the Olympic Village. "I think we can do something here," Schneider told him.

The United States followed with convincing triumphs over Norway and Romania, then got its quadrennial

headache from West Germany. This time the trouble commenced in warm-ups, Craig getting knocked out when a shot
from Eruzione hit him in the neck. Brooks told Janaszak
to get loose. Craig finally gathered himself, but he let in a
seventy-foot slap shot for one goal and a fifty-five-footer for
another, and the United States was still down two goals as the
game neared the halfway point. Right wing Rob McClanahan finally got the Americans on the board with a backhan-
der, and Neal Broten tied things up in the final 90 seconds of
the second period by jamming in a rebound. The United
States went on to a 4–2 triumph, and though the Americans
were hoping to win by more goals and thus move ahead of
the Swedes in the standings (goal differential is the main
Olympic tiebreaker), they couldn't complain too much. They
were second in the Blue Division, in the medal round, in the
Olympic semifinals. The next opponent would be the winner
of the Red Division: the Soviet Union, which, surprisingly,
had to come from behind to beat Finland and Canada in its
previous two games.

———

Poised over center ice in the hilltop arena, a Finnish referee
named Karl-Gustav Kaisla dropped the puck. The first
Olympic semifinal—the thirty-second game of the hockey
competition in the XIII Winter Olympics, and the most antic-
ipated event of the Games—was underway. The Field House,
with a capacity of 8,500, was completely overstuffed. Ten
thousand people? Twelve thousand? The turnstiles couldn't
keep up. Petrov won the draw from Johnson. The Soviets controlled the puck. Not even two minutes in, defenseman Valery
Vasiliev carried through center ice, passed to forward Viktor

Zhluktov, and kept on skating, getting the puck back to the right of Jim Craig, then threading a perfect pass to Zhluktov, who was charging in from the point. Already the Soviets were showcasing their intricate game, a defenseman in deep, a forward up high, the pieces moving seamlessly, the puck quickly. Zhluktov skated in on Craig, who moved out to cut down the angle. The Soviet wristed a lefthanded shot and Craig blocked it, blocked the rebound, and covered up. Craig knew it was critical that he get off to a good start. If you let the bear jump on your back early, you were done. Look at what happened at Madison Square Garden. The Russians were famous for their conditioning, another legacy of Tarasov's. Educated at the Soviets' sports think tank, the Institute of Physical Culture, Tarasov studied science and exercise physiology and developed novel ideas about training athletes to improve their lateral movement and agility, and to sustain a fast pace from start to finish. The conditioning regimen was practically year-round, consisting of everything from soccer to running on the beach to long, grinding rides on bulky, one-gear 1950s bicycles. "They were doing plyometrics before the rest of the world knew how to spell it," said Michael Smith, general manager of the Chicago Blackhawks and a Ph.D. in Russian Studies. Tretiak, the Hall of Fame goaltender, once said that he didn't take a day off training for twenty-one years, including his wedding day.

"You and the Canadians have the wrong approach," Tarasov told Lou Vairo. "You want to win games in the last period, but a well-conditioned team wins in the first ten minutes, maybe less. The opponent is destroyed not just on the scoreboard, but their will is broken when an opponent [comes out hard and fast]."

After Craig turned away Zhluktov, the Soviets were buzzing the goal again, Alexander Golikov forechecking hard, and rising star Sergei Makarov, a square-chinned 21-year-old winger with a wide face and a penchant for making wisecracks, right there with him. The night before, Makarov and Craig had played Centipede against each other in the Olympic Village video arcade. Craig wasn't much for video games, but he liked this one because it was a great test of hand-eye coordination. It was also free. "Isn't this great that we can stand here and play the game all night for nothing?" Craig said. They mostly communicated with nods and laughs. "The real game is tomorrow night," Craig said when they parted.

Makarov's linemate Alexander Golikov got the puck in front and was about to fire when Broten, backchecking assiduously, alertly got his stick on the puck and foiled him. Brooks's plan was to attack the Soviets and skate with them, but it was also to get all five skaters back in the zone when the Russians had the puck. You don't even think about containing the best forwards in the world with a pair of defensemen— a lesson that was reinforced for Brooks the night before when he dined with his agent, Art Kaminsky, and Ken Dryden, the Hall of Fame goaltender and ABC broadcaster, an erudite man who had extensive knowledge of the Russians. Brooks spent the meal peppering Dryden with questions, probing for a revelation, eighteen hours before game time.

Despite the vigilant defense, the United States was having trouble clearing the puck out of its zone. Just inside the blue line, Makarov flicked a pass to Alexander Golikov, who went in on Craig but backhanded it wide, and then it was

Makarov's turn, steaming past Mike Ramsey on the right wing, dangerously pushing the puck across center.

On the Soviet bench, Viktor Tikhonov was at his usual station, standing in front of his players, not behind them, the location preferred by Brooks and every other Western coach. He looked like a gatekeeper in a brown suit, jabbering constantly to his players, hair cemented in place. The Soviets were skating hard and passing crisply, and Tretiak had made a sprawling stop of the first American threat, defenseman Bill Baker making an end-to-end rush down the right side, getting in deep, and centering to winger Phil Verchota, who tried to ram the puck in from the doorstep.

Bill Baker had a poised and savvy approach to the game. He didn't carry the puck that often, but he could be plenty dangerous in the offensive zone. He had proved that ten days earlier when he had saved the Americans with his late heroics against the Swedes. The Olympic Field House was half-full then, the atmosphere so flat that right wing John Harrington thought to himself, *This is the Olympics?* The United States had missed a flurry of early chances and was on the verge of paying for it. As Jim Craig raced off in the final minute and Dave Silk hopped on, the United States forced a face-off in the Swedish zone. Center Mark Pavelich won the draw and got the puck back to Mike Ramsey, whose shot from the point was stuffed. Moments later, Buzz Schneider fought off a clutching Swede near the corner and steered the puck over to Pavelich, on the left boards. Pavelich spun around and centered it to Baker, who was open between the circles. The pass landed on his stick and Baker wound and fired, launching a slap shot no more than a foot off the ice, making sure he got it on net, beating Lindbergh low on the glove side. The red light came on and so did the entire American bench, engulfing Baker, a pile of blue shirts on the ice, the crowd roaring. *Now* it felt like the Olympics to Harrington, and everyone else. The goal turned out to be Baker's only one of the Olympics. Without it—and with the Czechs up next—the likelihood was that the Americans' Olympics might well have been over before Opening Ceremonies. "I knew if we could skate with that team we had a good chance to win a medal," Lou Vairo said.

———

In Grand Rapids, Minnesota, where the opener of walleye season is a holy day and the mighty Mississippi is more creek than river, nobody who knew Billy Baker was surprised by his nerveless game-tying feat against Sweden. Years before he became a blond-haired Olympic icon or a successful oral surgeon, Baker was a star without an attitude, a leader without locker-room histrionics, a tough guy without flaunting it. Baker was the kid you wanted to be like, a smart, good-looking athlete whose charisma was as understated as everything else about him. He had a gift for reading situations, deciding where he needed to be, on the ice and off. Baker was about 10 years old when he was trying to figure out whether he wanted to spend his winter playing basketball or hockey.

"How many basketball scholarships have come out of this area?" asked Gus Hendrickson, who would be Baker's hockey coach at Grand Rapids High School.

"None," Baker replied.

"I think you should play hockey," the coach said, with enlightened self-interest.

With his selection made, Baker would go down to Hernes-man's Feed Store with the other kids and get his skates sharpened, next to the railroad tracks by Highway 169, which comes 200 miles all the way up from the Twin Cities. Then it would be out to River View rink, a couple of blocks from the family's house. His routine was steady, his bearing humble, his achievements exemplary, whether as a two-way football player (he was a tight end/defensive end) or a single-minded student, or even now, as a husband, father, and doctor in Brainerd, Minnesota. John Rothstein was Baker's teammate on the Grand Rapids team that won the Minnesota state high school championship in 1975, Baker starring on defense, Rothstein up front, with two of the fastest skates anyone had ever seen. "He was always a leader in everything he did," Rothstein said. "He's blessed with so much God-given talent, but never stopped being a genuine person. He's still Baker. You would never know he has an Olympic gold medal."

Rothstein went from colleague to competitor in college, after Baker went to play for Brooks at the U, and Rothstein played with Mark Pavelich and John Harrington at the University of Minnesota–Duluth. That was when Rothstein truly began to appreciate how good Baker was, how resilient he was mentally. Not that he would advertise it, or anything else about himself. When he went to dentistry school, Baker told few of his classmates about what he'd done in his previous life. If you were out grouse hunting with Baker, or on a boat in Forest Lake, or hanging out with him at the lumberjack show during Tall Timber Days, the annual summer festival in Grand Rapids every August, you saw one side of Billy Baker. If you competed against him, you saw something else entirely, not fire and feistiness so much as skill and self-control and an unshakable faith that the job would get done. In Grand Rapids, kids felt good that they were his classmates. In Lake Placid, nineteen guys felt good that he was their teammate. Championship teams—in Grand Rapids, the U, and the Olympics—kept following Baker around. "I'm sure his forefathers led people into battle," said Dr. Bill Hoolihan, a childhood friend and Grand Rapids teammate.

Baker's contributions went far beyond his goal. Early in the Czech game, he took a slap shot in the neck, crumpled to the ice—and scarcely missed a shift. In the second period, he lined up Czech defenseman Frantisek Kaberle by the bench and checked him so hard Kaberle went head over heels and disappeared behind the sideboards. At six feet one inch and 195 pounds, Baker had the look of a kid who came off a Viking ship, and the work ethic of someone who might've built it. His father worked in the Blandin Paper Mill, the big employer in town, on the banks of the Mississippi. The mill produced the first coated stock in the country—glossy pages that were used by *Sports Illustrated, Time, Life,* and other magazines. Who knew Billy Baker would wind up *in* those glossy pages?

"He's one of those kids whose life was almost a storybook," said Mike Sertich, who coached Baker under Hendrickson. "He was destined to succeed, and he did."

———

Not long after Tretiak thwarted Verchota and Baker, the Soviet charge resumed. Petrov had the puck inside the blue line, saw an opening, and seized it, skating in and ripping a 25-foot shot just wide. Moments later, Mikhailov got caught hooking Rob McClanahan and was sent off for two minutes, the game's first power play. The crowd roared and did so again as Mark Johnson skated in on Tretiak, but Johnson couldn't get a shot off as the defense squeezed in on him. The Americans couldn't sustain the attack, the power play passing uneventfully.

After Craig made a splendid kick stop of a blue-line drive by Viacheslav Fetisov, the heralded young Russian defenseman, Tretiak turned away a wicked turnaround slap shot from U.S. left wing Buzz Schneider. The fleet-skating, hard-shooting Schneider had been superb throughout the Olympics and was on the go again, carrying down the left side and centering to Mark Pavelich, twenty feet in front of the net. Pavelich's wrist shot was blocked, and his rebound shot was deflected wide. With a bit over nine minutes gone, Schneider was behind his own net, looking to start up ice. Just as he got going, Soviet forward Vladimir Krutov whacked at his stick and sent the puck skidding ahead, right to defenseman Alexei Kasatonov at the point, a seemingly innocuous change of possession. Kasatonov let go with a shot and Krutov, about eight feet in front of Craig, extended his stick and got a piece of it, deflecting it downward, low on the glove side. The puck skittered under Craig's glove, into the net.

The crowd booed. One to nothing, Soviet Union.

The Americans had started slowly in just about every game they had played, but it was one thing to spot West Germany a lead and quite another to do it with the Soviets. The United States was a beat behind, giving the Soviets too much room to set up. Krutov briefly raised his arms. At 19, he was the youngest Soviet player and the most relentless, a five-foot nine-inch 195-pounder who was nicknamed Tank and would skate by you or through you—whichever was necessary. He got a quick pat on the helmet from forward Yuri Lebedev, and then it was off to the bench for more perfunctory congratulation. When the U.S. team scored, they looked like kids at recess, running toward each other, exulting, a group hug waiting to happen. The Soviets had emotions; they just didn't believe in displaying them. You didn't see them haranguing officials, reacting to fans, taking exception to every hard hit. They were artists on skates, with the demeanor of accountants. Celebrations were not their thing.

The crowd was similarly restrained. Even before Krutov's goal, the mood in the Field House seemed oddly detached, more tense than excited. This game had been more hyped than any Olympic event ever held in the United States. Out on the street, top-priced tickets were trading at four and five times the $67.20 printed price. Tickets were so in demand that to safeguard the distribution of media tickets, organizers needed six state police officers and a private security detail. Yet there was almost a sense that people were wary of rooting too hard, bracing for a blowout.

The mood around the offices of ABC late that week was not appreciably better. The network had paid $15.5 million for the right to televise the Games, a hefty investment at the time (though a broadcasting bargain by current standards: in 2002, the next time the Winter Games were held in the United States, the TV rights fee was $545 million). ABC desperately wanted to televise the U.S.–Soviet Union game live in prime time. Jim Spence, the network's senior vice president and the No. 2 man behind Roone Arledge, said that he had reached an oral agreement months ahead of time with Bob Allen, the chief of competition for the hockey tournament, stipulating that if the United States should make it to the medal round and play the Soviet Union, the network could move the game to prime time. Allen recalls no such agreement. "I didn't have the authority to change the time of the game," he said. Once the semifinal pairings were set, Spence reminded Allen of the conversation and said ABC definitely wanted to move the game. Allen said he didn't know if he could do that. Spence turned to Peter Spurney, head of the Lake Placid Olympic Organizing Committee. Spurney wanted no part of changing the game time. The local organizers had already been taking huge public-relations hits for the transportation fiasco at the start of the Games, when an acute bus shortage left people stranded all over the Adirondacks and very nearly forced the postponement of Opening Ceremonies. All they needed was for thousands of outraged fans who had tickets for the United States and the Soviet Union to show up at the arena and get Finland and Sweden instead.

Spence called Ray Pratt, sports director of the Games, and Pratt, heeding Spurney's orders, did all he could to stall him. At Spence's urging, Allen reached out to Dr. Gunther Sabetzki, president of the International Ice Hockey Federation, who said that if the network would pony up $125,000, the IIHF would switch the game time. Arledge and Spence weren't happy about a payment they considered extortion, but they agreed to pay it. In the meantime, Sabetzki checked with the four teams and apparently offered each $12,500 to agree to the switch. Three of the four teams agreed; the Soviets did not, not wanting to have the game start at four a.m. Moscow time, which is when it would have gone off with an eight p.m. start in Lake Placid. Spence was stymied. The game stayed at five p.m., as scheduled. ABC opted to televise it on tape delay; Al Michaels and Ken Dryden, the broadcasters, came on in their blue-knit shirts at eight p.m. EST. "It still bothers me that the game was not live when we had a commitment to do it live," Spence said.

———

After Krutov's goal, the anxiety in the building was almost palpable. The whole place seemed tight, American players and fans alike. Not even a minute later, Pavelich skated behind Tretiak and backhanded a pass in front, but nobody was there to do anything with it. The Soviets controlled, and controlled, the Americans going close to a half-minute without touching the puck. A shot by Valery Vasiliev went wide, and then Craig stopped a rebound shot by Alexander Golikov, who had scored seven goals already in Lake Placid, the most of any Soviet. The Americans had a fleeting chance when Neal Broten sped down the left side and centered to linemate Steve Christoff, but the long-legged Zhluktov, with a bushy brown mustache and a glowering countenance, caught Christoff from behind and poked the puck away.

Then Soviet defenseman Vasily Pervukhin launched a shot wide, and Craig briefly lost his footing and reeled backward, bumping into the goal. That was how most of the U.S. team looked, on its heels, reactive more than pro-active, the Soviets' increasingly dictating the pace and the play. With just under eight minutes left in the period, Krutov nudged a pass to Alexander Maltsev along the boards and Maltsev flicked it right back, Krutov alone on Craig, just missing from close range. The Soviets maintained the pressure. Vladimir Golikov, playing on the same line with his brother Alexander, carried toward the U.S. blue line, into traffic, then got stripped by Mark Pavelich.

At five feet seven inches, Mark Pavelich was the shortest player on the team, but he had legs as strong as a locomotive. Pavelich was a player that even his teammates loved to watch skate, and here he came, accelerating swiftly, veering right, into open space, tugging two defensemen toward him. Pavelich never said much, but if his hockey instincts could've talked, he would've been Churchill. Just a stride before he crossed center ice, he slid the puck across ice to the left wing, on to Schneider's stick. Schneider took it cleanly and skated a few hard strides, inside the blue line. He had room. Defenseman Zinetula Bilyaletdinov tried to close in on him, get a piece, but Buzz Schneider still had space. He was about forty feet out.

The best goal scorers are hard-wired with a sense of when it's time to shoot. Buzz Schneider was no different. He was at a sharp angle, but he'd gotten a perfect setup and could feel the Russians had not quite recovered. He let it fly. As he shot, Tretiak was still moving to his right. Schneider decided to direct his missile behind him, to the place the goaltender had just vacated. The puck rocketed over Tretiak's glove, into the upper right-hand corner.

The red light glowed.

Chapter Two

STIRRINGS OF BELIEF

Five minutes after his giveaway had put his team down a goal, Buzz Schneider evened it up, and there was a full-throated roar in the building to prove it. It was a nice time to continue his uncanny success against Tretiak. Schneider had scored a hat trick on him in the 1975 world championships, a claim few forwards in the world could make. "Buzzy owned Tretiak," Rob McClanahan joked.

After a tentative start, the U.S. players were skating with more conviction. They were tied with the greatest team on earth, and with the way the period had begun, that was not a bad thing.

William "Buzz" Schneider got his nickname from an aunt when he was a little boy. He had been getting up and down his wing for almost as long, skating as if he were turbo-powered. Schneider shot harder than anyone on the team. He needed a little room to get the shot off, but once he did, it was no fun for the goalies. Some guys drive their slap shot and the puck arrives light and unmenacing. When Schneider shot, the puck felt like an anvil. "It hurt to catch it," said Lefty Curran, the star goaltender of the U.S. Olympic team that won a silver medal in Japan in 1972 and Schneider's friend and former boss for Great Dane, a tractor-trailer company. "It was all in his timing. He's got a terrible golf swing, and I've seen him hit golf balls miles."

Without the overt edginess of a Dave Silk or the Olympic genes of a Dave Christian, Schneider was far from the biggest name on the team, but he was a superb athlete who may well have been a better baseball player than a hockey player. His other nickname was the Babbitt Rabbit, derived from his speed and his hometown on the eastern end of Minnesota's Iron Range, just down Route 21 from Embarrass. Home to 685 people, Embarrass proudly calls itself "The Nation's Cold Spot," a quirk of airflow making it a few degrees colder than neighboring towns. The official record low for Embarrass is −57, on January 20, 1996. It barely broke −50 in Babbitt that day. "In spite of our cold temperatures," Embarrassites like to say, "we are known for our warm hearts."

Buzz Schneider would pass through Embarrass on his trips to Eveleth, where his wife, Gayle, grew up. He was an out-of-towner, but everybody liked Buzz Schneider. He may have been the most popular and industrious player on the team; some guys were sure he would've been captain if the election had been decided by a truly democratic vote. The team *did* vote for captain, but Brooks wanted Mike Eruzione and nobody was sure how accurate the ballot count was. This was no knock on Eruzione, who turned into a terrific captain. It was just a testament to Schneider's immense likeability.

When Brooks was at the U, he was harder on Schneider than on anybody else. If practice wasn't going well and Brooks felt a rant coming on, he'd blow the whistle and call everyone in and then look disapprovingly at Schneider. Brooks had a lead vest he used as a discipline device. Buzz Schneider believes he wore it more than anyone.

"Buzzy, I don't know. You've got million-dollar legs and a nickel brain. You've got to think the game," Brooks would say. Or: "If this place didn't have boards, you'd end up out on the street." The quality that made Buzz Schneider attractive for singling out was that he could take it.

"To this day, Buzzy Schneider is one of the nicest people I've ever known," said Joe Micheletti, a Gopher teammate and former NHL defenseman who is now a broadcaster with the New York Islanders. "He always had a smile on his face. Herbie knew the strength of his personality, and knew that he could use that strength to get to the rest of the team and teach us about the game. It was tough to knock Buzzy off his stool."

Schneider played with his fellow Iron Rangers, Mark Pavelich of Eveleth and John Harrington of Virginia, all of them from the ore-laden precincts of northeast Minnesota, where lives and livelihoods were built around mines before the earth's bounty began to give out and foreign competition began to rise up. Their self-appointed title was the Conehead Line, named for the old *Saturday Night Live* skit featuring aliens who had heads the shape of construction cones and spoke in flat, mechanical cadence. The Iron Rangers often were spectators when Brooks was working on the power play, and during one such stretch Pavelich mentioned that the three of them were no more vital to the proceedings than the orange cones Brooks set up during practice. Brooks put them on a line together, reasoning that only wingers who grew up playing Iron Range shinny hockey—the Midwestern term for pickup games on lakes and ponds—could know what the freewheeling Pavelich might do next. Harrington once asked Pavelich what their breakout pattern was going to be.

"We're going to start at one end of the ice and finish on the other," Pavelich replied.

They had their own style of hockey—intuitive and organic and grinding—on the Range, and their own way of life, too. Before Play Stations and play dates and ultra-organized youth hockey, there was hunting season and fishing season and hockey season. Kids played on frozen lakes or makeshift rinks, eight to a side or ten a side or however many showed up a side. Goalie pads were more likely to be fashioned out of beefy magazines and rubber bands than anything you'd find in a store. Ron Castellano, a 32-year coaching veteran and the only coach Babbitt High School ever had ("People say I was the winningest coach in school history, but I remind them I was the losingest, too," Castellano said), played goal with a stick his father whittled from a hunk of wood. You learned to handle the puck and skate in traffic, and to find an open teammate, away from the posse chasing the puck. You would play for hours after school and all day on the weekends, and if you couldn't get to the lake or the rink, you'd do what John Harrington did—play road hockey in front of the house, the plows supplying snow chunks for the goals, and the walls of snow the au naturel sideboards. People on the Range are nice, so when they'd come by in the car, they'd slow down and maneuver around the goals. Why would anybody run over a kid's snow chunks?

You learned to be resourceful and self-reliant on the Range, and to stick together. Life was hard, money was scarce, and the cold was brutal. The average *high* temperature in January was 16 degrees. Entire towns would be picked up and moved if they happened to be sitting on a good-sized ore deposit. Warmth and community were virtues to be prized. When Eveleth Methodist Church was built in 1950, the funds that bought the bricks and mortar and everything else came from the $50,000 that was raised selling pasties, the hearty meat-and-potato pies that are as much a Range staple as bratwurst is in Milwaukee. When a man in Babbitt was stricken by a brain tumor, the fund-raisers and the church suppers came nonstop. The generosity isn't taken for granted in towns where, early in the twentieth century, a man wouldn't make much more than $1.50 for a full day of digging in the earth, about a third of what the average American laborer made at the time. "If somebody has a problem, everyone will stop and do whatever they can to help," said Matt Banovetz, a retired mineworker who spent thirty-five years working for Reserve Mining, until it went bankrupt in 1986. Banovetz's starting wage in 1951 was $1.19 an hour. He often worked sixteen-hour days. His wife had a big celebration the first time he earned $100 per month.

Time hasn't stood still on the Iron Range, but it has moved slowly, which is what being four hours from the Twin Cities and even 100 miles from Duluth will do for you. A season of youth hockey at Eveleth's historic Hippodrome—all fees included—costs $80. Two blocks away the Roosevelt Bar serves $1 drafts beneath a tin ceiling. In Hibbing, driving by Bob Dylan's childhood home doesn't cost a thing, and neither does traveling down the very Highway 61 that he sang about. You can play eighteen holes of golf in Babbitt for $18, and stay at the Red Carpet Inn for $25. After Reserve Mining shut down, you could buy a house for $10,000.

The Iron Range stretches for 110 miles, bordered by Grand Rapids on the west and Babbitt on the east. It actually comprises three separate ranges (Mesabi, Vermilion, and Cuyuna), the landscape pocked by open pits, huge and abandoned, and by scarred red hills built from the tons of rock and dirt that were extracted to get to the ore. The towns go by the names of Biwabik and Coleraine, Mountain Iron and Gilbert, and they all call themselves cities, even the places with only a few thousand residents. You know you're in the next town when you see its name on the water tower on the horizon. Most of the communities were built by the mining companies that set up shop there. Babbitt—all 108 square miles of it—was created from scratch by Reserve Mining in the early 1950s, from streetlamp to schoolhouse to the alphabetically ordered streets named for trees (Ash, Birch, Cypress, and so forth). It is a frontier fabrication that did not look kindly on any sort of interference or regulation. A sign near the edge of Babbitt said, "This town exists in spite of the following organizations: Sierra Club, Izaak Walton League, Friends of the Wilderness, Minnesota Public Interest Group and Minnesota Pollution Control Agency." The Schneider home on Birch Boulevard was a three-bedroom box that was more bungalow than house, with a tin detached garage. It was so indistinguishable from hundreds of other houses built by Reserve that it wasn't unheard-of for people to come home at night and walk in the wrong house.

The culture of mining courses through the Range like the ubiquitous train tracks that used to take hopper cars down to the Lake Superior ore docks. At the main intersection in Eveleth, Miners National Bank is on one corner and a steelworkers union storefront is across the way. On Central Boulevard in Babbitt is a nine-foot-high slab of gray-black taconite dedicated to Peter Mitchell, a prospector who discovered the ore deposits in the region. Every community has its ways, and each attracted its own subset of immigrant dreamers. There were a preponderance of Slovenians and Italians in Eveleth, Finns and Italians in Virginia, Croatians and Irish and Norwegians sprinkled here and there. All of them learned to deal with the vicissitudes of mining, the work hard but steady in good times, nonexistent in bad times. In the woeful economy of the early 1980s, unemployment exceeded 80 percent in more than a few Iron Range communities.

At its peak in the mid-twentieth century, the mining industry on the Range had hundreds of mines and employed some 17,000 people, producing about 80 percent of the country's iron ore. In 2004 it consisted of six mines, 4,000 mining employees, and a fraction of that production. On the outskirts of Virginia, an old mining site has morphed into an overlook where a short caged boardwalk lets you glimpse a massive pit with red banks and small bare trees poking up from the sides, the reforestation process slowly at work. The pit was once filled with hundreds of working men. Now it's filled with blue-green water.

With almost no high-grade iron ore left, Range mines have turned to taconite, a lower-grade ore. The production of taconite involves crushing the ore into powder, the iron extracted magnetically and then rolled into marble-sized pellets, a process that requires vastly bigger processing plants and investment. In Eveleth, mining cautiously awakened from a completely dormant state when shuttered Ev-Tac re-opened under a new name (United Taconite) late in 2003, thanks in part to a 30 percent ownership stake by a Chinese company. Taconite mining has saved the Range for a time, but it may be only a reprieve.

All over the Range, population is down and schools are being consolidated. Eveleth once had a population of 6,000 and is now down below 4,000. Steve Schneider, Buzz's brother, a gifted hockey player himself who went on to captain the Notre Dame team, was part of a graduating class of 140 students in Babbitt High School in the mid-1970s. In 2003 the senior class had 28 students. "People are leaving because there are no jobs," Bill Schneider, Buzz's father, said. Memorial Arena in Babbitt has a big photo of Buzz Schneider in his Olympic uniform in the lobby, and used to draw 1,500 fans for games against Ely or Eveleth or International Falls. Now Babbitt High doesn't have enough players to field its own team. Castellano started the program in 1959 and closed it in 1991. He coached kids who grew up and went to work in the mines and became fathers, and then he coached their sons. Then he watched entire families pack up and leave and try to find a job and build a life someplace else.

"It was brutal," Castellano said.

Like old ballplayers who lament that kids don't play baseball enough anymore, Iron Rangers of a certain age will tell you about the halcyon days of hockey on the Range: how Eveleth's John Mayasich, a two-time Olympian and Minnesota legend, would rack up goals and assists by the bucketful for the U in the 1950s; how Mike Antonovich dominated at Coleraine; and how John Rothstein would outrace everyone in Grand Rapids. It is not knee-jerk nostalgia. In the

early 1940s, the six-team era in the NHL, three of the starting goaltenders were from Eveleth. Eveleth High School has
won more state hockey tournaments than any other school in
the state, including four in a row between 1948 and 1951. On
Hat Trick Avenue, on a bluff overlooking Highway 53, sits
the U.S. Hockey Hall of Fame, which inducted the entire
1980 Olympic team in its fall 2003 class, commemorating the
occasion with a gala dinner with 1,000 guests. The plates
were rented from a place in the Twin Cities, and the Iron
Rangers who hosted the event honored their self-sufficient
ways. They woke up early the next morning and washed all
1,000 plates by hand.

Iron Range hockey rivalries used to run hot and deep. Friday night games would determine Monday morning brag-
ging rights in the mines. The Eveleth Hippodrome, a local
landmark at the corner of Jackson and Douglas, dates to
1919, a brown brick building with yellow walls and a hangar-
style roof and oversized photos of John Mayasich and Mark
Pavelich, Eveleth's gold medalists, that you see as soon as you
enter. Virginia's Memorial Arena has poster-sized photos of
its own Olympians, Steve Sertich and John Harrington, looking out from under a Dutch-boy haircut. When Virginia
High would make the four-mile trip to the Hippodrome, or
Grand Rapids would come from the west, the 2,800 seats
would invariably be full and the emotions overflowing. In
Grand Rapids, visits from Hibbing or Eveleth would draw a
standing-room crowd of 4,000. It wouldn't take much to get a
fight going, on the ice or in the stands. All season the Iron
Range Conference would be a boiling, competitive cauldron,
but whoever won and went on to the state tournament in
the Twin Cities for the finals—a statewide holy week, every

March—would have the whole Range behind them. The only thing better than winning the state title was doing it by beating a couple of the big schools from the south along the way. There's no Mason-Dixon line in Minnesota, but the differences between north and south Minnesota are as deep as any of the state's 15,000-plus lakes.

"There's a lot of pride in all those little towns up north, and a lot of respect people have for each other," Steve Schneider said.

After his games for Babbitt High, Buzz Schneider and his teammates often played shinny hockey on an outdoor rink. Schneider was always playing something. In football, he was a quarterback and defensive back and field-goal kicker. In baseball, he played third and outfield. He had an arm you didn't dare run on and a left-handed bat that could hit the ball into the next mine pit. Schneider practiced hitting constantly, studying cutouts of Ted Williams, standing in front of a mirror and swinging again and again and again. Baseball scouts are sighted on the Range about as often as palm trees, but they made it up to see the Babbitt Rabbit. The Pittsburgh Pirates invited Schneider to try out, and he might've done it, except that almost every big college hockey program was offering him a scholarship, including Minnesota and its new coach, Herb Brooks.

Brooks never saw Schneider play a high school game in person, but when you can shoot and skate like Schneider, coaches find out. Gus Hendrickson, hockey coach at powerhouse Grand Rapids, was so absorbed with trying to stop Schneider before playing Babbitt one year that he drove his pickup truck into a snow-filled ditch thinking about him. "He could beat anybody all by himself," Hendrickson said.

Before Schneider's senior year, Castellano decided he wanted to make Schneider, his leading scorer, a defenseman. It was a switch that would get him more ice time and give him a chance to rush as often as he wanted, but one that most forwards would have greeted with revulsion.

"Whatever you want," Schneider said.

That was Buzz Schneider, never one to make a fuss or let his ego get out of hand. He has deep-set eyes, thick eyebrows and lips, and a prominent nose. He exudes the sort of laid-back warmth and sincerity that makes you feel you've known him for ten years after ten minutes, his all-purpose affirmation "you bet" sprinkled through conversation. He used to sell tractor-trailers and now he sells real estate. You would definitely want to buy from Buzzy Schneider. Said his friend Lefty Curran, "I think he would've made a great pastor, because he has such a gentle way. He's always giving and thinking of other people." Steve Schneider still appreciates how Buzz encouraged him to go to Notre Dame, where Steve would be unencumbered by comparisons to his big brother. During the Scandinavian swing the Olympic team made in the fall of 1979, Schneider was thrown out of a game in Norway for getting into a scrap. The game ended in a 3–3 tie, the listless effort that triggered Brooks's now-infamous Herbies-in-the-dark session. Out of uniform, the ever-earnest Schneider turned to assistant coach Craig Patrick. "Should I go get my skates on?" Patrick told him not to worry about it.

Buzz Schneider was 25 in Lake Placid and is 50 now, and even as he talks about the debilitating back condition that ended his career and the misadventure his pursuit of pro hockey turned into, he does so without complaint or regret. The Pittsburgh Penguins wanted to sign him after he graduated from the U in 1976, but then the Internal Revenue Service locked the team down and off Schneider went to the Olympics in Innsbruck. A year later, he married Gayle, got cut by the Penguins, and wound up on seven more teams before the season was over, playing in places ranging from Hershey, Pennsylvania, to Oklahoma City to Hampton, Virginia, to Birmingham, Alabama, where Frank Mahovolich wanted him for his Bulls, a new World Hockey Association team. "It was the year I met everyone in hockey," Schneider said. A team in Germany wanted to sign him to a three-year deal, but by then it was 1979 and Brooks, who badly wanted Schneider on the Olympic team, thought he could get a better deal if he performed well in Lake Placid. So Schneider held off, scored five goals in seven games to tie for the team lead, and in fact got an upgraded offer and headed for Bern, Switzerland, where the money and playing conditions were better than the minor leagues in the States, and where he wouldn't have to worry about rampant goon activity.

Schneider played well in Bern and kept playing on U.S. national teams. In 1983 he was on the left wing again, even after Dr. Richard Steadman, Olympic orthopedist, took a look at the herniated disk in his back and said, "What the hell are you doing still playing?" The back got progressively worse, and Schneider, nearing 30 and by then the father of two boys, had decided not to go for a third straight Olympics. If there is a hole in his soul about the way his career played out, he does a great job hiding it. His oldest son, Billy, played Buzz in *Miracle,* the Disney feature film that came out in February 2004. Gayle Schneider cried when she saw her boy on the big screen, playing his dad. "He's better looking than I am," Buzz said.

Billy Schneider had his father's speed. He could run a 4.2 40-yard dash and skate by people as if they were mannequins, and he was the most valuable player on his American Legion team, which won the Legion World Series. Unfortunately, he had his father's back, too, his career done in by the same herniated disk—L-4—as Buzz's was. He appreciated the way his father never pressured him to play, never yelled. Whether he was watching Billy or his younger son, Neil, who played junior hockey in North Dakota, Buzz's preferred seat was in the corner of the rink. You would barely know he was there. "He always felt comfortable with himself. He didn't have to live through us," Billy Schneider said.

When they were selling tractor-trailers together, Lefty Curran used to tell Schneider all the time, "Buzzy, you've got to hang that medal around your neck once in while—let people know what you did." Schneider never would. He lives outside the Twin Cities, but when winter finally lifts, he and Gayle and family and friends spend as much time as they can in the family cabin on Hunter Lake, northwest of Grand Rapids, in the Chippewa National Forest. Buzz's grandfather bought it from a bootlegger during Prohibition. The price was $300. "I think he was in a hurry to get out of town," Buzz said. It came with a still, but the Schneiders were more interested in the stillness. The cabin is called Fugarwe, as in "Where the Fugarwe?" It has 10 acres and 1,500 feet of lakefront, and there are only two other houses on the lake. The nearest store is a half-hour drive. It has been the Schneider family retreat for three-quarters of a century, the serenity and the northern pike and the time together passing from generation to generation. They've made upgrades, added on, gotten plumbing, but the soul of the place is not much different from Buzz Schneider himself. It has never changed.

———

Schneider's goal sent a surge through the crowd and seemed to do the same thing to the Soviets. Not even two seconds later on the game clock, Soviet forward Alexander Skvortsov climbed on Schneider's back, a gratuitous mid-ice mugging that went unwhistled. Skvortsov took a drop pass from teammate Helmut Balderis, the only Latvian on the team and a player scout Lou Vairo said was the fastest skater he ever saw. Skvortsov eluded Christian and fired on Craig, who kicked the puck away with his skate. Balderis got the rebound but shot it wide with Baker strapped to his back, and Zhluktov missed on another good chance, Baker flinging himself on the ice in an effort to block it. Schneider astutely sensed that the Americans were scrambling and disorganized, and pinned the puck against the boards for some needed respite. On the ensuing face-off, Valery Kharlamov ripped a wrist shot low and hard to Craig's glove side. Craig made a spearing, sprawling grab and held on, Soviets swarming around him. The spool of black tape at the end of Craig's stick had unraveled, granting another moment of rest while Eruzione skated to the bench and got a replacement. The Americans were living dangerously. When play resumed, Broten's twenty-foot wrist shot from straight on was turned aside by Tretiak, and then here came Krutov again, sweeping around Eric Strobel and going in on Craig, who alertly dove from the cage and knocked away his centering pass to Maltsev.

More than sixteen minutes into the game, Krutov and

Makarov had unquestionably been the Soviets' most dangerous forwards, creating mayhem on almost every shift. The
legendary No. 1 line of Kharlamov, Petrov, and Mikhailov, by
comparison, had been unthreatening. It was surprising they
hadn't been more effective, but then, the Russians had had a
bizarre eleven days in the Olympics. After defeating Japan,
Holland, and Poland by a combined score of 41–5 in their
first three games, they needed third-period rallies to get by
Finland and Canada. They seemed strangely vulnerable.
"They didn't take a man and their power play, their passing, was not one hundred percent," said Jukka Porvari, the
Finnish captain. "They were just waiting. They had the same
guys, but they weren't playing at the same level."

Part of the problem may have been the absence of defenseman Vladimir Lutchenko, who had already won two
consecutive Olympic golds and dreamed of capping his career with a third. He never got the chance. Immediately after
the Soviets' victory in Madison Square Garden, Lutchenko
was informed by Tikhonov that he was being sent back to
Moscow, along with fellow defenseman Sergei Babinov. At
31, Lutchenko knew Soviet sports bosses had a history of
pushing athletes into retirement soon after they hit 30. Still,
he never saw this coming—and neither did his teammates.
"It was heartbreaking," Lutchenko said.

"Lutchenko was a superstar, and he was my mentor," said
Viacheslav Fetisov, who went on to become one of the first
Russians to play in the NHL and is now Russia's minister of
sport. "His experience and skill is what you need in a game
like that."

There were other issues, as well. In goal Tretiak had been
nowhere near his peak through the preliminary games, and

the offensive production was spotty enough that Tikhonov had even toyed with the notion of splitting up Petrov, Mikhailov, and Kharlamov. They had been together nine years. They talked him out of it. Mike Eruzione wondered out loud about the Soviets' level of motivation.

"You look at a guy like Mikhailov," the captain said in an interview the day before the game. "What does he care? I was watching him in 1972 when I was a senior in high school, and he was a champion. He was with the best team then, and he's with the best team now. He's done everything, won everything. Doesn't there come a time when it doesn't matter anymore whether you win again? If you're the Pittsburgh Steelers and you've won four Super Bowls, do you have to win a fifth to prove that you're good? I don't know. I'm only wondering. I've never been on a team like that."

Jim Craig hadn't either, but he wasn't worrying about the Russians' heads so much as his own body. He had been fighting a sinus infection and recurring headaches for most of the Olympics, and he couldn't even take an over-the-counter decongestant medication for fear of a positive drug test. But at least his ankle was behaving. He had a floating bone chip in it and could never be sure from game to game how much the chip would hurt; before the Garden game, he needed a cortisone injection in his bone. Craig didn't much care for uncertainty. He was particular about his routine, and his gear. His mask was white and angular and open in back, his long dark hair exposed, a jarring contrast to the whiteness in front. It was made for Craig by Ernie Higgins of Norwood, Massachusetts, mask maker for Gerry Cheevers, Ed Giacomin, and other NHL goalies. The masks cost upwards of $100 apiece, but the Olympics were no time to go comparison shopping.

He'd buy them himself and stay with what worked. Craig had one preferred skate-sharpener who knew just how he liked his blades. Before games he would go over every square inch of his equipment, like a surveyor poring over a land map. He'd get the jitters out of his system the day before, when he was snarling and short-tempered, working himself up to full competitive combustion.

Then on game day he tunneled in, kept quiet. He never wanted to send a nervous signal to his teammates. Not even a half-hour before the Russian game, he was sufficiently re-laxed to take care of a ticket request. A burly state policeman stuck his head in the locker room and told Craig that Andy Fila, Craig's goalie coach at Boston University, was outside and needed a place to watch the game with his daughter. Craig asked the cop to take good care of him and then re-turned to his tunnel. Brooks didn't even know this went on. "He would've flipped," Craig said. "If we had lost, it would've been the reason we lost."

When the game started, Craig was a different guy, locked into an almost trancelike concentration, always trying to be extra focused in the first and last five minutes of a game. The other fifty minutes, he'd break down into similar five-minute chunks. He never let himself think about throwing a sixty-minute shutout, just twelve five-minute ones. It was all a self-constructed mind game, Craig's one-save-at-a-time mantra.

After Craig broke up Krutov's pass, the Americans cleared their zone and tried to settle themselves. As Mark Wells, the fourth-line center, flipped the puck in, defenseman Jack O'Callahan skated hard and deep into the Soviet end, lining up Pervukhin along the boards and hitting him with a crushing check, the crowd roaring in delight even as O'Callahan went crashing to the ice. Pervukhin somehow stayed on his feet. O'Callahan got up and skated off.

"You okay?" a couple of teammates asked. O'Callahan gave a little nod. He wasn't okay. He was great. He was playing hockey again, and that was far from certain only a week earlier. O'Callahan had suffered ligament damage in his knee after absorbing a hard check from Valery Vasiliev in the Garden game, an injury that left him highly questionable for the Olympics. Brooks had to submit the final Olympic roster with twenty names on it less than forty-eight hours later, and there was no changing it after that. If he stuck with O'Callahan and he couldn't play, it would be a wasted spot and would leave the team with only five defensemen. If he called back Harvard's Jack Hughes, a defenseman who had been a late cut after spending six months with the team, and then O'Callahan made a quick recovery, he'd be depriving the team of a gritty and galvanizing back-line presence and capable puck-carrier. Brooks loved O'Callahan's toughness, and the depth of his commitment, and early on recognized he could use these traits, and O'Callahan's natural charisma, to reach other players. Brooks called O'Callahan during the beginning of the Olympic run-up and hatched a plan: "When I call you O'Cee and I rip into you, I'm really just trying to send a message to the team. When I call you Jack, then I am talking to you." O'Callahan made sure he listened well. The medical staff was optimistic O'Callahan could get back for the second week. Brooks decided to keep him.

O'Callahan and his three BU teammates—Eruzione, Silk, and Craig—were all descendants of Boston's long history in intercollegiate hockey, which dates to January 19, 1898, and a game between Harvard and Brown on a pond in the city's Dorchester section. Hockey took hold rapidly in Boston, its headquarters in Boston Arena, a drafty, two-tiered building with wooden seats and nonstop schoolboy games and wickedly parochial passions that mirrored those of the city itself. Boston is a forty-nine-square-mile seaside hub, the most compact major city in the country, smaller even than the Denver airport. It teems with ethnic pockets and educational institutions; with NASCAR-wannabe drivers and perhaps the worst signage of any urban road system in America; with citizens who do remarkable things to the letter R: in Bostonese, the BU coach's name isn't Jack Parker but Pahkah. Boston got its name, and its status as capital of Massachusetts Bay Colony, 350 years before Jack O'Callahan rehabbed his knee in Lake Placid. The year was 1630, the name derived from an English town called St. Boat Helper, a port town known for its kindly ways toward strangers. Boston was selected as the capital largely because of its supply of fresh spring water, the colonists having lost many family and friends to illness, and clean water being an essential element to good health.

It was on Greater Boston's frozen water that O'Callahan began to distinguish himself. He grew up in Charlestown, Massachusetts, a tough Irish-Catholic enclave across the river from Boston. His house was a short walk from the site of the Battle of Bunker Hill, where American patriots, outarmed and outmanned, twice repelled British troops before running out of ammunition in 1775. The British attacked again and the patriots finally had to retreat, though they managed to wipe out half the redcoat force before they did. The battle became an enduring symbol of the unyielding American spirit, and O'Callahan, Boston University captain and All-

American, most valuable player of the NCAA tournament in 1978, seemed to relive it every time he hit the ice. "Some of the talks he gave in the locker room, it was almost as if *we* were the ones getting ready to storm Bunker Hill," said Billy LeBlond, a BU teammate. "He would take no prisoners. He'd say, 'If we take this guy out then the rest of the team will follow.' You'd see him playing, with that toothless grin and the scar on his cheek (a souvenir of a broken bottle in a barroom fight) and it was a scary sight. He was a nasty, nasty player. There was no other option than winning. He played hurt a lot, lots of times when he shouldn't have been playing, when other guys wouldn't."

O'Callahan went to Boston Latin High School, a superb student who was fifth in his class and one of the only bespectacled hockey players around, because he couldn't afford contact lenses. O'Callahan was accepted to Harvard but chose Boston University instead, considering it his best chance to compete for a national championship. The headmaster of Boston Latin tried to explain to him that you didn't say no to Harvard. O'Callahan listened, then said no to Harvard.

Plenty of guys were bigger and stronger than the six-foot one-inch, 185-pound O'Callahan, but none were feistier. "There was always this dichotomy to him," said Jack Parker. "He was the kind of guy who could hang with the president of the United States or the Hell's Angels." He looked bookish and unimposing in his horn-rimmed glasses and street clothes; then the game would start and O'Callahan would turn almost demonic. When he was at BU, he estimated that he lost about a dozen teeth and ran his lifetime facial stitches total to between eighty and a hundred. "Some of them came from just growing up in Charlestown," he said once. "Some of them came from not keeping my head up. And some of them came from keeping my head up and not caring anyway. And with each one, I've learned a lesson." O'Callahan was a freshman in 1976 when BU and Minnesota got into their fabled brawl in the NCAA semifinals. He didn't pair up with anybody, Parker recalled. He just ran around the ice and tried to whale on people. An hour after the game O'Callahan was still in his uniform, frozen in front of his locker, the adrenaline rush of the fight fading against the finality of the outcome. The Terriers had lost.

After Lake Placid, O'Callahan played seven years in the NHL with the Chicago Blackhawks, then turned his competitive instincts to the Chicago Mercantile Exchange, where he trades stock-index futures and works with Jack Hughes, his Olympic teammate right up until Lake Placid. The company is called Beanpot Financial Futures, after the famed intracity hockey tournament held each winter in Boston. O'Callahan has a shaved head and a goatee, and a full set of teeth, and hasn't lost his ability to inspire. Years after Lake Placid, O'Callahan and Mike Eruzione made an appearance in Pennsylvania on behalf of the U.S. Olympic Committee, giving a talk to the workers for York, the refrigeration company and prospective Olympic sponsor. There were about 500 employees in the room. O'Callahan and Eruzione each made a short, impassioned speech and then they pulled out their gold medals and passed them all around, from one set of workman's hands to another, the whole place suddenly silent. "You would've thought you were in church and this was communion," Mike Moran, then the chief USOC press officer, said. "People were crying, holding the medals as if they were gold bullion." At the end, the employees gave O'Callahan and Eruzione a standing ovation. York became an Olympic sponsor.

———

With three minutes to play in the period, Makarov tested Craig with a hard drive that the goalie kicked away with his left skate. On his next trip down, Makarov got to the blue line and saw a space between Ken Morrow and Mark Johnson. He made a small leap and squirted through them. He was demanding attention every time he touched the puck, creating on the fly, and then he came again, taking a drop pass from Vladimir Golikov, carrying it in, looking to pass back to Golikov, to the right of the U.S. net. Makarov's pass deflected off Morrow's skate, right back to Makarov, who was in on Craig alone now, and he whipped a shot over Craig's glove into the upper right corner.

The net bulged. The crowd booed. Two to one, Soviet Union.

Craig's shoulders slumped, his discouragement detectable even behind his mask.

There were just over two minutes to play, and the Soviets were gunning for more. After Pavelich's pass for John Harrington, his Minnesota-Duluth teammate, was intercepted, Balderis skated in on the left side and drove a hard low shot that Craig kicked aside, a sparkling save. Skvortsov picked up the rebound and smacked another shot on goal. Craig stopped that, too, with a flick of his glove, popping the puck up in the air with his stick. Craig was almost four minutes into the last five-minute chunk of the period. He didn't want to think about going into the locker room two goals down. Another goal would take the crowd out of it totally. They had to try to stay close, and then see how the Soviets dealt with it.

That was the goal. It seemed a long way off.

The Americans weren't in awe of the Soviets the way they were in the Garden, but they were still giving them too much room to operate. The defensemen were effective at times in stopping the Soviets at the blue line, but once the red jerseys got inside the zone, they usually stayed for a while. With just over a minute to play, Mike Ramsey, the 18-year-old defenseman from the U, used his stick to take down Zhluktov in front, and then slammed Balderis and Skvortsov in the corner, as if he wanted to see if teenage brawn might slow the Russians down. It didn't. When Morrow lost his edge behind the net, Petrov picked the puck away from him and fed Mikhailov in front, another point-blank shot that Craig kicked away with his left skate. The score could easily have been 4–1 or even 5–1 at this point. Craig was keeping the Americans in it. The Soviets kept pushing, playing well but with no special urgency. Patience was as much their hallmark as the jets in their skates. "They would never shoot unless they had the perfect setup," said Warren Strelow, who played against the Soviets in the 1950s as the goaltender for a German all-star team. There was something else at work here, too, though, Makarov acknowledged.

"We believed we could score whenever we wanted," he said. "If we didn't score on a chance, it wasn't big deal because there would be others, many others." The only team the Soviets were concerned about coming into the Olympics was the Czechs. That the Americans had soundly beaten the

Czechs, 7–3, in the second game of the Olympic tournament hadn't seemed to change the Russian mindset.

After Craig turned away Mikhailov, Steve Christoff started out of the U.S. zone and threaded a nice pass to Broten, one of the fastest skaters on the U.S. team. Broten had just made a terrific hustle play, sprinting out to poke the puck away from Kharlamov, who was about to tee up the rebound of Mikhailov's shot. Now Broten was charging over center ice and carrying into the Soviet zone, faking a shot and drawing defenseman Zinetula Bilyaletdinov toward him, then switching to the backhand, centering it, Bilyaletdinov barely getting a piece of his stick on the puck. On the left side, Eruzione skated hard to the goal but couldn't catch up to the puck and it slid through the crease.

There were under thirty seconds left in the first period. On the next U.S. trip into the Soviet zone, Eruzione, at the left point, shot the puck toward the goal, but Christoff was tied up in front and Dave Christian, forward-turned-defenseman, skated in deep, hoping to pick up a loose puck that didn't come. Christian then turned and headed back on defense, the Soviets clearing the puck into the U.S. zone. Ken Morrow got the puck and with seven seconds left dropped it back to Christian, who skated across the U.S. blue line. Morrow shouted to him to shoot. The captain Mikhailov, the only Soviet player nearby, was offering little more than token resistance, seemingly ready to head into the locker room. One stride on the American side of center ice, about 100 feet out, Christian launched a slap shot, a hockey version of a Hail Mary pass. Put it out there and hope for divine intervention. Tretiak blocked it easily with his right pad but allowed the rebound to kick out some twenty feet in front of him, instead of steering it toward a corner. It was a careless bit of work, something you probably would never see him do except in the waning seconds of a period. The Russian defensemen, Pervukhin and Bilyaletdinov, had already begun to relax, straightening up, not much less stationary than statues in Red Square.

"Everybody thought the period was over," said Bilyaletdinov, now the coach of Moscow Dynamo. "We were all watching the clock. It was just a few seconds left." He was sitting in a chair on the second-floor landing of the Dynamo training center, about a half-hour out of Moscow. It was a sunny autumn day. Bilyaletdinov, 48, looked strong and fit, a handsome man with a warm smile and a smooth, deep voice, dark hair flecked with gray. He smiled faintly. "With so little time, you don't think anything can happen. What can happen?"

Chapter Three

BEAT THE CLOCK

Mark Johnson had just hopped over the boards, a late line change for Neal Broten. As Christian wound up for his hundred-foot shot, Johnson skated across the blue line. "I skated hard, because that's the way we were trained and taught. You skate until the horn goes off. If you get by the defensemen you never know," Johnson said. Suddenly, the rebound from Tretiak was coming toward him. Pervukhin and Bilyaletdinov, the defensemen, saw him coming, saw him splitting them, but couldn't mobilize fast enough to stop him. Johnson picked up the puck between the circles. Tretiak had come about eight feet out of his net, almost as if he were ready to skate off. Fewer than three seconds were left. Johnson did not shoot right away. For an instant the time went out of his mind. He was a goal scorer with a puck, one-on-one with a goaltender, and his instincts took over. Johnson stickhandled around Tretiak, deking him, sweeping left, giving himself an open net to shoot for. Johnson flicked the puck.

Tretiak sprawled backward and stretched out his stick, desperately trying to get a piece of it.

The puck shot into the net.

The crowd erupted. Johnson raised his stick and wheeled his right arm twice, bolo-punch style, but even as his teammates mobbed him, he was momentarily filled with panic, for the clock showed three big zeroes. *Did I blow it?* he thought. *Was I too patient?* Kaisla, the referee, huddled with the timekeeper and the other officials. Tikhonov briefly lobbied that the goal had come after time had run out, but the red goal light would not have come on if the horn had sounded. Kaisla ruled that the shot had beaten the clock and that one second remained in the period. Even in the box score, the digital digest of the game's action, the time listed next to Johnson's goal shrieks of its magnitude: 19:59. The game was tied at two. "It was not a question if there was any time left," Kaisla said. "It was a good goal."

———

Mark Johnson knew about Vladislav Tretiak and the Russians years before he faced them in Lake Placid. His entertainment of choice as a kid wasn't *Get Smart* reruns or *Rowan and Martin's Laugh-In* but endless viewings of his father's tape of the 1972 showdown between the Soviet Union and Canada, reel-to-reel inspiration of end-to-end action. On Sunday afternoons, in his father's weekly pickup games against selected University of Wisconsin Badgers in the Dane County Coliseum, he'd put what he saw into practice, wearing one of the red Russian jerseys his father had made for the designated opponents. Each week Mark would be a different magician, Valery Kharlamov or Vladimir Petrov or

Boris Mikhailov, a junior high kid in a Summit Series of his own. The games were intense, the experience invaluable. This was one of the things his father did best: make hockey games.

Bob Johnson was a warm and upbeat character in a sport known for missing teeth and dropped gloves. He grew up in a working-class neighborhood in Minneapolis, the son of a Swedish immigrant who changed the family name from Olars to Johnson upon passing through Ellis Island. Two decades before he would become a legendary coach, he was a 24-year-old Army lieutenant stationed in South Korea. He couldn't bring the neighborhood to Asia, but his passion was more transportable. He carved a rink out of rice paddy, flooded it with water, and got a hockey game going.

"He was like the pied piper. He could create a game of hockey anywhere," said Martha Johnson, his widow.

Bob Johnson died at age 60, late in 1991, only three months after he was diagnosed with inoperable brain cancer. The funeral was held in Colorado Springs, home of USA Hockey. Simultaneous memorial services were conducted in Pittsburgh, where Johnson coached the Penguins to a Stanley Cup only six months before; in Calgary, where he'd once coached the Flames; in Minneapolis and in Madison, Wisconsin, where he'd led the Badgers to three national titles. Badger Bob they called him, and he was renowned for his optimism and his personal mantra, "It's a great day for hockey." Johnson wouldn't look at a glass and believe it was half-full; he'd believe that at any minute it would get a refill. When he was coaching the Flames in 1985–1986, the team staggered through an eleven-game losing streak, the last of them a 9–1 drubbing by the Hartford Whalers. Every game was the one

Johnson was sure would end the drought. The Flames made it to the Stanley Cup finals that year.

Bob Johnson believed in enjoying the journey, and he clung to that philosophy even with the heartache that came when he and Martha became parents of a developmentally disabled child. There was no going back, no use plunging into self-pity. You change what you can and deal with everything else. In handling players, he tried to find the positive things they could do. The sign on the wall of Johnson's Penguins office said, "Never try to teach a pig to sing. It wastes your time and it annoys the pig."

Mark Johnson learned many hockey lessons from his father over the years, about creating open space and finding a goalie's soft spot, but the most enduring lesson he got was unspoken, conveyed in the daily laboratory of life. The lesson was about staying positive in the face of adversity.

"When one door closes here, another one is going to open over there," Mark Johnson said. He was behind his desk in his University of Wisconsin office, three stories up in Camp Randall Stadium, behind a door as red and glossy as a candied apple. "Women's Hockey," it said succinctly. More than a quarter-century after his last Badger shift, he remains the school's greatest player, its all-time leading goal scorer, with 125 goals in three years. He doesn't need his name on a door. Johnson was wearing a gray fleece vest and faded blue jeans and hiking shoes, a uniform that made him look no different from the thousands of students along the lakeside streets of Madison, a quintessential college town with the bicycles, bars, and backpacks to prove it. Situated between two lakes in the south part of the state, Madison has its columned state capitol and its sprawling state university down the street from one another and is equally diverse in its sociopolitical flavors—a place alternately flamingly liberal and ardently middle-American. It was Berkeley with more cheese in the 1960s and 1970s, and Mayberry with more snow the rest of the time, at once deeply progressive and staunchly traditional.

Johnson could fit in anywhere. He always had. He had a mop of brown hair in Lake Placid, over a hawkish nose. The center on Brooks's top line, he led the team in scoring with 11 points in seven games. The hair is much shorter now and swept back, but it is still brown and his body is trim and youthful looking, as unchanged as anyone's on the team. On top of a bookshelf was a photograph of Johnson's goal in the final second of the first period. Tretiak, good guy and a good sport, signed it.

Johnson has been the Badgers' head women's coach since June 2002, a career move he neither expected nor contemplated. Six weeks after the 1980 U.S. Olympic hockey team lit the cauldron to open the 2002 Games in Salt Lake City, Johnson was passed over for the Wisconsin men's job, a position most people assumed would be his. Mark wasn't merely Badger Bob's son, a Madison and Olympic icon. He had paid his dues after an eleven-year NHL career, working for six years as an assistant to the outgoing coach, Jeff Sauer. But athletic director Pat Richter opted to go with Mike Eaves, Johnson's teammate on the Badgers' 1977 national championship team.

Across four decades of a charmed hockey life, Mark Johnson had always been a star. He had won scoring titles, championships, and a gold medal, and nearly made the 1976 Olympic team at age 17. Rejection was something altogether new. Johnson was the captain of the Hartford Whalers when he was traded to the Blues in 1985, one year after scoring 87 points. That stung, but trades were part of NHL commerce.

This was different, personal, the first time Mark Johnson had in effect been told, "We like the other guy better." Richter delivered the news to Johnson in Sauer's office. Later Johnson cried.

"Did it hurt? Oh yeah, it hurt," Johnson said. "But life teaches you that you have to move on, and you try to do it in a fashion that you can walk away with your head held high. It's just like sports, like the final score of a game. It is what it is. It's no use feeling sorry for yourself. We can spend energy that we get nothing out of. No matter how much you complain or how much people think it's a wrong decision, you have to deal with it and move on. I've learned some things from it. I learned about the interview process, and some of the things you might do differently. As I move along, I know that I'll be better because of it. Could I have done a good job? Absolutely. Was I ready to do it? Certainly. I don't think the group was very big that thought I couldn't do it. But it just didn't work out. You just have to have confidence in what you are doing. It's not like it was the end of the world. It's not like I was going to have to get out of hockey."

In thirteen years as a pro hockey player, Mark Johnson lived in Pittsburgh and Minnesota and Hartford and St. Louis and New Jersey, and never found any place that compared to Madison. He was in no rush to go back on the road, or relocate, after he didn't get the men's job at Wisconsin, and neither were his wife, Leslie, his high school sweetheart, or their five children. Still, it seemed inevitable. "I didn't know where we were going, but I was sure we were leaving," Leslie said.

Then the Wisconsin women's job opened up, and Johnson applied for it. People in Madison were stunned when his name surfaced, and Johnson himself wasn't sure if it was a good move. The women's team was in disarray, having gone through three coaches in as many seasons. He wondered if it would stigmatize him in any way, if he would still be able to coach men if he chose to. Johnson talked with Ben Smith, coach of the U.S. women's national team, a man who had made the successful crossover from men to women, and whose assistant, Julie Sasner, used to coach the Wisconsin women. Johnson heard nothing but positives from Smith, about the players' passion for the game and their coachability.

He decided to take the job, and the impact was immediate. Johnson was the co-coach of the year in the Western Collegiate Hockey Association his first year, when Wisconsin finished 22–8–5. In his second year, 2003–2004, he led the Badgers to a No. 6 national ranking and a 25–6–3 record.

Johnson's salary and visibility do not compare with Mike Eaves's, but he insists it doesn't bother him. He has never made any effort to cash in on his Olympic stature or to get preferential treatment. He went to his first Green Bay Packers game with two of his boys and close friend Pete Giacomini late in 2003. Nobody in Lambeau Field recognized him. "It's exactly the way he likes it," Giacomini said. The Johnsons once had a garage sale at their house, and Giacomini was shocked to see Mark's hockey gloves from Lake Placid on a table. They were priced at $3.

"Are you nuts?" he asked Leslie.

"Who would want them?" she replied.

"Your kids are going to want them," Giacomini said. The gloves were pulled off the table. To underscore the value of such things, Giacomini got Johnson's permission to put a pair of game-worn Olympic hockey pants on sale on eBay.

They sold for $1,250.

The pants had been in the corner of the garage with a bicycle on top of them. That's how the Johnson home is, a bustling place thick with entropy, hockey gear strewn about, kids coming and going, plans made on the fly, with minimal worry and a conviction that things will work out. Leslie has about a thousand things going at once and balances them with joyful frenzy. "It's an interesting marriage," Giacomini said. "Mark's introverted, and he married a cruise director." Mark used two-by-twelves to build a backyard rink at the new house, thirty-two feet wide by fifty-five feet long. He's out there with the kids all the time. "There's not anything more pure than skating on a sheet of ice under the stars," Johnson said. "When I die and get to heaven, that's what it's going to be: skating all day and all night, just a pickup game forever."

If Johnson had initial doubts about coaching women, the feeling was mutual. Sis Paulsen was the Badgers captain in Johnson's first year. She played for a boys' team in high school in Eau Claire, Wisconsin, and used to watch footage of the U.S.–Soviet Union game in Lake Placid for inspiration. Paulsen didn't know what to expect from Johnson. The concern melted away in about the time it takes to resurface a rink, Johnson's first practice unfolding with briskness and creativity. "You can't make conditioning drills fun. And he made it fun," Paulsen said. "I learned so much from him in one year—more than I learned in my hockey career."

Johnson is much more teacher than screamer, and it has long been thus. His first head coaching job was in 1995–1996, when he coached the Madison Monsters in the Colonial Hockey League. The joke was that when Johnson finally got angry at the team and kicked a water bottle in the locker room, he made sure it was empty. The Wisconsin women had their own jokes and appreciated how Johnson—male coach surrounded by twenty-four young women—would take them and banter back. One sunny morning early in the 2003–2004 season, forward Jackie Friesen knocked on his office door and asked if she could get a copy of a tape from a game against Maine a few days earlier.

"You want to watch yourself score that goal again?" Johnson teased.

Johnson assured his team when he took over that this was not just a stopover until he could get a men's job. Six months later, his words were put to the test. Tony Granato, Johnson's friend, fellow Badger alum, and coach of the Colorado Avalanche, asked Johnson if he would be interested in joining his staff as an assistant. What would be a more ideal destination than Colorado, where his mother and two sisters live and where Johnson runs a summer camp? Who better to coach with than Granato? Johnson talked to Leslie, his family, a few friends. His kids wanted to go. After a few days, Johnson called Granato, expressed his gratitude, and said no thanks.

"I don't think I would've had the courage to walk into the locker room and tell these players I was leaving," Johnson said. "I've got signs on the wall that say, 'Commitment, Passion, Integrity.' If I am going to be a good coach and people are going to listen and respect me, I have to walk the walk, as they say.

"There was another, underlying part of it, too. I've coached two of the last four [men's] world championship teams, and NHL players. When a guy is making six, seven, eight million dollars a year, you can coach him, but are you teaching him, influencing him? On the men's side, if you're dealing with football, basketball, hockey, in the back of those kids' minds, they want to play for money one day. And that changes the parameters of a lot of things that we deal with, especially with the money that's out there now. On the women's side, their dreams are playing on the national team, in the Olympics. They're here for the right reasons. It's like when we played. Their dreams are similar to what ours were."

Johnson's 1980 teammates called him Magic for the things he could do with the puck. "He was our Gretzky, without the protection," Jim Craig said. Like his basketball counterpart, this Magic Johnson was utterly unselfish and made everyone around him better, an athlete whose eyes and hands moved in lockstep, with speed and unerring dexterity. When his father considered choosing him for the 1976 Olympic team, there were whispered objections of nepotism, much as there were later that year when Mark joined the Badgers as a highly touted freshman. Mark got pounded by upperclassmen during preseason, daily intrasquad gut checks. He never backed down, never stopped working. Soon he won them over. The coach's kid could play. "He was just one of those athletes who could do anything," Jeff Sauer said. "You put a golf club in his hand, and he could play golf well. Put a racquetball racquet in his hand, and he could play racquetball well. He wasn't a big, strong guy, but he could play anything."

Johnson's Olympic year did not begin auspiciously. He got food poisoning during the 1979 Sports Festival. Bob Suter, his roommate and Badger teammate, tried to nurse him back to health. George Nagobads, the team doctor, insisted it was nothing serious, but Martha Johnson wasn't convinced, and she brought Mark to the hotel where she was staying, feeding him clear liquids and Jell-O, working up to toast. Brooks didn't have a problem with the maternal interference. If there was any player who didn't need to audition, it was Mark Johnson. Brooks had seen plenty of him over the previous three years of Gopher-Badger games and knew all about his slick-skating, quick-thinking game, the way he braided creativity with a grit far greater than his five feet nine inches and 160 pounds would suggest. In the closing minutes of the 7–3 demolition of Czechoslovakia, Johnson suffered an injured shoulder when Czech defenseman Jan Neliba whacked him with a late hit, a play that sent Brooks into a rage. "You're going to eat that goddamn Koho," the coach shouted, referring to the Finnish stick that Neliba brandished. Brooks couldn't imagine life without Mark Johnson anchoring his No. 1 line. It didn't matter whose son he was.

Herb Brooks and Bob Johnson, the two most decorated college hockey coaches the United States has ever had, were not just fierce rivals. They were all but sworn enemies, the WCHA version of Alexander Hamilton and Aaron Burr, minus the pistols. When Johnson was assembling the 1976 Olympic team, two prime candidates for it were Reed Larson and Tom Vanelli, stars for Brooks's team at the U. Larson could well have been the top collegiate defenseman in the country. The pair never even tried out. Vanelli said he didn't know the team was interested in him and Larson said the first time he was approached was on Christmas in 1975, about six weeks before the Olympics. Some people around the Olympic team believed that Brooks held the players back because he was more interested in winning a national championship than helping Bob Johnson win an Olympic medal. "Herb didn't want [Vanelli and Larson] leaving," said Art

Berglund, the general manager of the 1976 team. "Certainly those guys were not encouraged to try out for the team." But people close to Brooks insist the coach would never do such a thing, that he would've let the players go if they'd been asked. Whatever happened, Buzz Schneider and Rob Harris were the lone Gophers on the team. When he was putting together his own team before 1980, Brooks was deeply worried that Bob Johnson might withhold Mark, an option that Mark Johnson himself says was never considered.

Part of the distaste between Brooks and Johnson was rooted in nothing more complicated than geography, two ferociously competitive men, each with his own hockey fiefdom, 300 miles apart on Interstate 94. Johnson grew up in south Minneapolis, Brooks in east St. Paul. Both were hard-driving but achieved their ends through vastly different means, Johnson gregarious and sunny, a master of positive reinforcement, Brooks remote and sometimes frosty, a master of motivating through fear.

Brooks may have been headstrong, but he was also pragmatic. He couldn't stand Badger Bob, but he needed Badger Mark. Ten days into the fall trip to Europe, Brooks called Johnson into his hotel room and basically told him that it was his team and that United States would go as far as Johnson could take it. Johnson was flabbergasted.

"If you looked at that whole group of players and looked at the coach and asked yourself, 'Who is going to have the toughest time?,' I would've been the one you would've picked," Johnson said. "But with all great coaches, they have a certain vision. It's just a matter of becoming a salesman and selling the player you're working with on what your vision is, and Herb was able to do that."

Brooks's words of confidence were empowering and liberating for Mark Johnson. He could play his game and enjoy the journey, the way his father always had. His memories of the road to Lake Placid are as vivid as his memories of the Games themselves: playing pond hockey with the guys in Burnsville, Minnesota; running the hill next to the Olympic arena in full gear, before and after practice; sitting by the campfire in the woods of Oolu, Finland, about 100 miles from the Arctic Circle. That was in September, and it was quiet and peaceful, and as the flames flickered, the U.S. Olympic team sat together and joked and told stories and drank some beer, a spontaneous gathering in the north woods, on the way to history.

Mark Johnson felt blessed. It made him wonder again why blessings aren't more evenly distributed.

Diane Johnson is 40 years old, the youngest of Bob and Martha Johnson's five children. She spent almost twenty-five years living in the Southern Wisconsin Center in Union Grove, Wisconsin, before moving to a small group home in Madison several years ago. She likes to go out to McDonald's and make crafts in her workshops. She is a happy person with a pleasant disposition. She does not use words. Diane Johnson has the functioning of an 18-month-old.

"It's part of the perspective we have as a family about fame and fortune," said brother Peter Johnson, a former scout for the Toronto Maple Leafs who now runs the rink in the town of Verona, outside Madison. "Maybe that's why our dad was so positive. Because he saw the other side of life, he took every day as a gift."

Jeff Sauer, who has known the Johnson family for most of his life, used to babysit for Diane. "It took a long, long time for Bob to accept it. I don't know if he ever did," Sauer said.

Diane was a beautiful baby, pink and perfect. There were no signs of anything being wrong until she was 14 months old and Martha noticed that she kept on trying to grasp things, not with her fingers but with the back of her hand. Again and again the baby tried to pick things up that way, even after her mother showed her how to open her hand. One day Diane got into the bathtub and turned on the hot water and let it run, burning herself so severely she needed to be hospitalized. It became increasingly difficult to care for her, especially with the needs of four other children to balance. She needed constant supervision. She needed to be in a safer place. When Diane was seven, Bob and Martha Johnson placed their youngest child in the Southern Wisconsin Center.

"I can't imagine how difficult it was for my parents to make that decision," Mark said.

He was 12 when Diane moved out. His mother doesn't believe it's a coincidence that around that time Mark was acting up in school, a high-energy, smart-alecky kid, more mischievous than naughty, a boy trying to find his way.

"Mark was one of the ones most affected when Diane left," Martha Johnson said. "He had a hard time understanding why we couldn't keep her. She was there and then suddenly she was gone. It was almost like someone died."

Diane was 16 years old when the U.S. hockey team became famous in 1980. She knew nothing about the specifics, of course, about her brother's starring role. Mark Johnson, a devout Christian, has long wondered why it was Diane who was different, why her world was so limited and tightly drawn while his has been so global and challenging; why a sister and brother from an identical gene pool can face such different fates, one life built around finger paints and Golden Arches, the other around international acclaim and Olympic glory.

"Sometimes you can't answer the why questions," Mark Johnson said. "You just have to trust God and be faithful. You have to be thankful and try to lead your life in a way that people can look to it as an example."

———

Thinking the first period was over after Johnson's goal, the Soviets retired to their dressing room, to drink their hot tea and lemon and brace for a certain reaming out from Tikhonov. When they were summoned back out by Kaisla to play the final second of the period, the only skaters for the Soviets at first were Mikhailov and Krutov. O'Callahan urged Kaisla to drop the puck and give the United States a chance for an empty-net goal. Then Makarov came out, the third and last skater. Not many people in the building noticed that No. 1 in red, backup goaltender Vladimir Myshkin, was skating toward the goal. The Field House rocked with the most raucous "U-S-A, U-S-A" chant yet as Kaisla dropped the puck for the face-off that restarted the game and ended the period. There was a huge cheer when the horn sounded. The U.S. team headed back to Locker Room 5. They had been outplayed, but the score was tied, the charge of Johnson's goal flowing through them like a current. "I've never, ever experienced that kind of emotion and the kind of adrenaline rush that I felt in that room after the first period," forward Eric Strobel said. "It was like your skates weren't even touching the ground. It was almost as if everyone was starting to believe, 'Hey, we can skate with these guys.' "

In the other locker room, Tikhonov was directing most of his tirade at Tretiak, the most famous goaltender in the world and owner of two Olympic gold medals. Tretiak certainly had not been at his best in these Games, and he had let in a couple of soft goals against Canada, and now he had wobbled in the first period against the Americans. But none of the Soviet players were worried about it. Tretiak's history and temperament made it a moot issue.

"Every goal for Vlady was like a tragedy," Makarov said. "If he let up bad goal, that was it. He didn't like to be screamed at. You didn't need to scream at him. He would slam the door. There wouldn't be any more. He would take responsibility for his mistakes and then that would be the end of it. No more goals."

Tretiak in fact yielded no more goals that night, but only because his work was finished.

Tikhonov, still irate, announced that Myshkin would be finishing the game. Myshkin had shut out the NHL All-Stars the year before, so this was no International Hockey League retread. Still, the Soviet players were stunned. It was akin to pinch-hitting for Babe Ruth in the seventh game of the World Series. Defenseman Sergei Starikov wasn't even sure at first he heard Tikhonov correctly.

"How do you do that?" Starikov said. He was in an upstairs room over the rink where he runs a hockey school in Union, New Jersey, a short, thick-bodied man, his voice still full of disbelief. "It's one thing to put me on the bench, or even to put Mikhailov on the bench, but to put Tretiak on the bench? It felt like a big hole had been put in our team."

Said Makarov, "The whole team was not happy when Tikhonov made the switch. It was the worst moment of

Vlady's career. Tikhonov was panicking. He couldn't control himself. That's what it was—panic." Bill Torrey, then general manager of the New York Islanders, was at the game with a host of other NHL executives. He went to get coffee at intermission and came back to see Tretiak sitting forlornly at the end of the bench. "I've known Tikhonov twenty-five or thirty years and I couldn't believe he did that," Torrey said. "I think Tikhonov totally wrote off the Americans after the 10–3 game. I think he thought they wouldn't be a problem and it wouldn't matter who was in goal. What he was trying to do was shake up his team. If he could replace the great Tretiak, that should send a message to the rest of the guys."

Tikhonov himself does not dispute that opinion. Years later, he sat in his office after coaching CSKA to a victory in its home arena, a boxy and indelicate place, grayish brown and hulking, on a Moscow avenue called Prospekt Leningradsky. His office was maybe three meters by four meters, a spartan space with a table, bookshelf, and pennants of all the teams he has coached on the walls. Videotapes were crammed into every available space. "The biggest mistake of my career was replacing Tretiak with Myshkin," Tikhonov said through an interpreter. "Tretiak always played better after he gave up a goal. The decision was a result of getting caught up in emotions. After Tretiak gave up the rebound and let in the soft goal by Mark Johnson, my blood was boiling. It was my worst mistake, my biggest regret." He paused. He smiled faintly when he was asked if he has watched a videotape of the game. "There's no need for me to see the game. I saw it once," he said.

Tikhonov had a wiry physique and a brisk splay-footed walk and, with his jerky head movements and slicked-back hair, looked like a cross between a rooster and Eddie Munster all grown up. His was a taut personality, one in marked contrast to the blustering ebullience of Anatoly Tarasov, and his system of play was just as different. Tarasov encouraged his players to be creative and intuitive, to think the game on the go. As long as the team was being aggressive, he was usually content. During practices, defensemen were actually punished for sliding the puck back and forth to each other instead of pushing the attack. The autocratic Tikhonov was more conservative and controlling. His gave the players' more criticism and less rope. He talked endlessly about the game's geometry and knew exactly how he wanted the angles to be.

"With Tarasov, no matter how much you worked in practice, you played," said Lou Vairo, one of the earliest American devotees of Russian hockey. "With Tikhonov, no matter how much you played, you worked."

Said Starikov, "There was constant pressure, pressure, pressure—every day, every minute from Tikhonov. He was always on us: 'Remember this, remember this, don't do this, don't do this, don't do this.' It was always negative. The creativity was choked out of us." Nearly everyone connected to the 1980 Soviet team considered it to be the strongest Olympic team the Russians had ever put together, yet there was a stiffness about the team's play, a puzzling lack of fluidity. "You could feel unrest in the air," Vladimir Lutchenko said.

Tikhonov took over CSKA and the national team in 1977 and was making his Olympic debut in Lake Placid. Lutchenko wasn't the last of Tarasov's former players to be weeded out. Tarasov hadn't been at the helm since 1972, but he remained a towering figure—Lombardi by Red Square.

"Tikhonov wanted to get rid of older guys," said Makarov, who went on to star on the celebrated KLM line on the Soviet national team in the 1980s. "The older guys were more powerful. They had been professionals for ten years. He was young coach. Nobody knew him. He wanted young guys so he could do what he wanted. He wanted Play-Doh players."

Tikhonov came to the Soviet national team from Dynamo Riga and had long since established a reputation for fanatical attention to detail. As an assistant to Tarasov in the 1968 Olympics in Grenoble, France, he was one of about twenty people in the stands for a game between Japan and Bulgaria. While other Soviet officials were hunting for a party with free food and drink, Tikhonov was dissecting Bulgarian breakouts. He had a little pocket notebook that he always carried with him. His wife, Tatiana, often woke up in the middle of the night to find Viktor sitting up in bed with the light on, jotting notes and thoughts into the book.

"Sometimes when you are sleeping you get great ideas that will not be there when you wake up," he explained once. "So I put it down in my notebook." Even when the Tikhonovs had company for dinner, he would have the book at the table. The joke among his players was that Tikhonov's job was hockey and his hobby was hockey. It wasn't easy when the national team would be holed up in its training camp in Novogorsk, about a half-hour out of Moscow. "You have breakfast with Tikhonov, lunch with Tikhonov, dinner with Tikhonov," Makarov said. "It could be too much. Guys would be relaxing at night watching television and when Tikhonov would come in, a couple of guys would slowly get up and leave. Then a few more would leave, and then a few more. Pretty soon Tikhonov would be watching TV by himself."

Viktor Tikhonov did not have an easy life growing up. His father died in World War II, and the family lived in a hardscrabble Moscow neighborhood. Viktor went to work as a bus mechanic to help bring in money. He became enamored of hockey and had a staunch backer in his mother, who viewed it as a way to help her son avoid the trouble other neighborhood boys were getting into. He was always playing, studying, and watching; being sociable or communicative did not come as easily. All through the 1980 Games he had a bout with the flu, his temperature spiking and then sinking, the team doctor finally hospitalizing him for observation a day before the game against the United States. Tikhonov never talked about it, and he never took antibiotics because he didn't believe in them. His mother was gravely ill during the 1994 Olympics in Norway. He visited her immediately before leaving but again shared nothing about it except to his closest friends. He doesn't talk about his successes much, either. Few of his honors or awards are on display in his Moscow apartment or in his windowless office in the CSKA Arena. Tikhonov grants no special treatment to himself or to any of his players.

Tikhonov left the Soviet national team in 1994 but was brought back in 2003 at the age of 73, his mission to restore Russian hockey to prominence. With the breakup of the Soviet Union in 1991, state support of the sports system crumbled and so did the staggering run of prosperity that had yielded twenty-three world championships between 1954 and 1993. His return came just six weeks before the death of Herb Brooks. Late one autumn night at the CSKA Arena, after his team had won an early-season game, Tikhonov was preparing to leave the arena when someone told him his appearance had changed little over the decades. "My wife says that when women want to keep meat fresh for a long time, they put it in the refrigerator," Tikhonov said. He pointed in the direction of the rink, about fifty yards away. "I have spent my whole life in the refrigerator." The coach smiled.

His spirits were not so buoyant at the end of twenty minutes in his first Olympic semifinal, as he stood and watched Mark Johnson tie the score while his cavalcade of hockey stars watched along with him. On the opposite bench, Herb Brooks smiled tightly, pumped his fist, and looked as if he'd gotten away with something. The horn sounded, and the ending was just the beginning.

INTRIGUE IN
THE WOODS

The mood in Lake Placid was not very placid at all as the Games began. On Saturday evening, February 9, hours after the Soviet Union trounced the United States in Madison Square Garden, Secretary of State Cyrus Vance addressed the eighty-second session of the International Olympic Committee at a reception at the Lake Placid Club. He warmly welcomed committee members and the world's athletes, then ended the feel-good portion of his presentation faster than you can say "boycott." This wasn't merely an Olympic year. It was an election year, and the Games offered President Jimmy Carter a chance—maybe his last chance—to stop his freefall in the polls. Traditionally, the opening of the IOC meeting is a politics-free forum, conflicts swept under the rings. It was the equivalent of dropping the gloves and yanking the sweater over the head as Vance, representing the president, addressed the Soviet invasion of Afghanistan and the upcoming Summer Games in Moscow:

From their beginnings in ancient Greece, the Olympics have symbolized some of humanity's noblest principles. Foremost among these is peace. . . . In the view of my government, it would be a violation of this fundamental Olympic principle to conduct or attend Olympics Games in a nation which is currently engaging in an aggressive war and has refused to comply with the world community's demand to halt its aggression and withdraw its forces. . . . To hold the Olympics in any nation that is warring on another is to lend the Olympic mantle to that nation's actions.

The United States' position on the Soviets' actions had already been emphatically staked out with a grain and trade embargo and U.S. support of the United Nations resolution condemning the invasion. Still, Lord Michael Killanin of Ireland, the IOC president, received an unwelcome surprise when he reviewed an advance copy of Vance's remarks. Killanin found them so offensive that he called the Soviet delegation and suggested they skip the affair. The Soviets, who had briefly considered a boycott of their own in Lake Placid, did just that. Amid the crackling of the fireplace and the tinkling of cocktail glasses, the tension in the room was thicker than a North Country snowbank.

Let the Games begin, and get ready to duck the rhetoric.

"That night was the only time in my life I've been embarrassed to be an American," said Phil Wolff, the chief of staff for the Lake Placid Games. "I spent three years fighting in World War II. Nobody has a deeper love of this country than I do, but that was not right to be so derogatory and political when we're supposed to be welcoming all our guests from around the world."

The Olympics had become vastly more security-conscious following the tragic massacre of Israeli athletes in the Munich Games in 1972, and the political climate added another level of vigilance. There were so many intelligence and counterintelligence personnel in town that at times the village looked like the set of a James Bond movie, with more pine trees. Top Lake Placid security officials went to an FBI training school prior to the Games and had briefings with the agency each morning. The Olympic security force numbered about 1,000, not including undercover federal agents. With surveillance cameras in the woods surrounding the Olympic Village, along with officers with guns, leisurely strolls were not advisable.

"There was a very strong FBI presence, that's for sure," said Mike Down, a retired sergeant with the New York State Police, the lead security agency for the Games. The same was true for the KGB. Steve Yianoukos, one of the Zamboni drivers for the Olympic Arena, recalled how a squadron of KGB men would materialize during Soviet practice sessions. On the Saturday morning after the U.S. game, Yianoukos saw a state trooper motioning to Tretiak. A look of panic crossed Tretiak's face; he apparently thought the officer's gesture was a suggestion that he defect. "All the guy wanted was to take a picture," Yianoukos said.

Soviet officials were sufficiently worried about the heightened tensions that they urged their athletes to stay close to the Village. When the Soviets were in New York City, there was a similar warning to avoid walking around. "They weren't so afraid of us defecting. They were afraid that someone would do something to us," said Sergei Makarov. "Before

1980 when we traveled we had maybe one KGB guy with us. When we went to America the KGB guys were everywhere."

You never knew where the undercover officers would turn up. The mayor of Moscow was provided a car and driver during his stay—a driver whose day job was as a federal agent, according to Wolff, the chairman of security for the organizing committee. Wolff didn't know whether the driver was FBI or CIA or who got him behind the wheel, but he did know that the mayor knew exactly what was up. One day early in the second week of the Olympics the mayor and a group of Soviet officials stopped by Wolff's office early in the afternoon. They brought out a bottle of vodka, as was customary; Wolff had his shot glass handy. "I want to thank you again for our driver," the mayor said with a twinkle. "He is doing an excellent job and we appreciate so much how he is helping us."

Agents on both sides were disguised in an assortment of ways. They might be interpreters or valets or delegation officials with a suspiciously fuzzy scope of responsibility. Sergeant Mike Down said that one of the most popular pastimes among top security officials in both camps at the Games was trying to figure out who the undercover officers were. It was usually easy enough to do. You told a joke and then you watched the faces for a reaction. If the guy smiled, you could pretty much know he was an undercover agent, because agents were the ones who knew English.

While the turbulence surrounding the Games had no direct bearing on the hockey tournament—Brooks never talked to his players about the Cold War or winning it for capitalism—the coach was completely comfortable with the notion of building a team into the enemy. He would regularly cultivate us-vs.-them scenarios to motivate his players, taking slights, real or imagined, and skating with them. His 1973–1974 Gophers—a team of American kids from Minnesota—heard Brooks constantly spouting about how nobody believed an American team could compete against Canadians (nearly all college hockey teams had sizable contingents of Canadian imports). "It was a steady drip on us all year: 'You guys are going to prove something to people,' " Don Micheletti, a standout forward on the team, said. "By the time the playoffs came around we were convinced we weren't going to lose." When the Gophers played Boston University in the NCAA tournament, the opponent wasn't just a school from the East; it was an arrogant bunch of Canucks and Preppies who thought you were lucky to be on the ice with them. Of the epic Minnesota-Wisconsin battles, Gary Smith said, "Herb had me so brainwashed about Bob Johnson that I thought he was the biggest ass on earth, and I never even met the man." Brooks always had a destination in mind, and if he needed to create bumps or ill-feeling to get there, it was no big deal. The coach was skewered in Lake Placid for ignoring Olympic protocol and not making his players available to the press after games, the suggestion being that he wanted all the attention on himself. The truth was that Brooks had spent months building the spirit and substance of a team, and he didn't want its bond getting loosened by having Jim Craig and Mark Johnson commanding all the headlines and everyone else getting ignored.

Brooks relished stirring things up and rarely had trouble finding targets for criticism. Few got more of it over the years than the powers-that-be at AHAUS, now USA Hockey.

"There are a bunch of big, fat, cigar-smoking people running hockey in this country," Brooks would say, a depiction that Walter Bush, the USA Hockey executive who gave him a shot at interviewing for the Olympic job, didn't care for: "I told him, 'Herb, I may be big and I may be fat, but I don't smoke cigars.' " Days before the Americans left Minnesota for their training camp and their pre-Olympic exhibition schedule in the late summer of 1979—an international itinerary that had been planned more than a year—Brooks told general manager Ken Johannson he wanted to chuck it all because it didn't give his players enough competition on the larger European-style rinks that they would play on in the Olympics. By the fall of 1979, it was Johannson who decided to chuck it, stepping down as general manager and being replaced by Ralph Jasinski. At almost every coaching stop Brooks made, he took on management and sometimes players and wasn't shy about going public, explaining in large measure why a coaching genius could have seven jobs in a ten-year span after the 1980 Olympics. When he was with the Rangers, Brooks called team captain Barry Beck a coward in the *New York Times*.

"Herb always loved a good scrap," Tim Taylor said.

——

The oldest of three children of Herb and Pauline Brooks, Herbert Paul Brooks grew up in a working-class neighborhood on the east side of St. Paul. His mother, by all accounts, was a stern and tough-minded woman who tolerated little nonsense from her three children. Even as a young man, friends said, Herb had a striking intensity about him, a quality that was in marked contrast to the way of his younger brother, David, who followed Herb to the University of Minnesota and was his 1964 Olympic teammate, an affable, life-of-the-party sort. Herb was an accomplished student and fine athlete, a left-handed kid who played a good first base and was a sweet-skating forward on St. Paul's Johnson High School team that won the Minnesota state title in 1955. He went on to study psychology and star in hockey at the U, where he played for John Mariucci, a pioneering force in hockey throughout the state, a man who was one of the few Americans to play in the National Hockey League in the 1940s and became one of the earliest champions of American players. It would be a cause that his pupil Brooks would devote his rinkside life to, though the devotion could manifest itself in peculiar ways.

Nobody on the 1980 team was more familiar with Brooks than Steve Janaszak, who was the goalie on two NCAA title teams for Brooks and MVP of the 1979 tournament, and who once went three months without hearing so much as a hello from Brooks. And he wasn't even in the doghouse. "Traumatic is the best way to describe playing for him," Janaszak said. Other players at the U took to calling Brooks "the Mute" for the way he'd wordlessly walk by them in the hallway. Dave Silk got on a hotel elevator on the thirty-fourth floor one morning in Finland, early in the European swing in the fall of 1979. On the twenty-fifth floor, the elevator stopped and in walked Brooks. The coach looked away, said nothing. Silk didn't know what to say or do. He stared straight ahead and watched the floor numbers go down. Finally they got to the lobby. "It was the longest elevator ride of my life," Silk said.

Restlessness came easily to Herb Brooks. Rest and relaxation did not. Meals were not something to savor; they were an annoying necessity, like putting gas in the car. "Eating wastes so much time," he used to tell his wife, Patti. His idea of downtime was spending a day planting around the house. Patti and the kids gave him a hammock one Father's Day, and they were all amazed when they actually caught him in it one day.

Brooks also could be maddeningly obstinate. When he was coaching the Gopher freshmen, the varsity made the Frozen Four in Boston and the Minnesota athletic director told Brooks that there wasn't enough money in the budget for him to make the trip. Brooks thought that was wrong, so he quit. Minnesota North Stars GM Lou Nanne and a host of others tried to smooth over Brooks's long-running rift with Wisconsin coach Bob Johnson but never got anywhere. Brooks would sometimes have spats with friends—Nanne among them—and not talk to them for a year or two. In the late summer of 1983, the next edition of the U.S. Olympic hockey team was in Lake Placid, training for the Sarajevo Games, at the same time that Brooks's New York Rangers were in town. Lou Vairo, who succeeded Brooks as Olympic coach, asked him if he would speak to the players. Brooks was at odds with USA Hockey—he usually was, often over player-development matters—and declined the offer, no matter that the roster included 1980 veterans John Harrington and Phil Verchota. In 1988, before the Calgary Games, he did the same thing, declining to say so much as "Good luck" to coach Dave Peterson's team.

"I've never seen anyone carry things as far as he would for a principle," said Glen Sonmor, a friend who was Brooks's freshman coach at the U in 1955. Sonmor knew Brooks for nearly five decades and still had a hard time figuring him out. "I used to say to Herb, 'Why do you always have to tilt at windmills?' He was always taking people on. Whatever I thought he wouldn't do, he would do. Whatever I thought he would do, he wouldn't do."

Sonmor wondered sometimes if Herb Brooks just couldn't stand prosperity. Nanne offered Brooks the North Stars job in 1978. Brooks would've been working for an old friend in his home city in the NHL, but he torpedoed it by demanding a three-year contract.

"Even I have a two-year contract," Nanne told him. "The owners don't want to go longer than that."

"I'm not doing it," Brooks said. Seven years later, Nanne was negotiating with Brooks again to coach the North Stars. A deal was reached, a flight booked to meet owner Gordon Gund, a press conference called. The night before the meeting with Gund, Art Kaminsky called Nanne and said Brooks wanted a $250,000 bonus if he were ever fired.

"Art, I can't pay a guy more to fail than to succeed," Nanne said.

"Call him. You know how he is," Kaminsky said. Nanne called Brooks, who would not back off—and wasn't hired. Two years later, Brooks and Nanne finally did reach a deal, but then Nanne left to accept an offer in the financial-services sector. In the throes of a horrible season, Brooks basically demanded a five-year contract from the new general manager—and was sent packing again.

In the summer of 2002, some six months after Brooks returned to coach the U.S. Olympic team to a silver medal in Salt Lake City (a team of NHL stars, not little-known collegians), Glen Sather, general manager of the Rangers, wanted

Brooks to come back to New York to coach the Rangers. After much back-and-forth, Nanne—now working as Brooks's agent—struck a multimillion-dollar deal. He, Brooks, and their friend and player agent Neil Sheehy opened a bottle of wine to celebrate at a St. Paul restaurant. The next morning, Brooks said he wanted stock options from the Garden's parent company, Cablevision. The deal fell through.

Said John Harrington, "It was almost like he was having a midlife crisis for the last twenty years. It was like he wanted to be doing something, but he didn't know what it was. He was searching for something, but didn't know what it should be."

Brooks and the Rangers talked again in the summer of 2003, but nothing worked out. Nanne said Brooks knew for sure that he wanted to get back in the league this time and was energized by the challenge of showing what his free-flowing style of play could do in an era when goals sometimes seem to come only a little more often than presidential pardons. "I think he was beginning to realize his own mortality and see that it was time to start enjoying things more," Nanne said. A day after their last conversation, Herb Brooks was gone.

———

Lake Placid organizers didn't have to deal with Brooks's sometimes mysterious ways, and it was a good thing; they had an abundance of international tension to occupy them. It was something that they had not bargained for when they won the right to host the 1980 Games. They were just looking to promote their hometown, a village of 2,800 people in the town of North Elba, which is 30 miles from the nearest interstate highway and more than 100 miles from the nearest domestic airport of any significance. As George and Stephen Ortloff note in their comprehensive Olympic history of the region, *Lake Placid: The Olympic Years,* it's possible to head southwest into the woods across from the village elementary school and hike 90 miles before you see another person—lots of deer and maybe a bear, but no people. Along the way, you would encounter a total of five roads, three of them paved.

Hugging the shoreline of two lakes, set among the High Peaks, the village is located in the middle of six and a half million acres known as the Adirondack Park, in a county (Essex) that is the second largest in New York State but the second smallest in population, with an estimated 35,000 residents. The first people to settle in Lake Placid were Mohawk Indians. In the early nineteenth century a loose procession of New England farmers headed west from Vermont, over Lake Champlain, traveling a rough wagon track called the Northwest Bay–Hopkinton Road. The farmers found land that was stunningly beautiful but hospitable to only those with the hardiest of constitutions. Indeed, the first recorded fatality in the area—a man named Arunah Taylor—died "by cold in the woods," according to records. The year 1816, the "Year without a Summer" in the Northern Hemisphere, brought more fierce cold, destroying crops and causing widespread starvation, prompting a mass exodus from the region. The town of North Elba remained almost completely unpopulated until the 1840s, when Gerrit Smith, a wealthy landowner and prominent abolitionist, began making land parcels available. Seeking to help black families gain a financial foothold, Smith gave away over 400 plots of 40 acres each to black residents of New York State. While not many black families availed themselves of the opportunity, Smith's generosity made the area well known among abolitionists, including John Brown, who settled a few miles outside the village of Lake Placid in 1849. Brown's slavery-fighting work took him to the South and Midwest and ultimately to Harpers Ferry, Virginia, where he was hung. He was brought home to his final resting place, and both his grave and his farmhouse in Lake Placid are among the area's most renowned historical attractions.

Perhaps no aspect of the XIII Winter Olympics spoke to Lake Placid's remoteness more than the Olympic Village, an eleven-building brick campus sited on thirty-six rolling acres eight miles out of town in the hamlet of Ray Brook. After the games, it was converted to—and remains—a federal minimum-security prison. Located in a forest, the Village was home to more than 2,000 athletes, a self-contained community complete with a chapel, post office, movie theater, game room, and discotheque, all of it guarded by double barbed-wired fences and a small militia of police. The rooms were slender little boxes with bunk beds and puny windows. The Russians took to calling it "Lake Placid Jail," and Tretiak, the goalie, was particularly appalled by the conditions and the isolation.

"The walls weren't exactly soundproof," he wrote in his autobiography. "When Petrov sneezed in the next room, my roommate, Krutov, would reply, 'Bless you,' without raising his voice. The nights were awfully cold, we had to sleep under three blankets, and the annoying howl of the ceiling fan kept us awake. To me, it all looked like torture." The Americans had it a bit better: they were housed in double-wide trailers that Lake Placid organizers had to bring in to supplement the permanent rooms, and the accommodations were well appointed by comparison, with bigger rooms and less austere décor.

The strong likelihood is that no Olympics will ever be staged in such a remote place again. Four years after the Lake Placid Games were contested on a budget of $200 million, the Summer Games in Los Angeles had a *profit* of $268 million. Between worldwide corporate sponsorships and global television rights, the Olympics have become a billion-dollar business, a five-ring brand that is purportedly built on the purity of international competition and stirred by patriotic fervor but is as driven by economic imperatives as Microsoft or General Motors.

The first winter resort in the nation, Lake Placid had successfully hosted the 1932 Games, but the scale was so much smaller then—17 countries and just over 300 athletes—that it hardly qualified as a reliable indicator that the community could do it again. Local leaders were unfazed, and starting in 1949, they bid for every set of Winter Games, beginning with the 1956 Games, which would go to Cortina d'Ampezzo, Italy. Despite earnest and at times far-sighted efforts, the Lake Placid group, led by postmaster Ron MacKenzie, might never have succeeded were it not for a rabid band of environmentalists in Colorado.

Denver had won the right to hold the 1976 Winter Olympics but had neglected to consult its citizens, who were growing increasingly concerned about the clear-cutting that would have to be done to prepare for the Games. On Election Day 1972, as President Richard Nixon was being voted in to a second term, the Denver Games were voted down, the environmentalists persuading Colorado voters to say no to a referendum on whether to finance the Olympics. Denver had to back out, and though Lake Placid was spurned in its pitch to pinch-hit for Denver, the village's perseverance was finally rewarded in Vienna in October 1974, when the IOC executive board awarded it the 1980 Games. A victory party was held that night with the day's other big celebrant, the winner of the 1980 Summer Games: the city of Moscow.

Even with the Cold War pall that shrouded the Games and in spite of the nasty transportation snafus that gridlocked the village over much of the first week, these Olympics had an endearing, small-scale quality. The Opening Ceremonies were held on the Lake Placid Horse Grounds, with a ring of temporary bleachers and a thoroughly low-tech production. The press center was in the high school, and the greatest speed-skating performance of all time was produced by Eric Heiden on a simple outdoor oval right in front of the school. A friend and former youth hockey teammate of Mark Johnson's from Madison, Wisconsin, Heiden swept every event in his sport, from 500 meters to 10,000, capturing an unprecedented five gold medals. Figure-skating pair Randy Gardner and Tai Babilonia provided their own poignant drama, hinging on whether Gardner's bad hamstring would hold up long enough for them to compete for the gold. (It wouldn't.) Ed Lewi, the press officer for the Games, would drive reporters to venues if they couldn't find a shuttle bus. "It was the last of the small games," said Mike Moran, who spent a quarter-century as the press chief for the U.S. Olympic Committee. "We'll never see a Games like that again. It was almost like elementary school compared with the way the Olympics are now."

There were no cell phones or beepers or Palm Pilots in Lake Placid, no doping scandals, and not even live television for what turned out to be the greatest sports moment of the century. There weren't entourages the size of small armies around the biggest stars. Dream Teams were still a pipe dream. In Lake Placid, you didn't have athletes looking for their sponsor or chemist. You had Jim Craig looking for his father. You had twenty players who were the youngest Olympic hockey team the United States has ever put together, eighteen of them still in college, kids who maybe were known in Williams Arena in Minneapolis or Dane County Coliseum in Madison, Wisconsin, or Walter Brown Arena, just off Commonwealth Avenue in Boston, but scarcely anyplace else. You had kids who put their lives and hockey careers and studies on hold for six months for the opportunity to get tormented and tongue-lashed and improved by a hardass coach; who were playing for their country and couldn't imagine anything better, except when they wanted to kill him. To the U.S. players, Lake Placid was neither too remote nor too small, and the sharp words from Cyrus Vance and the hide-and-seek games played by FBI and KGB agents were not a factor, either. Lake Placid, New York, was exactly where they wanted to be.

THE SECOND
PERIOD

Chapter Four

"IT WAS TEAM"

If you were a hockey player anywhere in the world, you knew about the legend of Vladislav Tretiak. He was the sort of goaltender who made you look at the net and wonder how you were ever going to get the puck past him. Maybe he hadn't been in peak form in Lake Placid, but he was still Tretiak, tall and regal looking even in the tired red sweater. The Americans were shocked when they came out to see Myshkin scuffing up the ice in front of his goal, and Tretiak, No. 20, parked at the end of the bench.

Sergei Makarov sensed his team was dealing with another big change as well. The last time he'd seen the Americans in New York, they weren't much more engaged than window shoppers across the street at Macy's, the world's largest store. *What is going on with these American guys?* he thought. *How can they be so different from games in Madison Square Garden?* Said Makarov, "Their eyes were bright. Their eyes were burning. It was team."

Flying into the U.S. zone in the opening minute of the second period, Valery Kharlamov didn't like what he saw and circled back to center to regroup. Harrington circled with him but wound up hooking him, the two of them spilling to the ice, the whistle coming seconds later. The Soviets had their first power play. Brooks sent out Mark Johnson, Ken Morrow, Mike Ramsey, and Rob McClanahan, who was considered the best two-way college hockey player in the country. After Craig stopped a high drive from the left side by Vladimir Golikov, McClanahan blocked a shot by Bilyaletdinov at the point and then froze the puck along the boards. The guys on the team liked to tease McClanahan about his upper-crust background, his chiseled looks, the fastidious manner in which he prepared his sticks, folded his clothes, put his false front tooth in a Tupperware container. He may have been from North Oaks, a tony St. Paul suburb, and may have had more eclectic intellectual interests than some of his rink-rat teammates, but he skated hard and fast and had as much appetite for grunt work as for glory, his style much more proletarian than patrician. There was a lot that was deceptive about McClanahan. He had an unimposing upper body, and his shot didn't scare much of anyone, but you underestimated him at your own peril. He was a beautiful skater and he never stopped, his legs as thick as his arms were thin, getting him around the ice as fast as just about anyone. "Sometimes when people first met him they'd think he was a cocky, snooty guy, but when you get to know him you realize he's totally the opposite," said Don Micheletti, who lockered alongside McClanahan at the U. "He's a guy who would do anything for you, always pumping you up, picking you up if you had a bad shift. He was definitely a player any coach would want to have on his team." He was also tightly wound and unrelentingly intense. When he was with the New York Rangers, McClanahan participated in a charity tennis tournament with players from the Islanders and Devils, among them Barry Beck, Steve Janaszak, and Chico Resch. A decorated high school tennis player, McClanahan played it as if it were the Wimbledon finals, not a hit-and-giggle exhibition. One night at the U, he and some friends—among them a laid-back Gopher football player—went out drinking. Loosened by a few brews, McClanahan began to tease the football player about his mellowness, daring him to take a swing at him. McClanahan did not let up; he never let up, in anything. Before the night was over, he had a shiner as a souvenir of his persistence.

"Mac was the kind of guy who would go 110 percent brushing his teeth in the morning," Janaszak said.

That was why it was such a jolt to the players when Brooks went at him in the locker room after the first period against Sweden. McClanahan had suffered a deep thigh bruise in the period and was in considerable pain. He had removed his equipment and was getting an ice treatment from Smith, the trainer. Brooks checked with Doc Nagobads and found out McClanahan couldn't harm himself if he played on it, though it would be acutely painful. Then out of nowhere Brooks started to spew, berating his first-line winger for being a candy-ass and a pretty boy, a white-collar coward. McClanahan lashed right back and stepped toward Brooks as Brooks stepped toward him, his ice pack flying, tears coming down his face, people shouting, mayhem and bad feelings spilling everywhere, out into the hallway. A few players wanted to rip Brooks's head off. Mike Eruzione, the captain, jumped in to get the coach out of the room. "I remember sitting there thinking, 'Twenty minutes into the Olympics, and we've already imploded,' " Ken Morrow said. "Herb's lost it." McClanahan wound up getting dressed and playing with his injury. The players on the U.S. team barreled out of the locker room, incensed that Brooks would make such a cheap-shot attack. It felt like a violation, a verbal sucker punch. McClanahan stood between shifts for the rest of the game because the leg hurt more when he sat. "Herb knew exactly what that would look like, singling out Robbie that way," Janaszak said.

Brooks's attack provoked the desired outrage and a tie, but wrought questions along with it. In the service of motivation, is any tactic fair game for a coach to invoke? Does the end always justify the means? Depending on your viewpoint, Brooks was either a genius for finding the right button yet again, or he was heading toward diabolical for calling out an injured player who gave as much as anyone on the team—and deserved better than to be used like a rat in a laboratory experiment. There is no record of Brooks ever apologizing, or even explaining himself to McClanahan. McClanahan, for his part, has publicly never strayed from the high road, even before Brooks's death, saying to anyone who asked that Brooks was able to get more out of his players than anyone he has ever seen. Still, McClanahan's friends said that it took years before he could forgive Brooks for what he did, that the wound was agonizingly slow to heal. He would sometimes joke to people that they should set him straight if they ever heard him waxing on romantically about the joy of playing for Herb Brooks. One of Rob McClanahan's enduring regrets is that he never really got closure on the incident before Brooks died, never sat down with him and officially forgave him and told him that he understood what his purpose was, even if McClanahan didn't like it.

"It cut very deep with Robbie for a long time," Don Micheletti said.

Brooks was a complicated man, one who teemed with contradictions, beginning with the way he braided new-age ideas with an old-school demeanor. He was iron-fisted yet gave his players as much freedom—and room to create—as any coach in the country. He pounded them into shape but left them on their own, with no curfew, in their downtime. He was an unrepentant taskmaster yet was profoundly intuitive in his judgments of people, character, and competitive makeup. Many NHL scouts were not completely sold on Jim Craig—one general manager said he had a half-dozen other college goaltenders rated ahead of him—but after getting to know Craig and seeing him rise to the moment in the world championships in Moscow in 1979, Brooks was convinced he had that skill and swagger and resilience to give him his best shot at a medal. The same snarling man who would regularly demean his players could be one of the funniest people around. On his flight to Nagano, Japan, in the winter of 1998, when he coached the French Olympic team, Brooks was seated next to a woman with a baby. At one point she began to breast-feed the infant.

"I hope you're not offended, sir, but it's the only thing that will stop his ears from popping," the woman said.

"I'm not offended, but all these years I've just been chewing gum," Brooks replied.

Brooks had lots of friends, yet he could sometimes be elusive to even those closest to him, as if he were afraid to be pinned down, to get too close. His mind moved fast, and his body followed suit. "I sometimes got the feeling that Herbie was never comfortable in his own skin," said one old friend. "He was a great guy, but it was as if he wasn't always present when you were with him."

For all his planning, Brooks could be as impulsive as a preschooler. He once had a beautiful home overlooking Turtle Lake, north of the Twin Cities; Brooks sold it because he didn't like a new neighbor—or the monstrous house he was building. Stopping back in Minnesota from a West Coast trip while he was coaching the Rangers, he found a frozen pipe, immediately brought out a torch to thaw it, and wound up burning down the entire kitchen. The family had to move out while the damage was repaired.

Brooks would routinely treat the players as if they were German shepherds, then would turn around and bring sandwiches and express his thanks to behind-the-scenes people like equipment manager Buddy Kessel and trainer Gary Smith. During the second period of the Soviet game, Neal Broten was hopping over the boards for his shift, unaware that Ken Morrow had just come out of the penalty box. Noticing the United States had six skaters, Smith reached out and grabbed Broten, sparing the United States a possible two-minute penalty.

"Way to stay in the game, Smitty," Brooks said. It was more of a compliment than he gave any of his players that night.

———

Not even two minutes into the period, the Americans were effectively killing the clock. Dave Christian controlled the puck through center ice and passed back to Baker, who started out, skating on the left side. He passed to Broten in the middle, but the puck hit a Soviet stick and deflected to Vladimir Krutov, who took it in the midsection and quickly dropped it to the ice and flicked a pass to an onrushing Alexander Maltsev. Christian, skating backwards, couldn't hope to stay with him, and Baker had no shot, either. One of the things Brooks admired most about the Russians was their ability to play at an elevated pace and sustain it for an entire game. Sometimes sooner, sometimes later, that pace would cause opponents to break down, shredding their comfort zone as if it had gone through the Zamboni. To compete with them, Brooks knew his team couldn't merely move fast. It had to think fast. The way he wanted to play the Russians put tremendous demand on players to read plays, anticipate, move without the puck. One of Tarasov's favorite sayings was "Speed of hand, speed of foot, speed of mind. The most important of these is speed of mind. Teach it." Brooks taught it, and he had "Cardiac" Jack Blatherwick, sports physiologist and his strength and conditioning coach at the U, to help him. Brooks and Blatherwick were hockey soulmates, spending countless hours studying Russians on film, constructing drills, creating practice plans that were scripted to the minute, the pace fast, the emphasis on quick movement and quick reaction. Games had a clock, but hockey brainstorming sessions rarely did for Brooks. When Warren Strelow was coaching goaltenders with Brooks for the Utica Devils in the American Hockey League in upstate New York, his hotel phone rang at 2:30 one morning. It was Herb Brooks, genius and insomniac.

"What are you doing?" Brooks asked.

"I'm sleeping."

"Got a pencil?"

"Why?"

"Write down these line combinations and let me know what you think," Brooks said. Brooks was no different with old friend Lou Nanne. "When Herb wanted to talk hockey, it would go on forever," Nanne said. "He would talk to the door if he thought the door would talk back to him."

Joe Devaney is the visiting locker-room attendant for the Rangers, in his fourth decade of working Garden hockey games. He became close to Brooks during the coach's tenure in New York. After Ranger defeats, Brooks would hunker down in the locker room for hours, stewing about what went wrong, replaying the game in his head. Devaney and a colleague would go in to clean up, and Brooks would invariably go over to the chalkboard to give them a richly detailed, X-and-O breakdown of where the Rangers had fallen short. "We wouldn't have a clue what he was talking about," Devaney said. "We'd just stand there and nod our heads."

Now Maltsev was in alone on Craig, and nobody was going to come close to catching up to him. He swept left and clanged a low shot off the post, into the net, a hard metallic sound followed by a hush, a power-play score that came with 40 seconds left in John Harrington's penalty and just over two minutes gone in the period. Baker disdainfully cleared the puck out of the net while Craig was still sprawled on the ice. Maltsev stayed stone-faced as he accepted a few helmet taps.

Three to two, Soviet Union.

Craig got up and shook his head. Despite all he'd done the Soviets were on an eight-goal pace and pushing for more. After Helmut Balderis barreled down the left wing, into the

American end, Ken Morrow did a superb job riding him off and poking the puck away. Eric Strobel recovered it behind the net and started to stickhandle out to Craig's left, a risky play that got much riskier when Alexander Skvortsov deflected the puck away, and Balderis—*Eliktritchka*, the Electric Train—gathered it and swung behind the cage and tried to center it through the back door, Craig stopping it with his stick. Zhluktov tried for the rebound but got sandwiched by Phil Verchota and Mark Wells. With the scare survived, Dave Christian, in front of the U.S. net, batted down a pass from the point with his left glove and spotted Rob McClanahan streaking up the middle. Christian threaded a perfect pass straight ahead, on to McClanahan's stick. McClanahan sped in on goaltender Myshkin, but Valery Vasiliev hustled back to check him and Myshkin steered aside a tepid backhand.

Moments later, the United States controlled off the face-off in the neutral zone, and the puck went to Mike Ramsey, at 19 the youngest American player. Ramsey was hounded by Maltsev and lost the puck to Yuri Lebedev, who flicked it across ice to Krutov, at 19 the youngest Soviet player, who already had a goal and an assist in the game. The first generation of Soviet players typically were dazzling artists and playmakers who tended not to be very physical. Krutov, a man his teammates later said should've gotten significantly more ice time than he did, was an altogether different breed, a barrel-shaped body who was equal parts artist and bullrusher. At the blue line, Krutov was about to surge into the U.S. zone when Morrow skated up and crunched him, a clean open-ice check that stopped Krutov cold. The hit knocked Morrow down but extinguished the threat. This was Kenny Morrow's specialty.

Morrow was a man of few words and no wasted motion, a back-line Hemingway with a darker beard. He had a great ability to read plays as they unfolded, to know where he should be. It didn't look hard until you tried to do it yourself. Bill Torrey of the Islanders, the general manager who drafted Morrow out of Bowling Green, watched the game next to Al Arbour, who would be the next man to coach Morrow after Herb Brooks. Near the end of the game, Torrey turned to Arbour and said, "We got ourselves a defenseman."

———

Don Morrow was a six-foot five-inch shortstop, long-limbed and low-key, Cal Ripken before Cal Ripken. He got to everything without even seeming to be in motion and threw just as deceptively. "I was 212 pounds and he could turn me upside down when he threw a baseball," said Gale Cronk, an old friend. Don Morrow played against Hank Aaron in the minor leagues once. He was one of the best athletes in Flint, Michigan, and probably would've made the Detroit Tigers but for the baseball mindset of the 1950s, when clubs weren't much more inclined to embrace six-foot five-inch middle in-fielders than they were to hire players who did not have white skin.

Don Morrow went to work at an automobile parts plant, just as his father and brother did, on the line for Chevrolet. He passed on his size and athletic ability and disposition to his younger son, who never heard his father talk about his playing career or complain. "He did what most people in Flint did then," Ken Morrow said, sitting in a suite high above the Arena at Harbor Yard in Bridgeport, Connecticut. The Islanders were playing the Boston Bruins in a preseason game, and Morrow, the team's director of pro scouting, was watching alongside general manager Mike Milbury and other club executives. The suite cleared out after the game, and Morrow had the faux leather couch to himself. His trademark beard has been trimmed back to a mustache, his hair short and spiky and retreating, his body as straight and strong as a lumberjack's. He had olive slacks and a dark double-breasted blazer and print tie, creased and color-coordinated. "You went to high school and hoped to get a job in the factory and then twenty-five years later, you would be counting down the days to retirement."

Morrow lived the factory life himself, once. For a few summers in college he punched out dashboards and bumpers, making good money but learning quickly that the line wasn't for him. He found the sameness stultifying. Ken Morrow made his office the blue line, and maybe it wasn't surprising that he patrolled it with a clock-puncher's reliability and shift worker's anonymity, no fuss, no theatrics, just results. Gale Cronk, who was a major force in junior hockey in Michigan, used to joke that Morrow's slap shot was so slow you could read "made in Canada" on the puck as it went, but darned if a big percentage of his goals seemed to come at critical moments. He was a player Brooks knew he had to have. Just to make sure his no-beards rule didn't get in the way, Brooks made an exception for preexisting beards, like Morrow's. When a game was spiraling out of control, Ken Morrow could always be counted on to restore order. Brooks almost never got on him; there was never a reason to. "If you had twenty-two guys like him, you'd never hear about general managers or coaches getting fired," Torrey said.

"If you were going to build a prototypical defenseman,

it would be Kenny Morrow," said Gordon Lane, Morrow's longtime defensive partner with the Islanders. "You never noticed him, but he was always there."

Blending in was always Morrow's specialty. He won four straight Stanley Cups with the Islanders, the first of them coming four months after Lake Placid, making him the first man to capture Olympic and NHL titles in the same year. Yet he always kept the profile of a fifth defenseman on a minor-league team. He doesn't wear a Stanley Cup ring or any other ring. As Lake Placid was convulsing in patriotic merriment that Friday night, Morrow iced his shoulder and slipped out the back door of the arena. "I wasn't trying to shun anything. I didn't even know all that celebration was going on," Morrow said. When the Islanders would go out after games, Morrow would be the quiet one in the corner, enjoying a beer, not shy, not antisocial, just content to take it all in with his low-volt steadiness.

"He's always been really comfortable with who he is," said Greg Morrow, Ken's older brother, a part-time scout for the Islanders and former player for Ohio State.

At six feet four inches and 210 pounds, Morrow may have been the strongest player on the U.S. team, but he was as understated about that as about everything else. He had long arms and legs of granite and knew how to use his stick to thwart attacks, how to position himself to ride guys off the puck. Greg Morrow knocked Ken out cold once during an Ohio State–Bowling Green game but never had to worry about retribution. If guys wanted to fight, Ken would just clinch up. He was plenty tough but never mean.

"You got the feeling that when he took you into the corner

he wanted to say he was sorry," Neal Broten said. "He'd never give you the extra elbow the way a lot of guys would."

Morrow isn't much for off-ice confrontation, either. Sometimes his wife, Barbara, will gear up for an argument and get even more worked up because her husband will refuse to engage. They got married in August 1979, and there was no time for a honeymoon, Ken having to go off to Europe with the team. Barbara went to Disney World with her sister. They'll get to the honeymoon one of these years.

Morrow's meticulousness and his fondness for routine were as much his signature as his beard. In the pros, every night on the road he would call room service at 10:30 to get apple pie with vanilla ice cream. "Rooming with him probably cost me twenty pounds over my career," Gordon Lane said. Morrow's Christmas tree has to be perfectly symmetrical, with no gaps or wayward branches. He has his way of loading the dishwasher, and if someone loads it differently, he'll unload it and do it again. When he's home he vacuums every day. In the locker room, game after game, year after year, he would methodically tape his socks and his stick, each row of tape overlapping by the same width, and it might take fifteen more minutes to tie up his skates because he wouldn't think of having laces that were not taut and perfectly straight. He's the same way now when he helps his son, Evan, put his skates on. Someday Barbara Morrow figures she may see her husband get flustered or impatient, but it will take some doing. After the gold-medal game, Ken Morrow passed four sticks around the locker room and had the guys sign all of them. He put them under the bus as the team left to board Air Force One to fly to see President Carter in Washington.

When the bus arrived at the airport, the sticks were gone. Even being a crime victim didn't really faze him. Lane laughed when he heard the suggestion that a video of Morrow's life be shown to young NHL players as a model for how to conduct themselves. "People would fall asleep halfway through it," Lane said.

The Islanders are the only NHL organization Ken Morrow has ever worked for. Drafted on the fourth round in 1976, he stayed in Bowling Green and didn't even consider signing until 1979, when the Islanders offered him a $35,000 contract. He had a 1972 Camaro and was tired of having no money. Signing, of course, would mean no Olympics. Brooks quietly lobbied Cronk to persuade Morrow to hold off. "We'll fix the car up and keep it going," Cronk said. "One more year is not going to make or break you."

Long before the team ever got to Lake Placid, Brooks took steps to ensure that the top players—all of whom had been drafted by the NHL—would not be lured into turning pro before the Games. In those days, once a player signed and took NHL money, he was done as an Olympian. By contrast, players in the IHL, such as Mike Eruzione, could retain their eligibility because the IHL was technically classified as an amateur league, though players received small salaries for playing. AHAUS officials worked to convince NHL clubs that the pre-Olympic schedule under Brooks would be so rigorous that, far from losing a year of development, the players' games would prosper. Players were persuaded that the Olympics not only offered a chance to represent their country but would improve their games and raise their visibility along the way—and that their tax-free stipend of $1,100 per month wasn't much different from what they'd make in the minors. Art Kaminsky, a lawyer who would ultimately represent most of the players on the team, worked closely with Bill Torrey, among others, to facilitate an arrangement whereby NHL clubs and AHAUS shared the cost for a player's insurance coverage. Morrow was perhaps the closest to turning pro; his father had died in his freshman year at Bowling Green, and he was about to be married. But with a $250,000 insurance policy in place, Morrow opted to hold off joining the Islanders, and other top players—Dave Christian, Mark Johnson, Rob McClanahan, Jim Craig, and Mike Ramsey—followed suit. The only player whom Brooks really wanted who didn't play was Joe Mullen, the Boston College star and former street hockey player from New York City, and the top scorer for the United States in the world championships in 1979. Joe's father was ill and the family needed the money, so he signed with the St. Louis Blues.

It was not as if pro hockey were a long-held dream for Morrow. He just loved to play and was grateful for the chance to do it. "The way I viewed it, at every level I played at I'd think, 'If this is as far as I go, I'll be very happy,' " Morrow said.

Morrow started playing at age six, on a rink his father built in the backyard. Don Morrow put up low boards at first, then floodlights, then four-foot boards. He had a shopworker make goals out of metal pipe, and he cut the core out of the pucks so they weren't so heavy. The games would go on morning, noon, and night. The brothers became expert at digging pucks out of snowbanks by studying the angle of entry. "What better way to spend a winter in Michigan than playing hockey in your backyard?" Ken Morrow said.

Eighteen months Ken's senior, Greg Morrow played a

more physical, grinding style than his brother. Hours before games, Greg would be restless and energetic, getting his bag together, checking his equipment. Ken would be flopped on the sofa, watching TV. Greg and the other kids they played with would spend hours training in the summers. Yet when it was time for preseason conditioning, Ken would crank out one wind sprint after another while guys all around him were collapsing. "I dare say that if you were honest, if anyone thought either one of the boys would've made it, it would've been Greg," Loretta Morrow, their mother, said. "He worked so hard at it. Ken was so laid back it looked like he wasn't even trying."

"He ain't human," Greg said. Ken Morrow laughed, a hearty, staccato sound.

Greg and Ken were on the Detroit Junior Red Wings together before splitting up for college. Greg had two knee operations coming out of juniors, and after a stellar freshman year for Ohio State, he ripped up his other knee as well as his chance of making the Olympics and the NHL. There were times he felt sad and envious. His brother helped him through it. "He never said anything to make me feel like he was doing something superior to what I was doing," said Greg, now superintendent of a golf club in Flint. "He has always been very humble about it and sensitive to how I felt."

Not even a week after the Olympics, Ken Morrow was on the blue line for the Islanders, showing at 23 the poise of a man of 33. The seamlessness of his transition enabled Torrey to trade popular veterans Billy Harris and Dave Lewis to the Los Angeles Kings for Butch Goring, a deal that was widely credited as being a key component to the team's subsequent run of Stanley Cups.

Like the careers of most of his Olympic teammates, Morrow's career predated the explosion of NHL salaries. He made $50,000, $55,000, and $60,000 in his first three years. When a bad knee forced him to retire, his top salary was $1.9 million. He negotiated the way he played, preferring to avoid acrimony. He was content with where he was and what he had. People have reversals in life and ask "Why me?" Ken Morrow has good fortune in life and asks the same thing: "Why me?"

"I think about that all the time," he said. "I don't want to get too philosophical about stuff, but I was drafted by the Islanders in 1976. What if the timing had been different? What if I hadn't made the Olympic team? What if we hadn't won the gold medal? What if the Islanders hadn't won four Stanley Cups? There are a lot better players in this game who haven't had that success. People say success is where preparation meets opportunity. Maybe I did prepare myself, but still, so much of it is in the timing."

For Don Morrow, the timing was not nearly so kind. Around Thanksgiving 1975, he wasn't feeling right. During a Junior Red Wings scrimmage, he passed out on a chair. He underwent tests and they revealed the worst: a brain tumor. That winter, he made it down for an Ohio State–Bowling Green game to watch the boys play against each other. He wore a knit cap that had the red and gray of Ohio State on one side, and the orange and brown of Bowling Green on the other. "He was on Cloud Nine, being at that game," Gale Cronk said. Don Morrow got much sicker in the spring and was hospitalized at the Hurley Medical Center in Flint. He was starting to slip away. The children were there, and so were a few other close friends and relatives. At about three in the morning, Ken Morrow was saying his final goodbye to his father. Don Morrow looked up from the bed. "If you ever get a chance to play in the Olympics, for your country, make sure you do it," he said. Don Morrow died a few hours later, four years shy of seeing Ken crunch Vladimir Krutov by the blue line.

During the mid-1990s, the Islanders trained in Lake Placid. Ken Morrow would sometimes go up to help out. One year he decided to work with the young defensemen. He tied up his skates, methodically as ever, and went out on the Olympic Field House ice for the first time since February 24, 1980. He skated a solitary lap. It started to come back. He saw the benches and the penalty box and remembered the corners where certain things happened, and what the feeling was like. The building was unchanged, with the same red seats and the same flat blue roof, the same white girders and black tracks of lights. It hadn't been junked up with neon and overcommercialization. He was grateful for that. Morrow had heeded his father's parting words and lived a hockey life he never imagined possible. Elaborate sentimental excursions are not his style, but Ken Morrow knew just where he was and what it meant.

"It was pretty neat to be out there," he said.

———

Morrow's hard check sprang the puck free from Krutov, and not long after a sustained American possession yielded sharp passing but no shots on goal, Mike Eruzione picked up a loose puck and started out of his own end. Eruzione, who had not been involved much offensively to this point, crossed the red line and spotted Christian, who had sprinted to catch up to the play and surged into an open space on the left wing.

Eruzione backhanded the puck to him, and Christian moved into the Soviet zone and swept toward center and dropped it for Broten, who ripped a slap shot wide, five and a half minutes into the period. The crowd let out a collective groan of disappointment and had the same response on the ensuing U.S. push, which ended when Mikhailov, Stan Laurel–lookalike, hustled back to prevent McClanahan from getting off a straight-on shot from forty feet out. The Soviets broke out quickly, and Viacheslav Fetisov hit a streaking Alexander Golikov. Mark Johnson skated with him and took Golikov down with his stick and then quickly pulled it back, as if to conceal the evidence. There was no whistle. The Russians were stepping up the pressure. Fetisov found Alexander Golikov again, and this time he took the puck behind the American goal, where it was picked up by brother Vladimir, who backhanded it right across the crease, just inches ahead of a speeding Makarov, who had most of the net to shoot into but couldn't get a good shot off and poked it inches wide. Fetisov teed up from the point, another dangerous chance that was blocked in front. Scrambling to calm things down, Silk lifted the puck into the seats.

The Soviets were playing at an astonishing pace. This was why Brooks was so adamant about having good skaters. If you couldn't keep up, the Russians would bury you. In the U.S. end, Mark Pavelich, one of the fastest U.S. skaters, dug the puck from along the boards and slid a perfect breakout pass to John Harrington, shooting up the middle, both Soviet defensemen caught up ice. Harrington took the puck at center ice and found himself alone. Fetisov scrambled futilely to catch him. Harrington crossed the blue line. Fetisov swung his stick wildly, as if it were an ax, but caught all air and no

Harrington. Harrington moved in on Myshkin but looked tentative, the puck not obeying his stick. His best shot was top shelf, right side. That's where he aimed, but the puck sailed far to the right and into the endboards. Once more the crowd groaned. When you are a counterpuncher trying to take down a heavyweight, you have to not only pick your spots judiciously, you have to convert them. The Russians knew they were going to get ample scoring chances, because they always did. The Americans had no such assurance. Harrington was disheartened but kept skating and caught up to the puck along the sideboards. He'd been playing catch-up for years. It was no time to stop.

With a strong, handsome face, tidy salt-and-pepper hair, and a Kirk Douglas chin, John Harrington looks more like a U.S. senator than a U.S. gold medalist. Most everyone knows him as Bah, a nickname he's had since he was an infant. His older brother, Joe, tried to say "Baby" and could only get out "Bah." It stuck. "Nobody who has known him a long time ever calls him John," said Mary Harrington, his mother.

A retired history teacher, Mary Harrington was a high school valedictorian at 16 and a college graduate at 19. She already had two master's degrees when she turned down a fellowship to Yale to marry her husband, Charles. She does crossword puzzles in minutes and can name every king and queen of England since the Norman Conquest in 1066. She once handed John a copy of her favorite quotation: "Perseverance and discipline are omnipotent." Her son built a life around it.

Harrington was part of the U.S. Olympic hockey team for eight months and spent seven of them living in fear of being cut. It wasn't until mid-January, after he'd played strong back-to-back games against the Winnipeg Jets, a team that was considering signing him, that Craig Patrick told him that he didn't need to sign; he would be going to Lake Placid.

"I felt like a grand piano had been lifted off my back," Harrington said.

Harrington grew up in the Iron Range town of Virginia, four miles up the road from Eveleth, the hub of Range hockey. He was a lunch-pail winger, a hard-skating, ultra-dependable kid who outworked most everyone and always had. He'd look around and see better players, then try to find a way to be better than they. When he set a goal, it almost always got met. He was the kind of player coaches love, because he elevated the whole team's work rate.

"I don't think you're pushing us hard enough," Harrington would tell Gus Hendrickson, his coach at the University of Minnesota–Duluth. "We need to do more."

Harrington came by his grit honestly. His parents had been in Lake Placid for the first week, but his mother had to return home under threat of being docked her $300 salary, notwithstanding that a clause in the teachers' contract in Virginia said that if a teacher were absent because of an event of school or community interest, he or she would not be penalized. "I don't know what could be of more local interest than having a boy from Virginia going for a gold medal in the Olympics," she said. The Minnesota Education Association sent her a lawyer. Mary Harrington fought hard for her rights. She was mortified when the *Duluth Evening News* ran a headline when her son came home that said, "Hero's Welcome Dimmed by Mother's Plight," but she didn't back off.

Ultimately, no penalty was assessed. For Mary Harrington, it was the principle. "She's got one of those wills that doesn't let go," said Tom Harrington, John's younger brother.

The Montreal Canadiens were Harrington's first hockey heroes. He loved their flair and their French names but learned pretty early that he was no Guy LaFleur. There's a home movie of John on the ice at six years of age, falling down, getting up, falling down, getting up. He was a second-line center in peewees, an unspectacular forward in high school, a walk-on at UMD who saw the eighty kids at tryouts and wondered if he should even bother. In his first game he scored an overtime goal to beat the 1976 Olympic team, a squad that featured Steve Sertich, another Virginia guy, but even as late as his junior year at UMD, Harrington wasn't making every road trip. Brooks regularly told him he might not be good enough to play on this team.

"I had been hearing it my whole life," Harrington said.

Diligence and dedication were as much a part of daily life in the Harrington home as sticks and skates. Like a lot of Range towns, Virginia had its share of saloons (54 at one count for a town that then had about 12,000 people), the miners getting their paychecks and heading for Main Street, a wide boulevard with old brick storefronts. But that wasn't the routine for Charles Harrington, a locomotive engineer who made runs from the hulking mines in Virginia to the ore docks in Duluth. He worked in the post office when the mines were slow. Plenty of nights he'd come home from the train, sleep in a chair for a few hours, then go off to sort mail, though he turned down lots of overtime shifts driving his engine so he could be at his kids' games. "I can always work, but this game will never be replayed," he'd tell anyone who asked. Mary Harrington worked late, too, often typing out three different 100-question tests for her history students, in the years before computers. John and his brothers helped with the construction when the family moved into a new colonial on First Street North in Virginia. The summer before he became an Olympian, John built a deck for his mother in the back of the house, complete with flower boxes. She told him he'd never have to buy her another Mother's Day present. He did anyway.

Charles Harrington grew up poor, moving from place to place, troubled by the chronic instability. Having a home and providing for his family meant everything to him. After the Harringtons moved into the new house, Charles told Mary, "I don't want to move anymore. I hope they carry me out of here." And twenty-two years later, in 1995, they did. Charles Harrington got kidney cancer. Mary Harrington got a hospital bed and set it up in the family room. The family had six months to say goodbye, to share feelings. Even in the face of his own mortality, Charles Harrington didn't want any slack. Two days before he died he made sure the recycling was out. He felt lucky to have the family he had, the life he had. The feeling was very mutual.

John told his father once that he regretted not being able to spend as much time with him as his siblings had, because he was away so much, training for the Olympics, playing in Switzerland, coaching. "You're living your life," his father told him. "You've done a lot of things and gone a lot of places. That's good."

Harrington's current place is Collegeville, Minnesota, where he is the head coach at St. John's University. He is the only player on the 1980 team who coaches men's college hockey, a man with a plan, and perfectionistic proclivities. He makes out his tidy to-do list every night before bed, folds the laundry a certain way, likes his clothes crisp and pressed. Even when he wears jeans and a knit shirt he looks dressed up. His kids and players tease him about his lawn, which is something out of a turf magazine, crosscut and carpet-thick, all but manicured with tweezers.

"He mows it in certain ways and certain days, and we don't even walk on it because we're afraid he'll yell at us," said Chris Harrington, John and Mary Harrington's oldest son, a star defenseman for the University of Minnesota. "He's definitely one of the obsessive-compulsive people when it comes to order. He pays serious attention to detail. I guess that's what makes him a good coach."

Harrington plays an hour of half-court basketball just about every day in the St. John's gym and still outworks people. He gutted out an impressive three-hour, thirty-six-minute time in the Twin Cities Marathon once, though he had never gone farther than twelve miles in his life before. He wanted to die with two miles to go, but he had set a goal.

Harrington has a military man's approach to life, and it seemed to be a good fit when he enrolled in the Air Force Academy out of Virginia High School. On Day 1, he got a haircut, got hollered at by his first upperclassman, and was out of there. "I stayed two days, because it took one day to get processed out," Harrington said. "I was a small-town guy. To me the earth was flat outside of Minnesota, and I was sure I would fall off. I didn't even give it a chance."

Harrington was the team chronicler of Brooksisms, the coach's favorite sayings, duly recorded in a little spiral note-book. He collected them all: "You're not talented enough to

win on talent alone." "The legs feed the wolf." "You're playing worse every day, and right now you're playing like it's the
middle of next month." "We went to the well again and the
water was colder and the water was deeper." He took them
all in, and now has his own sayings: "Hard work beats talent
when talent doesn't work hard." In his tidy office, the sign on
his bulletin board says:

St. John's Hockey: Old School
Not Guts, No Glory.

Harrington signed with Scotty Bowman and the Buffalo
Sabres after the Olympics, but he never made the NHL and
never was paid his $20,000 signing bonus, either. In his sec-
ond pro game, with the Sabres' AHL affiliate in Rochester,
he got welcomed by a goon and wound up in the hospital, a
bunch of teeth knocked out and his jaw wired shut. He was
set to return to Lake Placid—the Sabres' training-camp
site—when Pavelich called him from Switzerland in the late
summer of 1980 and said his team had an opening for another American player. Unconvinced that there would be a
place for him in Buffalo, Harrington headed for the Alps. He
and Pavelich became the most prolific scoring tandem in the
top Swiss league.

Life after Lake Placid wasn't easy at first for Bah Harrington. He felt adrift at times. Ever since Steve Sertich had made
the 1976 team, the Olympics had been Harrington's mission
in life. It was what drove him. After it had been achieved beyond all measure, it was almost as if he'd lost his direction,
his adrenaline supply. The NHL had never really been a big
dream of his, so he never went after it in his full-bore way. He

regrets that now. He got into coaching and started as an assistant at the University of Denver, where one of his players was Danny Brooks, Herb's son. Harrington had some of Herb in him. He'd berate kids and motivate them by keeping them guessing, and he would live and die with every game to the point that Jeff Sauer, coach of Wisconsin, told him, "You've got to learn how to lose."

Harrington got the head job at St. John's, a Division III school, in 1993. He was almost maniacally intense at first. In between periods of one game he lit into his captain with such a string of curse words he cringes to think about it even now. He slammed one of his wingtip shoes so hard into a rack of water bottles he almost broke a toe. Harrington still isn't a blithe spirit after a loss, but he has mellowed. Coaching his son, Chris, in a couple of off-season tournaments helped him to realize he wouldn't want anyone hollering at his son that way. Slowly, haltingly, he began to lighten up.

When he started coaching, Harrington spoke frequently with Brooks and had Brooks-like goals: to be a big-time NCAA coach and win a national championship. Now he is not so sure. Harrington was a finalist for three Division I jobs—at Alaska, Notre Dame, and his alma mater, Minnesota-Duluth—and was passed over each time. He went into the UMD interview thinking the job was all but his. He was crushed when he didn't get it, and blames himself for his hubris. At St. John's, Harrington gets great kids who are serious students, kids he can teach and whose lives he can impact. Collegeville is a wonderful community. He's had great success—St. John's was 22–4–1 and No. 6 in the country in 2003–2004—and he doesn't have to sweat out whether he's going to get fired if the team doesn't make the NCAA tournament, and he gets to see much more of his wife and daughters, as well as many more of Chris's games, than he would if he were in Division I. Harrington appreciates everything he has, says he's "100 percent content," yet there is a sense you get from him, more implicit than explicit, that there is still a yearning to test himself at the highest level of college hockey.

"I've always thought that winning the gold medal was the best and worst thing that ever happened to him," brother Tom Harrington said. "The best because he achieved the pinnacle, the worst because he climbed the mountain at twenty-two, and he's spent the last twenty years trying to get back up there. He's got a great gig at St. John's, and he knows it. But when you've been to the mountaintop I think it's hard not to have part of you want to get back there."

With Harrington's breakaway going awry, Myshkin, behind his caged mask, had still not been tested. Harrington chased down his errant shot and swung it behind the goal, where Schneider got the carom and tried to stuff it in, switching from forehand to backhand, but he couldn't get enough of it to angle the puck into the goal. It shot across the crease. The second period was approaching the halfway point, and so was the game. The players knew they had to forget the missed opportunities and keep skating, but it was hard. The Soviets came down and after Maltsev got bodied off the puck by Buzz Schneider, Mike Ramsey ducked an onrushing Krutov behind the net and skated out. Pressing on was the only option.

Chapter Five

HOLDING
PATTERN

Mike Ramsey had spent much of the first thirty minutes hitting all things in red, but now he was cruising, not bruising. He charged up ice, legs churning, 75 inches and 190 pounds in high gear, the son of a bread deliveryman, making a run of his own. He carried the length of the rink and looked sure and strong. Ramsey loved to put his fluid, big-shouldered body to use. He was a wonderful physical specimen, an athlete who won a state tennis title and was an all-city football player for Minneapolis's Roosevelt High School. Scotty Bowman liked him so much that he made him the Sabres' first pick—No. 11 overall—in the 1979 NHL draft. Ramsey was the first American-born player ever to be taken on the first round. It made for a lot of headlines and an equal amount of grief from his coach. Brooks was fond of calling him "an eighteen-year-old prima donna." When Ramsey asked him once what he would be the next year, Brooks said, "A nineteen-year-old prima donna."

Ramsey played in the NHL for eighteen years, a four-time

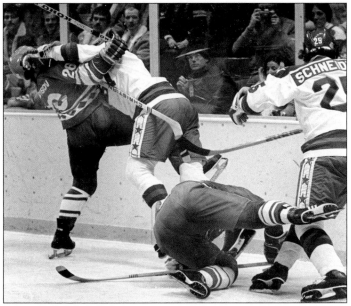

U.S. winger Rob McClanahan mixes it up along the boards with Alexander Skvortsov of the Soviet Union. Buzz Schneider and an unidentified Russian are also in the fray.

U.S. goalie Jim Craig turns away a shot by Helmut Balderis.

Russian forward Viktor Zhluktov gets triple-teamed by Schneider (25), Dave Christian, and Jim Craig.

Mark Johnson is about to beat Russian goalie Vladislav Tretiak with one second to go in the first period.

Alexander Maltsev beats Craig for the Soviets'
third goal of the game early in the second period.

Vladimir Petrov is bodied off the puck by
Mark Johnson *(left)* and Bill Baker.

John Harrington (28) is at the doorstep as Mike Eruzione's
game-winning goal slips by backup Russian goalie Vladimir
Myshkin with ten minutes to play, putting the U.S. up 4–3.

Herb Brooks sweats out the closing minutes from behind the U.S. bench.

With the clock at 0:00, let the delirium begin.

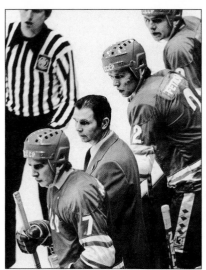

The clock is ticking, and Alexei Kasatonov (7), coach Viktor Tikhonov, Viacheslev Fetisov (2), and Vladimir Krutov don't look happy.

Two teams, one line, and a couple of patriotic gate-crashers.

Out on Main Street,
Lake Placid, flags
were plentiful and
elbow room was not.

After beating Finland
for the gold medal,
Jim Craig has the
American flag.
Now if he can only
find his father . . .

Bruce Bennett Studios

A day after the Olympic Games were over, President Jimmy Carter and his wife, Rosalynn, are surrounded by cowboy-hat-wearing heroes, including Mark Wells *(far left)*, Dave Silk *(left of the podium)*, and Mark Johnson *(right)*.

Bruce Bennett Studios

Mike Eruzione, Jim Craig, and Ken Morrow are happy civilians, framed by the Boston skyline.

All-Star and relentless hitter whose ferocity earned him the ire of the entire Edmonton Oilers organization in 1986 when he flattened Wayne Gretzky in the NHL All-Star game. Ramsey's hockey passion ran so hot that when he finally retired, he'd look at the box scores in the morning paper and literally feel a wave of nausea come over him: his name was not in there, and it would never be again; there would be no more forwards to punish or rushes to make. Ramsey, now an assistant coach with the Minnesota Wild, wasn't the most disciplined of the American defensemen in Lake Placid, but it was impossible not to love his energy and his attitude, a man's body melded to a child's enthusiasm. He never wanted to be out of the action and rarely was, even if it meant chasing Soviet forwards into corners instead of stationing himself in front of the goal.

Fetisov, his future NHL rival, finally stopped Ramsey's rush by tying him up along the boards. The crowd cheered Ramsey's effort. The face-off was to the left of Myshkin, and at the other end, Craig wondered when he would be tested again. He didn't have to wait long. The puck squirted free behind his net after the Russians carried it in, and Craig wandered perilously behind the net, trying to freeze it. Vladimir Petrov jabbed at the puck with his stick. You don't do that to Mike Ramsey's goalie. Ramsey cross-checked Petrov in the head, crashing him into the boards. Petrov pushed back and the sticks went up and then Ramsey dropped his, as if he were ready to go. Kaisla blew his whistle, rushed in to calm things down, and skated over to the official scorer to tell them Craig would be getting two minutes for delay of game.

There were just under ten minutes remaining in the period. As the Soviets tried to set up their power play, Johnson took the puck away from Fetisov at the blue line and raced down the right side, faked a shot to freeze defenseman Valery Vasiliev and Myshkin, then slid a pass over to a wide-open Schneider. He fired wide to the left, another big chance gone. Johnson was everywhere on the penalty kill. Fetisov took a slap shot, and Johnson blocked it. Petrov got a superb feed from Kharlamov and blasted at Craig from ten feet out, and there was Johnson again, anticipating the play brilliantly, dropping to his knees and extending his stick, getting a piece. The Soviets had still another scoring chance from close range as Johnson lay on the ice, but Petrov shot it wide.

After a harrowing two minutes had been survived and the teams were back at even strength, Ramsey and Krutov exchanged a couple more hits deep in the U.S. end. Then, with under seven minutes to play, the Americans settled down. Starting out from behind the U.S. goal, Jack O'Callahan snapped a pass up the middle to Eruzione but it was intercepted by the mustachioed Zhluktov. Eruzione swung his stick to spring the puck free once more, nudging it ahead to Christoff. Here came the Americans, passing, moving, the puck zipping around as if it were on a string, as if they were Soviets: Christoff to O'Callahan, back to Christoff, over to Broten, out to O'Callahan, back to Broten. Broten slid the puck to a pirouetting Christoff, an artful pass into the slot. Not unlike Pavelich, his fellow north-country centerman, Broten lived to set people up. He had broken John Mayasich's assist record when he registered 50 as a Gopher freshman. This was precisely how.

———

Eight miles from the Canadian border in northwest Minnesota, the manufacturing hub of Polaris Industries sprawls over 24,000-square feet on the west side of Highway 89, not even a half-mile from the heart of Roseau, Minnesota. The plant produces thousands of snowmobiles and all-terrain vehicles annually, employing 2,400 people in a community of 2,700, and is such a vital economic engine in the area that when the worst flood in 100 years deluged the town in the summer of 2002, the school and Polaris were the first two places rescue workers tried to spare. Polaris snowmobiles are the city's second most well-known export. The first, of course, is hockey players.

As the Ice Age ended and the glaciers receded a few million years ago, melted water filled 15,000 lakes inside the borders of Minnesota, a name deriving from the Native American words *Minne* and *Sota*, or "Land of Sky-Blue Waters." Ultimately a new ice age took form, one marked not by glacial expanses but by kids with sticks. Minnesota has produced more Olympic and professional hockey players than any other state, and Roseau has provided its share. It has been a hockey hotbed ever since the game was introduced 100 years ago by two brothers from nearby Hallock, Art and Arch Alley, who fashioned sticks from tree branches and watched a game break out on the Roseau River. By 1920, the city had a lighted rink. Another rink went up not long after, and when it blew down in a terrific windstorm in the early 1940s, Roseau Memorial Arena was built, a wooden hockey barn with the smell of history and old beams, and a roof that looks a bit like an upside-down canoe. Memorial is still the home of the Roseau High School Rams, who have been to twenty-nine Minnesota state tournaments and won six of them. Roseau has produced seven NHL players, among them Brian Erickson, who used to be a Washington Capital and now owns a used-car lot. He still answers to the nickname Butsy. His father, the former mayor of Roseau, goes by Binky.

"Usually if you play in the National Hockey League you are the best player in your town, your region, or maybe even in your state," Butsy Erickson said. "I was only the third-best player on my *block*."

Erickson grew up on Third Avenue, one house down from the Broten residence, home to a family of 100 percent Norwegian stock and three future NHLers: Neal, Aaron, and Paul. Newell and Carol Broten and their five children lived in a tight, three-bedroom house. Neal and Paul slept in the same bed for years. One year Newell grossed $4,400 driving a propane truck. Later he worked for the Roseau department of public works. He'd take a five-minute lunch hour and get back in his truck. You made do with what you had and dealt with what was. Having one bathroom tended to make for a morning logjam, so Neal would often go off to school and shower in the locker room. As a kid he would use one of his mother's old girdles and garter belts to hold up his hockey socks, with no apparent self-consciousness. In first grade he was already so polished as a hockey player that he regularly played with fourth-graders, with the understanding that there would be no whining about aches and pains. "If you get hurt, don't start crying, unless you broke your arm," his father would tell him. Neither Newell nor Carol made the trip to Lake Placid. It was going to cost $2,500, and besides, Aaron was playing for the U, Paul for the Roseau Rams. Newell Broten says if he'd known what was going to happen he would've quit his job and scraped together the money, but he says it more for a chuckle than anything. He likes to be amused. He loved the story Herb Brooks told about the time he asked Neal what he'd had for dinner the night before.

"Pizza," Neal replied.

"Anchovies?" Brooks asked.

"No, I think it was Domino's," Neal said. Newell Broten laughed. "We've had a good life," he said.

"I was brought up right," Neal said.

He was wearing faded blue carpenter jeans and a fraying, gray NHL Players Association shirt, and was sitting at a rustic kitchen farm table, overlooking the back of the seventy-five-acre horse farm in River Falls, Wisconsin, he shares with his wife, Sally, and their two daughters. The land has a benign roll and deep quiet. A rusty iron horse welcomes you near the start of the driveway, before you pass a stand of pines and wind up at a modest brown house that seems almost at one with the land, earthy and open. Way out back there's a Native American sweat lodge, an igloo-shaped, back-to-earth sauna where you can heat up stones and bask in warmth all year-round. The horses that Sally raises are in the barn next to the house. Inside, the decor is early-American horsey, with tack hooks and hardware in the bathroom, and antiques and Native American rugs throughout.

"This is a comfort house," Neal said. "If you have mud on your boots, it's no big deal. If something spills, you wipe it up. I love it out here. It's nice and private. No one ever bugs you. We don't get reporters or people who write books, and if one comes, you just beat them away with a stick." He smiled. His face is still cherubic in his forties, and his perpetually tousled hair makes him look younger still.

Understatement is Broten's way. When he and Sally got engaged in February 1981, a year after the Olympics, there were no rhetorical flourishes or bent-knee entreaties. "Maybe we should get married. I'm going to go buy a ring," he said to 18-year-old Sally. She met Neal in the Roseau school parking lot. She had pulled up in a horse trailer to pick up her little sister at a softball tournament. Black flies had the horses making a twitching, kicking racket.

"Need any help?" asked Neal, standing nearby.

Sally Miller knew who was making the offer. Everyone in town knew Neal Broten. He had just finished his freshman year at the University of Minnesota, a five-foot nine-inch, 155-pound prodigy who had helped the Gophers to the 1979 NCAA championship, giving Brooks the perfect sendoff before he went off to the Olympics. Brooks would later call Broten the finest player he ever coached at the U.

Hockey was a way of life for Neal Broten almost from the start. Games would break out on the kitchen floor, three brothers batting around a rolled-up pair of socks. Out front on the street they'd play boot hockey, using two snow chunks for goalposts and walls of plowed snow as sideboards, the same as kids would on the Range and all over northern Minnesota. Most of the games, though, were on North Rink, an oversized metal shed with ice that the kids' fathers would take turns staying up all night to make. If it was 30 below outside, it was 20 below in North Rink. Kids would play for four or five hours after school, and maybe twice as long on weekends, days starting with hot chocolate and Cream of Wheat and lunch usually being skipped, and sometimes dinner, too. Newell Broten was in the house one night around 8:30 and realized Neal, eight at the time, hadn't come back yet. It was clear and brutally cold, maybe 25 below, the kind of night when sounds were unmuffled and seemed to travel for miles. Newell could hear the faint cry of a child coming from the far side of a nearby field. He found Neal in the middle of it, almost chest deep in snow. He'd taken the shortest route home and run out of gas. His overalls were as stiff as planks. Newell lifted his boy out of the snow and carried him home. "To this day I don't know if he would've froze to death if I hadn't heard him crying," Newell Broten said.

Broten learned the game playing shinny hockey, with as many guys per team as would show up. You learned to stick-handle and control the puck, because you might not touch it again for twenty minutes if you lost it. He had quick feet and hands and extraordinary balance and could maneuver the puck with alarming agility. Passing was the essence of Roseau hockey. Always, the puck moved. When your best player is as eager to move it as everyone else, something special happens. The whole team feels included and good. Even as a kid that was Broten's style of leadership. There were not many words. A pregame speech? Butsy Erickson never heard one. He never heard Broten get on someone who was less gifted, either. He made everyone feel important. By his demeanor you couldn't tell whether he'd scored six goals or gotten shut out. His teammates liked him so much that they wanted to make him happy. As much as Broten revered Herb Brooks—he would get goose bumps when he would see him even two decades after Lake Placid—Broten much preferred the carrot to Brooks's oft-used stick. He was generous without thinking about it. After the Olympics Neal went back to the U and won the first Hobey Baker Award as the nation's top collegiate player. Neal's first comment was that his brother Aaron should've won it because

Aaron had had a better year. A year behind Neal at the U, Aaron nearly went to Lake Placid himself; he was one of the forwards—along with fellow Gopher freshman Tim Harrer—whom Brooks brought in for a look in January. The team was incensed at Brooks for toying with them this way, and if Broten hadn't been so well liked and laid-back, it could've been an impossible spot, being torn between wanting his brother to play with him and not wanting to see a teammate get screwed. Neal kept quiet and kept skating.

"He was just a guy who brought everybody along," Erickson said. "Instinctively, he needed and wanted other people around him."

Said Neal, "I loved going to the rink. I loved practicing, passing the puck. The most fun thing about hockey is when you get a group of guys and you play as a team and everyone works in the same direction and you get your goals done. That's what it's about. It feels good to do that."

Roseau youth teams won three state championships when Neal was coming up. One of their biggest games as pee-wees was in Grand Rapids, on the western edge of the Iron Range, another community with deep hockey roots. The buzz beforehand was that there was no way the Roseau boys would be able to compete. Roseau won, 14–0. Neal had nine goals and five assists. "It was just one of those amazing, magical nights," Erickson said. Broten had a lot of those, in a career straight out of a border-town storybook. About the only thing Brooks would ever say to Broten was, "How do you feel?" or "Do you have your legs?"

Broten played thirteen seasons for his home-state team, the Minnesota North Stars, becoming as much of an icon downstate as he'd been in Roseau. In 1985–1986 he became the first American-born player to have a 100-point season in the NHL. He made four NHL All-Star teams. He had his No. 7 jersey retired and he got to hold up the Stanley Cup— huge highlights, even if neither happened where he wanted it to. The Stars moved to Dallas and Broten was traded to New Jersey and won the Cup as a Devil, in 1995. He'd just been named captain before the trade. Broten felt completely out of place in his new environs, a country kid dropped amid the tangle of highways and refineries that clog north Jersey, but he was a two-way force on the ice, playing as unselfishly and creatively as ever. He had 8 goals and 20 assists and was plus-9 in 30 regular-season games. He had 19 more points— 7 goals and 12 assists in 20 playoff games. He followed Ken Morrow as the only 1980 Olympian to have his name on the Stanley Cup. "The Devils don't win that Cup without him," USA Hockey executive Lou Vairo said.

Broten retired from the NHL after seventeen years in 1997, the end more bitter than sweet. He got hurt early in the 1996–1997 season and wound up being sent to Albany in the AHL by the Devils. He was traded to the Los Angeles Kings, finished up back with the Stars. He felt jerked around, was sure he could still play, but decided it was time to go home to Wisconsin and help Sally with the horses, even as he was honored with the NHL's Lester Patrick Award for his contributions to American hockey.

Some guys have trouble with life after the limelight. Broten liked it. Simplicity is best, and fame sometimes isn't simple. He came out of retirement briefly in 1998–1999 to help the United States qualify for the world championships (playing with his brothers for the first time on a national team, he had six points in three games), but that was just being a hockey patriot. He doesn't watch hockey on TV, doesn't read about it in the paper, and skates about a half-dozen times a year, usually in charity games. The only hockey keepsake on display in the house is the replica of his No. 7 jersey the Stars gave him.

"We've done our time in hockey," he said. "Now our life is horses."

Pro hockey is ruled by the clock, the schedule tight and unforgiving, over games, practices, travel. Broten relishes that his time is his own again, the ice sheet of his life awaiting his next move. Soon he would be out in the barn, moving 180 bales of hay to make room for a new shipment. A horse sale was coming up in a few weeks, and he and Sally would be off to that. "Neal's someone who will go whichever way the wind blows," Aaron Broten said. "He's a happy-to-be-alive person. He pretty much doesn't know what's going to happen next week or next month or the next hour, and that's how he likes it."

When Neal was inducted into the U.S. Hockey Hall of Fame, he asked his father to introduce him. Newell Broten is not much keener on speeches than his son. He got some mild sedatives from his local pharmacist and got through it fine, except for the choking up at the end when he called Neal "the greatest son a father could ever hope to have."

"It's not like you're up there talking about duck-hunting," Newell Broten said. "You're talking about your kid, and that kind of gets to you."

———

A stiff backcheck by Zhluktov spoiled Christoff's prime opportunity via Broten, but he had another chance, O'Callahan steering a superb cross-ice pass from the point. On the left side of the goal now, Christoff wristed a shot but Alexei Kasatonov picked it right off his stick. Five minutes remained and it seemed as though it had been a fortnight since anyone had scored. The Russians were charging again. Morrow and Ramsey doubled up to thwart a streaking Kharlamov as he swept down the left side, and then Craig turned away Vasiliev's slap shot and kicked away Petrov's attempt to stuff the rebound. Time was starting to get short. Craig had been brilliant and the United States had done a solid job containing the Russians, but you wondered if the Americans didn't need to commit more to the attack, put the wheels in fast-forward, and not worry so much about having sufficient numbers back to fend off the next Russian wave. It was time to see if the legs really do feed the wolf.

With under four minutes remaining, Ramsey started out of his own end and nudged the puck ahead to Strobel. On the right side, long blond hair poking out from beneath his blue helmet, Strobel started to fire up, cruising past Lebedev, the crowd sensing something good might be unfolding. Strobel had been a football standout in high school in Rochester, Minnesota, but he always seemed to do better in open space than in high-contact zones. Brooks had known Strobel for most of the kid's life. Art Strobel, Eric's father and a one-time New York Ranger, used to play with Brooks on the Rochester Mustangs, a semipro team. Brooks recruited Eric for the U, and more than a few people shared the coach's opinion that Strobel was the best pure skater in the country. He had the biggest thighs this side of Eric Heiden, and jet fuel in his skates, a fluid, straight-up style that came with the ability to lean into turns and stay at full speed, making defenders look as if they were skating with ankle weights. "He was so smooth, so fast, so good," said Don Micheletti, his roommate for two years at the U. "He had the most talent of any player I ever played with."

Strobel's nickname was Electric at the U, but his demeanor was definitely unplugged, laid-back, the current coursing at its own rate. He was unfailingly pleasant and utterly unflappable; his amiable detachment left you wondering at times what was going on within. Brooks knew that Strobel had precisely the sort of high-torque game he needed to attack the Soviets; the only question was whether all the torque would be there and would be revving in the right direction. From the time he was in peewees, Strobel could take over games seemingly at will. His coach, Don Lecy, once asked him before the third period of a big game if he could get a couple of goals; Strobel got him the goals. In the 1979 NCAA semifinals, Strobel wrecked New Hampshire all by himself, scoring a hat trick, leaving coach Charlie Holt to say, "If we could've stopped him, we had a chance." On each goal, Strobel streaked across the blue line, faked to the inside, swept wide, and went in on the defenseless goaltender. The next night, in the final against North Dakota, the Gophers won without much contribution at all from Strobel, and that always seemed to be the rub with him. You knew he could do it, but would he? His inconsistency drove Brooks crazy, but it wasn't about laziness or willful indifference. Strobel just didn't burn with the white-hot intensity that so many of his teammates did. His was an artful, almost whimsical game, a palette full of speed and skill, but the finished canvas varied. "You never knew if he was going to get back on defense, or be doing pirouettes in the neutral zone," trainer Gary Smith said.

Strobel had missed a breakaway in the opening minutes of the first game against Sweden, backhanding a shot high and wide. He'd started the Olympics on the first line with Johnson and McClanahan—as fast a skating line as the United States has ever put on Olympic ice. But Brooks wound up switching things up, putting Dave Silk on the first line, and putting Strobel with Mark Wells and Phil Verchota on the fourth. Strobel never seemed to be on his game offensively in the Olympics, putting most of his energy into stopping goals rather than scoring them. It was okay, the same way it was okay when Brooks moved him from center to right wing and back again when he was at Minnesota. "Some days are better than others," Strobel said. "If you get on a roll, you get on a roll. Hockey is a funny game. Things bounce funny all the time. I think everybody fit into a role during the Olympics. Going into it, I had a lot of chances early. Things didn't seem to be clicking for me offensively. I kind of fit into the role of protecting. That's where I saw myself in those games. Make sure when they are out there you're not going to get scored on. That's where I thought I could be most effective."

It's hard to get Strobel worked up. It's one of the reasons the parents whose kids he coaches in peewees in Apple Valley, Minnesota, appreciate him so much. When the 1980 team was inducted in the U.S. Hockey Hall of Fame in October 2003, Strobel's team took out an ad to congratulate him in *Let's Play Hockey*, the bible of Minnesota hockey. In a world populated by coaches who are over-the-top intense, Strobel keeps it low-key and fun. "Last year we only lost two or three games all year and this year we've only won a couple of games," said Lynn Freeman, one of the team parents. "He's exactly the same coach this year as he was last year. I have never seen him riled up."

Like Bah Harrington, Strobel was drafted by the Sabres and started his pro career with the Rochester Americans. One of his teammates was Dave Schultz, the notorious Broad Street Bully for the Philadelphia Flyer teams of the 1970s. Strobel joked to Schultz that he should teach him how to fight. "You're not here to fight. You're here to make plays and score goals," Schultz said. Strobel's plan was to do his goal scoring in Germany the following season, thinking that the bigger rinks and more open European style would suit him better than the more physical NHL. Then, in an Americans' playoff game, he went into a corner to get a puck, got rammed from behind, and broke a bone in his leg. It was the last competitive hockey game Eric Strobel ever played. He reported this with neither regret nor wistfulness as he sat on a sectional sofa in his spotless and comfortable contemporary colonial. Located in an upscale subdivision south of St. Paul, the house is done in whites and earth tones, with big windows, soothing in a monochromatic way, like Eric Strobel himself.

He went back to the U and got his degree, met his wife, Kim, at his favorite Minneapolis bar, Sergeant Preston's. He became a partner in a computer and telecommunications firm, and he and his sister took over the family office-acoustics business. He and Kim had two daughters ten months apart, Strobel sliding into career and fatherhood as effortlessly as he used to wheel up the ice. He's invariably accommodating if people approach him for an autograph or a conversation about 1980, but he has never had any desire to seize the spotlight or relive the glory. "We came home, people slapped us on the back and said, 'Way to go,' and they had parades for us. And that was it. That's the way we are in the Midwest. Obviously people were proud, but they didn't go overboard, and that was fine. It was a great moment, but where is it going to get you? You just get on with your life."

———

Strobel deftly avoided a hip check and headed toward the blue line, but his open ice closed quickly, and so did his options. He got jammed up by the defense and he and his left wing, Phil Verchota, almost collided. Strobel somehow slid the puck cross ice to Wells, who wound up tying up Pervukhin and forcing a face-off. Strobel, Verchota, and Mark Wells skated off, replaced by Broten, Christoff, and Eruzione.

Christoff's first contribution was a defensive one, bodying Krutov off the puck as he bolted through the U.S. zone. The ubiquitous Krutov regained control and whipped a pass out to Kasatonov, who wound and fired, a low, hard drive that Craig stopped and smothered. Krutov charged toward the goal and again tried to scavenge the puck loose, and this time it was Morrow who was the policeman, cross-checking him from behind. The force of the shot sent Krutov barreling into Craig, his helmet crashing into Craig's mask, the goaltender falling backwards to the ice. As tempers flared and scrums were breaking out all around the goal, Jim Craig lay prone in the crease. He covered his mask with his blocker. It may have been the scariest moment of the Olympics for the Americans, the star goalie on his back, the crowd booing, the anxiety palpable. In front, Morrow, Christoff, and Eruzione bumped with Krutov. Behind the net, Ramsey was entangled with Lebedev. At the end of the bench, Steve Janaszak, who hadn't played since the Madison Square Garden game thirteen days before, wrestled with the possibility that it might be his time.

Apprehension mounted as Craig remained down. Slowly, he shook his head and pulled himself up to a seated position. He flipped the puck from his glove to Kaisla and clambered to his feet. The crowd cheered, thinking the Americans were getting a power play, but Kaisla sent off both Morrow and Lebedev. Craig dropped to his knees and rechecked his pads, then stood up and rapped his stick against his leg. Baker and Johnson skated by to make sure he was okay, tapped his pad with their sticks. On the bench, Janaszak stopped wrestling.

Steve Janaszak had his routine while his teammates slept, and he kept to it. He and Craig Patrick would get up early and go to the rink, and Janaszak would strap on his gear and get in the net, and Patrick would shoot pucks at him in an empty arena. Janaszak was a two-time national champion with the University of Minnesota Gophers. He was the most valuable player of the 1979 NCAA finals, eleven months before Lake Placid. Those solitary sessions with Patrick were the only ice time he would get in the Olympics.

There were 12 hockey teams at the Olympics, 20 players per team, 240 players in all. Steve Janaszak was the only one of them who did not play. The closest he got to action was when Craig got dinged by a Mike Eruzione shot in warm-ups before the West Germany game—and then allowed two soft goals in the first period. Janaszak had the hardest and most thankless role on the team, having gone from standout goalie to spare part, All-American to skate sharpener. Brooks had forewarned him that this could happen, and Janaszak appreciated the heads-up. He stayed ready and positive, the epitome of a team player, putting aside his own agenda for the larger good. One of the first things Jim Craig did in the final press conference was to publicly thank Janaszak and acknowledge his contributions to the team. Then the two Olympic goaltenders, the Olympic poster boy and the answer to a trivia question, embraced.

"In his own way, Janaszak was as important as Craig, because of the way he handled not playing," Lou Vairo said. "The way he supported him and the team and the coach's decision was something special. Imagine if he was a whining, miserable creature in that position? He was perfect."

"I had the best seat in the arena and in the locker room for the greatest sporting event of the twentieth century," Janaszak said.

Larry and Betty Janaszak, Steve's parents, had a harder time dealing with his role than their son. It hurt them to see the big computer printout all the Olympians got of the results in every sport, and to note that their son was the only athlete in the Games who never got to compete. They both sent angry telegrams to Brooks after the Olympics, the coach getting them before the team went to see President Carter in the White House. Larry Janaszak had played hockey a few years before Brooks at St. Paul's Johnson High School. They shared the same hockey roots, the same east side background. It was hard to understand why his boy, who had done so much for Herb Brooks, couldn't get him in for so much as a period in a five-goal rout of the Romanians. Was that too much to ask? Betty didn't think Larry's words were strong enough, so she sent her own telegram. She is a devout Christian woman; the Janaszaks stayed in a lakeside Bible camp during their one week in Lake Placid. She now is sorry for what she did.

"Herb Brooks made Steve a better person," Betty Janaszak said. "He made him stronger, and gave him what he needed to bear up under the whole thing."

Said Steve Janaszak, "The guy had a bigger influence on my life than anybody outside of my parents. It wasn't easy playing for him, because he pushed you beyond what you knew to be your limits. But it was the same thing that made him a great coach. He taught you a lot about yourself, and what it takes to succeed.

"As a competitor it was very difficult for me to play the role of a backup. I'm basically not wired for that. I would like to believe that I provided a good, challenging incentive to Jimmy to perform, but the fact is that this is something which is impossible to measure, and it would be foolish to claim any impact for this. Jimmy was the best amateur goaltender in the world at the time, and the results proved it. And the results are all that matter."

Janaszak came out of White Bear Lake, Minnesota, north of St. Paul, the son of an electrician. He started playing hockey at age five, a fifth-line center on a team that carried three lines. "I spent a lot of time sitting on a snowbank with a frozen butt," Janaszak said. The goalie on the team was a kid named Pee Wee Peliquin, who liked to blow bubbles with his gum, the trouble being that they would stick to the inside of the mask and then freeze. One day Pee Wee got fed up with the bubbles and the stickiness and bolted from the goal, never to return. Steve volunteered and never played fifth-line center again. His father would come home from a long day of wiring and take Steve out to the rink at the local junior high school, where they would play by the headlights of Larry's old Rambler. Steve would skate and skate until it was time to go, and then they'd drive home together, cold and tired and happy. In a lifetime of playing hockey it may be Steve Janaszak's sweetest memory.

Janaszak came to the U from Hill-Murray, a private school in St. Paul, an athlete who wasn't big—five feet eight inches and 160 pounds—but versatile enough to letter not only in hockey but in football, golf, and soccer as well. He was bright and funny and self-deprecating, a math major with a Fu Manchu mustache and a steady-going disposition. He spent summers doing electrical work with his dad and fishing from the dock by a boatyard called Johnson Boat Works, and he spent his winters between the pipes. In three seasons following the Olympics, Janaszak appeared in three NHL games, one with the North Stars and two with the Colorado Rockies. He floated around the minors, to Fort Wayne, Fort Worth, Wichita. In Texas he worked as an electrician on the side. On the first night of his pro career, his Baltimore Skip-jacks of the Eastern Hockey League provided an unforget-table initiation: Nickel Beer Night. The Zamboni broke down twice, and there was a full-scale brawl after the winning goal was scored. "I stepped onto the ice and got a bucket of beer dumped on my head," Janaszak said. "And all I could think was, 'A week ago I was with the president.'"

More than most, Janaszak would learn that life can defy all expectation. A short walk from the team's trailers in the Olympic Village was an entertainment complex with a small theater. One day a bunch of U.S. players came in to watch a movie, rearranged the furniture, and got a stern talking-to from an interpreter who was working in the complex. Several days later, Janaszak went down to Main Street and purchased a ceramic heart for Valentine's Day, when the United States beat the Czechs and the backup goaltender was beginning to become very interested in this interpreter. He gave her the heart. Her name was Jackie Minichello, and she would become Mrs. Steve Janaszak. After the Russia game, he and Jackie and her family went out to eat in a little place on the outskirts of town. It was the first time he met his future in-laws.

During his hockey journeys, Janaszak met a top executive with an investment firm and wound up getting into the world of finance. He is a bond trader who lives in the village of Babylon, on the south shore of Long Island, a short walk to Great South Bay, a world apart from White Bear Lake. He is a contented husband and father of two daughters. When he thinks of Lake Placid, his memories go far beyond the spectacle of the game against Russia or the joy of scrambling onto the podium and having a medal put around his neck and hearing the national anthem. "I met a person who became my wife, my best friend, and who was able to turn a conceited young jerk hockey player into a productive husband and father," Steve Janaszak said. "In the vocabulary of my current business, the whole thing is a trade I would do again in a heartbeat."

From his spot on the bench, Janaszak watched the teams skating four-on-four with just under three minutes to play in the period. Brooks wanted the best-skating foursome he could come up with at such a critical time—players who could cover all the open space and not let the Soviets set up one of their passing clinics. Mark Johnson was set to take the face-off, joined by McClanahan, Christian, and Baker. The Soviets went with Petrov, Mikhailov, Vasiliev, and Starikov. To the left of Craig, Johnson and Petrov faced off, and the draw was a draw. Baker rammed Petrov into the sideboards and rode him down, Petrov bounding up angrily but thinking better of exacting revenge. Johnson started out of his zone but he was pickpocketed by Mikhailov and, moments later, pickpocketed the puck right back, off the stick of Vasiliev. Johnson started up ice and pushed the puck ahead to a streaking McClanahan on his left, a two-on-one taking shape, the crowd letting out an expectant roar. But Starikov played McClanahan superbly and Vasiliev raced back to hound Johnson, and the Soviets escaped without so much as a shot on goal being taken.

The Soviets controlled again after O'Callahan's centering pass in the Soviet zone was blocked by Starikov, who looked up and found Balderis cruising through center. There were under two minutes to play. Brooks had been keeping the shifts short the whole game to keep his players fresh, and was still at it, Pavelich, Schneider, and Harrington coming on, Schneider immediately making a fine hustle play, catching Balderis from behind with a lunging poke-check that loosened the puck over to Ramsey. It was a simple play in the fast flow of the action, but it was just what Makarov was talking about when he said the Americans' eyes were burning. Their offense in the game was sporadic, but the effort was consistently full-bore. The U.S. players were contesting everything, making it difficult for the Soviets to sustain their attack. Now if they could only find a goal somewhere.

Chapter Six

STICKING
AROUND

Hemmed in by the sideboards and with Helmut Balderis all over him, Mike Ramsey cleared the puck out of his zone. The teams would be back at full strength in a half-minute. Vasiliev fed Balderis as he circled back in the neutral zone. Balderis pivoted to go on the attack, but just as he did, Mark Pavelich dropped low to the ice and stripped him at the Soviet blue line and Buzz Schneider reacted instantly, filling his wing with a few explosive strides. Without even appearing to look, Pavelich passed the puck behind him, dropping it for Schneider, the pair of them reading each other superbly just as they had in the first period, and indeed, through the entire Olympics. If you got to an open patch of ice, Mark Pavelich would find you. He never wanted the fuss and the spotlight that came when he scored himself; when he did, his revelry was invariably brief and self-conscious. He almost never raised his stick, the way most other hockey players did. Pavelich probably spent as much time on ice in his life as the rest of the team put together, and it showed, not only in his skating but in his instincts. If you didn't find him on a lake back home in Eveleth, it was usually because he was up the hill at the U.S. Hockey Hall of Fame, watching videotape of Bobby Orr.

"That was his hero," John Harrington, linemate and fellow Iron Ranger, said. "Even though Orr was on defense, that's what he wanted to do, how he wanted to play, the spin-a-ramas, coming down on the defense, playing a game of chicken, daring them to stop him. Pav was spectacular."

Long after the 1980 Olympics, someone asked Herb Brooks how to locate Pavelich, his undersized, underrated, and overwhelmingly gifted center. Brooks suggested heading for the north shore of Lake Superior, in the northeast corner of Minnesota.

"You'll need some luck, and some good snow tires," the coach said.

Pavelich had a game all his own, and a style all his own, too, forged through all those hours on Ely Lake out the back door of his little brown house. He wasn't much good at any other sport but was like a windup toy on skates; you put him on the ice and watched him go. Pavelich could change direction and create at full speed, a dynamic talent who made more impact with less acclaim than anyone else in the locker room. It was the way Pavelich preferred it. The people of Eveleth honored him with his own float on the Fourth of July parade five months after the Olympics, a festive occasion except that Pavelich didn't show. He was the only 1980 player who didn't go to Salt Lake City for the 2002 Olympics and the cauldron-lighting. He had thick lips and straight brown hair that flopped on his forehead, and he was maddeningly elusive on the ice—"He's by far the best skater I've ever

seen," said longtime friend, teammate, and current Eveleth
High School coach Craig Homola—and the same way off it.
Pavelich would rather have root canal than do an interview.
He'd rather play than deal with the repetition and dissection
of practice. He'd rather hunt and fish more than anything
that didn't involve a stick and a puck. Outdoors was his fa-
vored environment, and when he retired after six-plus seasons in the NHL, he lived without electricity and plumbing
while he and his wife, Kara, built their house. The night he
scored five goals for the New York Rangers on Winston Hat
Night was Pavelich's worst nightmare—thousands of hats on
the Garden ice and no place to hide. His Ranger teammates
joked that the only way you'd ever get him to agree to being
on the postgame show was if you promised him a fishing pole
as the payoff.

When he was at the University of Minnesota–Duluth,
Pavelich and a teammate decided to go hunting before practice one day. They moved their rifles from one car to another
in the Duluth Entertainment and Convention Center parking lot and set off about twenty miles up the road. Trouble
was that Vice President Walter Mondale was in town to give
a speech at the Convention Center and Secret Service men
on the rooftops had seen the two young men with the guns.
Soon there was an all-points-bulletin out for Pavelich and his
friend, and the highway patrol, two county sheriffs, and federal agents were combing northern Minnesota. The man-
hunt lasted most of the day.

"They were all searching for a guy who was going to
assassinate the vice president," said Gus Hendrickson, the
UMD coach. "They didn't know it was just Pav out partridge
hunting."

When Pavelich reported for practice, he was apprehended by authorities, who took him into a room and interrogated him. When he came out, assistant coach Mike Sertich asked him if everything was okay.

"I didn't even know the governor was in town," Pavelich said, in complete innocence.

Pavelich's taciturn ways were almost as legendary as his playmaking, and he would often drive Brooks mad. Brooks's psychological wheels never stopped turning, and he loved the challenge of concocting ways of pushing players to get better. He'd been doing it successfully for years at the U. Phil Verchota heard nonstop about a hotshot high school winger the coach was supposedly recruiting. "He's six-four and 220 and can shoot the puck through the boards," Brooks would say and then skate away. The recruit never materialized, but the message did: Verchota had better bring his A game or his spot on the wing might belong to someone else. Before a big game against highly regarded Bowling Green in the national championship year of 1979, Brooks pulled aside Verchota and Don Micheletti, two of his biggest and best forwards. "When [Ken] Morrow gets the puck, I want you guys to stay away from him. Just back off. I don't want either of you guys getting hurt." Brooks, of course, wanted Verchota and Micheletti to be all over Morrow. And they were. Brooks hated it when his tactics did not work, and they did not work on Pavelich. When the Olympic team played an exhibition game in Hibbing, Minnesota, eight miles from Eveleth, Brooks made a point to track down Gus Hendrickson.

"I need you to go talk Iron Range to Pavelich, because he won't listen to me," Brooks said. Hendrickson found Pavelich and told him Brooks was upset and that he needed to start listening to him.

"Oh."

"He's really getting mad."

"Oh."

"He says if you don't start doing what he wants, you won't play hockey again in the world because he'll blackball you."

"Oh."

"So what's going to happen?"

"I don't know."

Said Hendrickson, "It wasn't insubordination. He would never do anything intentionally to be a smart-ass. That's just the way he was."

Before a road game against Michigan Tech, Minnesota-Duluth coach Hendrickson stopped in a Houghton, Michigan, diner for a cup of coffee, and there was Pavelich, his star center, eating a couple of pasties. Game time was about an hour and a half away.

"What are you doing, Pav?" Hendrickson asked.

"I'm eating."

"Why?"

"I'm hungry."

"The game is in ninety minutes."

"OK," said Pavelich. He kept eating, and had a hat trick that night.

Pavelich had a simple, well-defined universe—and didn't much care about anything that was beyond it. Symbols? He donated his gold medal and Olympic warm-up suit to the Hockey Hall of Fame. "It's better off here than in the back of my closet someplace," he said. Reporters were nothing but people you don't know asking about things they don't know, resulting in exposure he didn't care about. Clothes were a complete afterthought. A friend from Eveleth visited Pavelich in New York when he was playing for the Rangers. After the game there was a celebrity-laden party on the Upper East Side of Manhattan. Ron Duguay was there with a couple of models. So was All-Star defenseman Barry Beck, lots of pretty people. Pavelich showed up in jeans and a flannel shirt with holes in it. During one college road trip to Notre Dame, Hendrickson mandated that everyone have a jacket and suitcase. Pavelich wore a hunting jacket. Somebody opened his suitcase to find a toothbrush and a pair of underwear and nothing more. Nick Fotiu, a Rangers teammate, once took him out shopping to get some decent clothes so he wouldn't be in such flagrant violation of Brooks's Rangers dress code.

"He dressed like a mountain man from the backwoods of Minnesota," Fotiu said. "Then he would come out on the ice and play his heart out. He was an unbelievable player."

Undrafted out of college, Pavelich became one of the elite centers in the NHL. He loved the fraternity of the locker room and was a complete rascal when he was in it. He once put a grouse in Mike Sertich's pants leg. He'd routinely saw guys' sticks in half, then retape them and watch for the reaction when the bottom went flying. In New York, a fellow Minnesotan named Tom Younghans was excited about his Rangers debut and his first home game in the Garden. "You've got to lead us out there tonight," Pavelich told him. Younghans was honored. Pavelich went off and put Scotch tape on his blades. Younghans indeed led the Rangers onto the Madison Square Garden ice—and fell on his face.

Even with his antics, Pavelich's teammates loved him everywhere he played. Not only was he absolutely unselfish and wanted no credit, he made everyone around him better, a full-speed freelancer in a five-foot seven-inch body with steel-cabled wrists and forearms that made him as strong a 160-pounder as you will find. He was the guy who set up Baker for the huge goal in the final half-minute against Sweden; who might've been the best player on the ice against Czechoslovakia; who had two more assists against the Soviets. He never got tired and still doesn't. Joe Devaney, the visiting locker-room supervisor at Madison Square Garden, is a close friend of Pavelich's. Devaney has seen Pavelich paddle a canoe an entire day without letting up. Teammates swore they never saw him take a deep breath.

"As a wing, all you had to do was get open, and the puck would be there," said Bob Hallstrom, who teamed with Pavelich at Eveleth High School before going on to play for Cornell.

The son of a carpenter, Pavelich was never much for the books or formal functions. Even when he was around his closest friends, he was quiet. He was like that even before the tragedy that happened the summer before he enrolled at UMD. Pavelich was out hunting with friends in the woods not far from his house. The guys fanned out, Pavelich fired his gun at a bird, and the next thing anyone knew, Pavelich's neighbor and best friend, Ricky Holger, was dead. The funeral was at a church in Eveleth, and the whole town turned out. The boys' parents didn't blame Pavelich; they knew it was a terrible mistake. Pav's friends were there for him, their support and compassion strong but unspoken.

"I think we all tried to treat him the same, because we were kind of nervous about not wanting to say the wrong thing," Hallstrom said. "We didn't really want to bring it up.

We were pretty scared that he would do something to himself. I guess we were too dumb to intervene, or talk to him." Friends said the loss made him even quieter and more reclusive. Each year around the time of the accident, Pavelich often would withdraw even more.

Hallstrom paused. "Pav would never hurt a soul," he said. "Never." People closest to him know the immense burden of guilt he felt, and they have great admiration that he could get through it and carry on and give himself a splendid hockey career and a fulfilling life. John Rothstein roomed with Pavelich for a time at UMD. "He is as wonderful as wonderful can be," Rothstein said.

Pavelich has a teenage daughter and still lives in the handsome, woodsy home he and Kara built, with windows on a lake in Lutsen, Minnesota, a couple of hours east of Eveleth. It takes a lot to get him out of the woods. He shocked his teammates by showing up for the reunion game they had in Los Angeles before the 2002 Olympics, driving out from Minnesota. He camped on his way home, took his time, stopped and bought fishing lures. Pavelich surprised everyone again by driving out for the Hollywood premiere of the 2004 film *Miracle.* Soon it was back to his life in the woods, to his land and his backhoe and bulldozer, and to the privacy he cherishes.

"Not too many people in life can say they are doing exactly what they want, and Pav is," Devaney said. "He's completely happy and content with what he does. He marches to his own drum, and it's a great drum."

———

With the period and the twin penalties winding down, Schneider took the feed from Pavelich and was deep on the left wing without much net to shoot for. He ripped a shot that went through the crease. The puck shot along the boards to the point and Jack O'Callahan shot it back in. Schneider fought for it behind the net, but the Soviets got control and Balderis backhanded it up the wing to Makarov, who charged through center into the American zone and centered to Vasiliev, who tried to backhand a shot on Craig but was foiled by O'Callahan.

The teams were back at full strength as the clock went under the one-minute mark. Nearing the Soviet blue line, Christoff tried to stickhandle in when Krutov stole the puck off his stick and was off with startling speed, bearing down on Craig, a two-on-one with Yuri Lebedev, a sandy-haired forward with No. 11 on his back and the dashing looks of a TV anchorman. There were thirty seconds remaining in the second period. A foreboding quiet filled the building as Krutov and Lebedev came in on Craig. A two-goal deficit would probably be too much to come back from against this team. Krutov came down on the right and then pulled up slightly, preparing to pass; he had a good piece of the near side to shoot for and probably should've taken the shot himself. Krutov centered the puck for Lebedev. O'Callahan hustled back and dove at Krutov to try to break up the pass, and then Ramsey was diving, too, extending his stick, impeding Lebedev's path, and preventing him from getting off a shot.

The puck skidded all the way across the ice. Nobody in the building was more relieved than Steve Christoff.

It had not been an easy go of it in Lake Placid for Christoff. He had been the leading goal scorer in the pre-Olympic season, with 35 goals in 56 games, but had scored just once—late in a 7–2 trouncing of Romania—through the first six games. He had had chances but wasn't converting them, and that was never easy for someone as accustomed to scoring as Christoff, who had averaged almost two points per game in his sophomore and junior years with the U—and was named the team's MVP as a sophomore.

Christoff was raised in Richfield, Minnesota, a suburb of Minneapolis, an All-American center of few words and many goals (he was only the third thirty-goal scorer the Gophers had ever had) who would achieve his own sort of renown quite independent of the Lake Placid miracle, having served as the model for the Hobey Baker Memorial Award. Every year, the top male college hockey player in the country gets a 40-pound sixteen-inch-high bronze and acrylic likeness of Steve Christoff, who shot hard and skated fast; a forward who had size and agility and eyebrows that looked like a hedge. For all his gifts, Christoff also had a penchant for self-criticism, his face turning into a glower when things weren't going right. "Steve could have a great game, but if he wasn't scoring, if he wasn't getting goals or assists, he was real hard on himself," said Don Micheletti, a Minnesota teammate. "That was how he measured his success."

Hockey, for a long time, was Christoff's life. When he was in ninth grade, he interviewed the president of the Minnesota North Stars, Walter Bush, for a school report. The report had nothing to do with the North Stars' decision to draft him on the second round after his sophomore year at Minnesota, in 1978. Christoff signed with the North Stars after the Olympics and was a major factor in the club's run to the semifinals of the NHL playoffs in the spring of 1980, scoring eight goals—a rookie record for the postseason. When a reporter remarked on how grounded and single-minded he seemed barely two months past the Olympics, Christoff said, "You can't live your life on what was in yesterday's newspaper."

At six feet one inch and more than 200 pounds, Christoff had perhaps the quickest release on the team, a snap shot more than a slap shot. It was his greatest weapon, and when a debilitating shoulder injury early in his pro career robbed him of some of the snap, the goals slowed dramatically. "It was like a great pitcher who suddenly loses his fastball," said Glen Sonmor, Christoff's coach with the North Stars. "It was a sad case after he got hurt, because he could really rifle the thing. He had this great, great asset, and then it was gone."

Christoff had 55 goals in the 1981–1982 and 1982–1983 seasons and a total of 17 goals the next two years, making an almost instantaneous transformation into journeyman, getting traded three times in five NHL seasons. He got tired of moving around, and then decided to enroll in flight school and move around for a living. He is a pilot for Mesaba Airlines, flying short hops around the Midwest, apparently suffering no permanent psychic scars from the night the team's pre-Olympic trip to Warroad, Minnesota, featured not one but two takeoffs aborted when the pilot taxied into a light pole. Christoff has successfully avoided all light poles as a pilot, and done likewise with the celebrity that comes to 1980 Olympians, content to let others be the more visible team representatives. These days he gets his sporting kicks vicariously, through his wife, Anna, one of the elite female handball players in the world.

———

After the diving defensive efforts of O'Callahan and Ramsey wrecked the Russians' two-on-one chance, Krutov regained possession and pushed the puck back to Valery Vasiliev at the left point. The game had the frenzied feeling of the final seconds of regulation, not the second period. Vasiliev swung it to Pervukhin on the right. Pervukhin fired a slap shot into the S of USA on Craig's chest. Craig held on and took a little skate out of the crease.

Broten faced off with Lebedev and gave hard chase after Christoff backhanded the puck into the Soviet end. As the clocked ticked toward zero, Broten, the slightest player on the ice, skated hard into the corner and drove the Soviets' brilliant young defenseman, Fetisov, into the boards. The horn sounded. The teams headed off and Jim Craig skated slowly out of goal, unstrapping his mask as he went. He looked up at the scoreboard. Someone rubbed him on the head. The goaltender looked over his shoulder at the goal, a hint of displeasure on his face. He'd seen 30 shots in two periods and stopped 27 of them. The Americans were behind by a goal, against a team that had dominated third periods for decades. In five previous Olympic Games, the Soviets had outscored their opponents, 14–4, in the final period. The U.S. team had won its third periods by a score of 11–3 in these Olympics. For months Brooks had been saying that while he wouldn't guarantee a medal, he would guarantee that no team would be in better condition than the United States. His team's goal was to be in a game with the Soviets with twenty minutes to play. The team had gotten its wish, and nobody knew better than Warren Strelow that it would be Craig who would be spending the third period under the most competitive duress. Nobody knew much of anything better than Warren Strelow when it came to playing the goal.

"He's probably as outstanding a coach in understanding

the fundamentals of goaltending and making goaltenders better as there is in the game," said Sonmor, the former North Stars coach who brought Strelow in to work with his University of Minnesota goalies in the mid-1960s.

Strelow was working as a high school English and social studies teacher at the time, coaching the school team in Mahtomedi, Minnesota. He would go on to become the first full-time NHL goaltending coach, with the Washington Capitals in 1983, and he has been helping goaltenders stop pucks ever since.

More than a half-century has passed since Strelow played his first game in goal and learned a lesson for a lifetime. The debut came at an outdoor rink in St. Paul with goal judges stationed behind both goals. Strelow's team outshot the opponents 56–3 but lost 1–0 because Warren let in a goal when he was talking to one of the goal judges. He has never needed another reminder of the perils of wandering focus. His team won the city championship the next year with Warren in net.

Strelow grew up by the railroad tracks in east St. Paul, an only child, a banker's son. He lived down the hill from Brooks, and they played countless hours of hockey together at Phalen Park, taking turns jimmying the lock of the warming house so they could turn the lights on and keep playing. They both went on to star for St. Paul's Johnson High School, Strelow graduating in the class of 1951 as an all-state goaltender. The Johnson team played outdoors then, drawing sometimes as many as 2,000 spectators. Strelow was a big, quiet kid who wasn't inclined to date or socialize or make small talk. Sports were his passion, and there was one for every season: football, hockey, and baseball. Strelow was never happier than when he was in the net, or behind the plate, catching. He liked strapping on equipment and going to work. He once got behind the plate without a mask and had his cheek broken by a foul ball ("I looked like a squirrel with nine million nuts in my mouth"), but neither that nor a series of pucks in the face could persuade him to wear a mask in goal. Real goalies didn't wear masks in the 1950s.

Strelow relished the responsibility that came with playing goal. He coaches the same way he taught. In the classroom, he preached patience and doing your best, and if he had to correct or critique a student's work, he would always try to finish with something positive. Goaltenders are fall guys in a rectangular cage, scapegoats waiting to happen. Screw up and a red light goes on. Screw up and your team loses. What's the gain in beating up a goaltender after he lets up a soft goal? It may be more important to minister to a guy's psyche than to refine his technique.

"The position is negative. Why put any more negativity on it?" Strelow said.

Working with goaltenders is like building a house, Strelow believes. You begin with a solid foundation, with fundamentals such as balance, being square to the puck, knowing how to read and react to certain situations. When the foundation is in place, you build up from there. But underpinning everything is self-confidence and the ability to cope with good things and bad things with the same emotional stability. One of the first things Strelow admired about Jim Craig was his ability to bounce back. If he made a mistake he wouldn't wallow in it. Outwardly he'd stay supremely confident, even if he were going through a rough patch. After Craig gave up the two long goals in the first period against West Germany, Brooks thought about pulling him and putting in Steve

Janaszak. Brooks told Janaszak to get loose and get ready, then talked to Strelow.

"No," Strelow said. "He hasn't lost a game. We have to stay with him. He'll play his way through this and be a better goalie because of it." Strelow has always been his goalies' staunchest ally, a rotund and outsized advocate in thick glasses and street shoes. He doesn't believe in embarrassing them or humiliating them. He plays to a guy's strengths. He never says, "Do it this way." He says, "I have something that may help you." His approach inspires profound loyalty from people such as San Jose Sharks' goaltender Evgeni Nabokov, who won the Calder Trophy as the NHL's Rookie of the Year under Strelow's tutelage, setting franchise records of shutouts and victories.

"It's hard to describe what this guy does for us, how helpful he is," Nabokov once said. "You've got to see him with us day after day. This guy gives up all his heart—everything that he has—to hockey. His life is hockey. He's watching the tapes all the time. He's talking to you. Anybody can coach. Any goalie who retires can tell you what to do. It's not that hard. But it's harder to go deeper, to get to know the goalie as a person and to understand them. Nobody is able to understand you like Warren does."

Strelow wanted to be an Olympic goaltender himself, once. He tried out for the 1956 team, but was No. 3 on a team that was only going to keep two goaltenders. In the summer of 1955, he had another tryout. Strelow was working a summer construction job with a guy who was a bird dog for the Boston Red Sox. He arranged for Strelow to have a workout when the Red Sox minor-league affiliate in Louisville, Kentucky, visited St. Paul. Then about six foot two and 200 pounds, Strelow stepped in the cage and knocked the first five pitches he saw over the fence. The bird dog was astounded. The club's head scout came in a little later in the summer and invited Strelow to come to spring training. One month later Strelow heard from his draft board. He didn't go to spring training in 1956. He went into the Army.

After his hitch was done, Strelow returned to Minnesota and reconnected with Brooks. When Brooks got the job at the U, Strelow was one of his first hires. When Brooks got the Olympic job, it was a foregone conclusion who would be coaching the goaltenders in Lake Placid. Before the tryout at the National Sports Festival in the summer of 1979, Brooks told Strelow that a panel of top coaches would pick the players.

"And you will pick the goalies," Brooks said.

"What if I pick someone you don't like?" Strelow replied.

"I don't care who you pick, you just better be right."

Strelow paused and laughed faintly, remembering. "Herbie believed in me. He gave me a chance. He was my best friend," he said.

The fall of 2003 and winter of 2004 were some of the saddest and loneliest times Warren Strelow ever had. Seriously overweight and suffering from a kidney disease, Strelow was waiting for a kidney transplant when Herb Brooks died. He had been on the list for eight months. Nine days after the funeral, Strelow's wife had a dream that Brooks had come over to the house, concerned about Warren's health and inquiring about the transplant. The next morning, Strelow got a phone call from his doctor. A kidney had been found. It was a perfect match in all six of the critical categories. The doctor told Strelow he had better odds of winning the lottery than of getting such a match. The doctor called it a miracle. Strelow hung up and wondered if Herb Brooks was still looking out for him. He had a transplant operation a day later.

It took well, but there were complications with medication, requiring him to recuperate at home in Minnesota. The goaltending coach for the San Jose Sharks, Strelow found himself apart from a team for the first time in nearly twenty years, not happily immersed in the minutiae of stopping pucks but wearily trying to get his body right. As grateful as he was for his miracle kidney and the chance to be with his wife, Carlene, it was hard to be away, and harder yet to fathom that his best friend was gone. Strelow talked to his goalies every Monday through the season, watched game tapes constantly, and conversed almost daily with Wayne Thomas, former NHL goalie and the Sharks' assistant general manager. The phone can accomplish only so much. "This is a guy who loves his job and loves being around the players," Thomas said. "I think it would be hard on anyone."

For decades Strelow has talked to his pupils about being patient, not expecting improvement to come instantly. He has an artificial hip and an artificial knee. He has diabetes. He has struggled with his weight problem. The nurturer of netminders, Strelow hasn't been too successful in getting himself to be patient. He keeps reaching for the phone to call Herbie, keeps thinking it might be Herbie on the line when someone calls him. Mostly the house has been quiet. The Sharks made it to the Western Conference finals in the 2004 playoffs. Maybe that would be something to build on for the following season. For Warren Strelow, it was a nice thing to think about.

THE PUCK
STOPS HERE

Jim Craig had the corner seat in the locker room, closest to the door. As his teammates charged in, Craig kept to himself and did what he always did, taking off his skates, his pads, his chest protector, all his gear, and then methodically putting it all back on again. He had started doing this at Boston University, finding it a good way to occupy his time between periods, to ready himself for another twenty-minute test. He lived period to period when he was in the net, breaking them down into four five-minute installments, and his ritual equipment-shedding was one of the ways he calibrated the time.

"Whether I had a good period or a bad period, that was my signal that it was time to start over," Craig said.

Goalies are different from other human beings. By workplace location and mindset, they occupy their own distinct space. A goal cage is six feet wide and four feet high, twenty-four square feet to keep the puck from penetrating. You are quite literally the last line of defense, the ultimate determinant of who wins and who loses. You need a special sort of self-reliance to play the goal, and a willfulness that borders on defiance: *You are not getting this puck past me.* Jim Craig had both in abundance. His self-confidence was staggering at times. If somebody scored on him, it was an aberration, a screwup by someone, somewhere, and one that wouldn't be repeated. When Craig first got to Boston University, the incumbent goalie was Brian Durocher, and a heralded recruit named Mark Holden was on the way. Craig told Jack Parker, the Boston University coach, "I've seen Durocher and I've seen Holden, and I'm going to be your goalie." Never mind that Craig was not hotly recruited coming out of Oliver Ames High School in North Easton, Massachusetts, or that he came to BU from Massasoit Community College, nobody's breeding ground of big-time hockey players. Parker was stunned at the kid's cockiness. It made the coach think of Paul Newman's line in *The Hustler:* "When you're good and you know you're good, it's the greatest feeling in the world."

Jim Craig was good. He was very good, and he picked a wonderful time to be even better than that. In the first period alone, he faced 18 shots and stopped 16 of them, kicking, gloving, sprawling, an acrobat in a white mask. He faced 12 more shots in the second period and turned away 11 of them. He had first caught Brooks's eye the previous spring in the world championships, stifling Czechoslovakia in a 2–2 tie. Craig could skate, had a good knack for cutting down angles, and at six feet one inch and 190 pounds did not give opponents much net to shoot at. "Jimmy had the fastest glove I've ever seen," said Randy Millen, a high school teammate who went on to play at Harvard. "He'd just steal goals from guys with that glove."

The only time the United States had won a hockey gold medal in the Olympics, in 1960, it had gotten a superb effort from the man in goal, Jack McCartan. The two times the Americans had won silver, Willard Ikola (1956) and Lefty Curran (1972) had likewise delivered big plays in the net. Brooks and Strelow both believed that Craig was the man best equipped to face the crucible of Olympic pressure, no matter that backup goalie Steve Janaszak had been the most valuable player of Brooks's 1979 championship team at the U.

Craig started playing goalie at age 11, in borrowed skates with cardboard toes. The invitation came on Holmes's Pond in North Easton, Massachusetts, forty-five minutes south of Boston, not far from the snug, roadside colonial where he grew up with his parents, Don and Margaret Craig, and seven brothers and sisters. It was a house where the ashtrays were usually full—both parents were heavy smokers—and affection was present in equal bounty. Don Craig was a warm-hearted man, huggy and kissy in a time when a less secure guy would not have been so. Before Jim left for school each morning, he would write a little note to his mother— "Have a great day, Mom, I love you"—and leave it in the porchway mailbox. Margaret Craig saved every note. A few times when Jim got mad at his parents, he tried to storm off to bed.

"I could never do it," Craig said. "I'd always have to come back down. I couldn't go to sleep without kissing them good-night."

Phil Thompson, the Craigs' postman, encouraged Jim to try out for the local youth hockey league. On Holmes's Pond one day, Craig heard kids talking about a team called the Aces. Craig decided to give it a go, though he didn't know the red line from the blue line, and thought offsides was a rule from football. A catcher in baseball, he immediately liked the idea that the position of goalie came with a bunch of gear and an assurance that he'd be on the ice the whole time. None of this shift-to-shift stuff for him. At Oliver Ames High, the only time Craig exchanged words with his coach, Gerard Linehan, was when Linehan pulled him from a game. Ames was up 8–0 and Linehan wanted to give the backup guy a chance. "He wanted to play every minute of every game and every practice," Linehan said.

Playing goal quickly took center stage in Craig's athletic life. He and his brothers beat up the basement of the house, blasting slap shots at each other with a street-hockey ball. At 13, he'd make early Sunday morning trips to Boston Arena to play the goal against 16- and 17-year-olds. He'd want Linehan to shoot 200 pucks a day at him after practice. He loved to challenge people, and to accept challenges back. Dave Silk had the same hypercompetitiveness, and their practice battles were a BU staple, Silk saying he was going to put a puck in the upper corner and Craig telling him he had no chance and taking it away. "There was nothing Jimmy wouldn't take on," said Billy LeBlond, a defenseman and BU teammate. "He was as hard as stone in goal." In his spare time as a young teenager, Craig would draw pictures of rinks and goals and practice signing his autograph. Craig was a relentless worker and knew exactly where he wanted the work to take him.

"He truly believed in himself," Linehan said. "This wasn't just another kid from a small town who was going to be a businessman like his father or an accountant like his brother.

He was going to be a hockey player. He set his goal and he was going to do whatever he had to do to get there."

Craig grew eight inches in his last year in high school and once he got acclimated to his body, his goaltending career took off. After Craig's one-week stay at Norwich Academy, a military school in Vermont (he couldn't stand the regimentation any more than John Harrington could at the Air Force Academy), and part of a year at Massasoit, Parker brought him into BU. Craig went 25–1–1 in his sophomore year, then went undefeated (16–0–0) as a junior in 1977–1978, helping BU capture the NCAA championship, doing it with his usual swagger. Craig played Boston College a total of 15 times in his BU career and won 14 of the games. Midway through his senior year, before the annual Beanpot Tournament—the midwinter intracity competition among BU, BC, Harvard, and Northeastern—Joe Concannon, the late *Boston Globe* sportswriter, asked Craig how he wanted to remember his last Beanpot.

"I want to play BC in the finals, be up by a goal, look at the scoreboard, and shake their hands as losers one more time," Craig said. Concannon wasn't taking notes or taping when Craig was talking, and Craig wasn't sure if the interview was on the record or off. But he said what he said and didn't back off it when his comment showed up in the *Globe*.

Craig had a penchant for stirring things up, getting people riled, whether with his stick or his mouth. He talked constantly to his teammates during games and practices, a not-always-welcome stream of pleas, admonitions, and critiques. "He never shut up," Mark Johnson said. "You just had to tune him out." Even in no-check adult leagues, Craig, now a forward, not infrequently gets embroiled in heated exchanges, sometimes egged on by opposing players wanting to record their own Olympic moment by making a run at the miracle goalie, sometimes by his own chatter and stickwork. A few years ago, Randy Millen, an adult-league teammate, urged Craig to tone it down. "The goal for this year is not to score the most points or win the most games. It's for you to win the Lady Byng," Millen said, referring to the sportsmanship trophy the NHL awards each year. Craig throttled himself back. Millen admired his behavioral adjustment.

Craig has never been one to worry about editing his thoughts or feelings. He is unhesitatingly forthright. If he feels something, he says it; if he is angry, he vents it. Just as quickly, the feeling and anger pass. Hugh Gorman III, Craig's longtime friend and agent, jokes about how Craig can be hollering one minute about some business deal and turn around the next and say, "Where are we going to have lunch?" It's the same when Craig has a disagreement with his wife, Sharlene. You get it out and move on. Craig lost his mother to cancer when he was 20, two and a half years before the Olympics. He lost his oldest sister, Ann, a couple of years after. He's sure there's a connection there in his desire not to hold on to things.

"In our household, you didn't waste your time being mad at someone you loved," he said. "You can be mad, but get over it. You don't want to be mad at someone and wish you had said something that you didn't."

Craig wasn't overly chummy with most of the guys on the Olympic team. It just wasn't his priority. The dozen Minnesotans were from a different universe. Even his three BU teammates on the Olympic squad—Eruzione, Silk, and Jack

O'Callahan—were different, raised in more urban environments in and around Boston; North Easton had much more of a small-town feel. Craig didn't mind going off on his own. He was one of eight children, and like a lot of children from large families, he learned self-sufficiency early, learned how to carve out his own space and his own routine. "He was a loner," Warren Strelow said. When his BU teammates headed off to throw back some Molsons at the Dugout, the team's office headquarters on Commonwealth Avenue, Craig wasn't often among them. Nineteen guys on the team use one agent to represent their marketing and promotional interests; Jim Craig has his own. Brooks had the players take a 300-plus question psychological profile in the summer before the Olympics. One of the few who didn't take the test was Craig, who didn't see the point. Brooks could've taken his refusal as insubordination or as a sign that Craig had some latent vulnerability he didn't want exposed. Instead he took it as evidence of Craig's take-on-the-world mentality, which the coach had liked so much in the 1979 world championships.

During the pre-Olympic tour, the players moved into apartments together in the Twin Cities area; Craig lived in the basement of Doc Nagobads's house. It not only spared him from paying rent and left him more money to send home each month, but it was the homier, family environment he preferred. Craig missed his mother profoundly and became especially fond of Velma Nagobads, Doc's wife. He was much more inclined to spend time at the kitchen table with the Nagobadses than to go out with the guys. "He was like our own boy," Nagobads said. "We became very, very close."

Craig doesn't forget the people who have been there for him. After coaching him in the National Sports Festival, Tim

Taylor got a kind note from Craig thanking him for his work. When BU goalie coach Andy Fila was stuck and needed a ticket a half-hour before the Russian game, Craig didn't hesitate. Loyalty is something he prizes. "If you were Jim's friend, he absolutely could not do enough for you or say enough to make you feel good," said Billy LeBlond, his roommate at BU. LeBlond would go home with Craig for weekends, and he still fondly recalls how Don Craig would greet him with a hug, a pat on the back, and how he would be completely embraced into the family fold.

Family meant everything to Jim Craig, and it still does. "He's a wicked homebody," Sharlene Craig said. "He'd rather be home than anyplace else." Craig now lives in a handsome, three-story gray colonial in an upscale subdivision four miles and quite a few income brackets from where he grew up. Don Craig's salary as a food service manager for Dean Junior College had to stretch a long way for eight kids. Clothes were handed down, allowances didn't exist, and the food bill was trimmed when Don would pull up in the driveway with a perk from his work: cartons of fish, milk, bread, and other groceries. The boys would scramble out to carry them inside.

The Craigs did most everything together, in good times and otherwise. When his mother got very sick his first year at BU, Jim took the Green Line on the T to Massachusetts General Hospital almost every night after practice to be with her. He would dab her lips with Q-Tips and keep her company. She would ask about his life at BU and his hockey and tell him how wonderful it would be if he could play in the Olympics one day. Margaret Craig lost her hair, suffered from shingles, a dignified woman being robbed of her dignity. It was a horrible process to watch. She dropped to forty-seven pounds. Early in September 1977, before returning to BU for his junior year, Craig was at his sister Maureen's house in the coastal town of Mattapoisett, near Cape Cod, where his mother was living out her last days. He went swimming with his brothers that day and remembers jumping into the bay off a place called Peanut Rock and plunging toward the bottom. The water was cold and dark, and as Jim Craig moved through it he heard a voice tell him that his mother was gone, that her suffering was over. He swam to the surface and got out and grabbed his two little brothers' hands. He started walking down the dirt road. He looked up and saw his brothers-in-law walking toward them.

"They were coming to tell me my mother had died, but I already knew," Craig said.

Craig had a much happier premonition six years later, in Salt Lake City. He was playing for a minor-league affiliate of the Minnesota North Stars. There was a fashion show in Craig's hotel, and one of the models was a young woman named Sharlene Pettit. Craig had been a major heartthrob ever since the Olympics, with letters, come-ons, and overtures coming faster than pucks on a Russian power play. Once in a Chicago hotel he walked into his room to find a naked woman on his bed. "Please leave," he said, which was also what he said to the redhead who showed up in his office one day, after mailing a series of photos of herself in various stages of undress. The moment Craig saw Sharlene he was smitten. He approached her awkwardly after the show. "Are you from Salt Lake City?" he asked.

"She looked at me like I was an idiot," said Craig, who's embarrassed by the lameness of his opening line even now.

He saw her again later and didn't do much better. He went up to his room and called a friend. "I just found my wife," Craig told him.

Sharlene Pettit knew nothing about the 1980 Olympics or the U.S. team's heroic goaltender. Jim Craig liked that. He didn't have to worry about whether she liked him or his stardom. There wasn't an image that he felt he had to live up to. It wasn't always easy being Jim Craig after Lake Placid.

"He had a hard act to follow, which was himself," Andy Fila said.

Six days after the Olympics, Jim Craig was in net for the Atlanta Flames, the patriot in pads who would save a reeling franchise. A sellout crowd turned out for his debut, ice storm be damned. Craig won, 4–1. For a time he was more famous and popular than Wayne Gretzky. His introductory press conference was held in a shopping mall, 2,000 people stuffed into a rotunda. The governor declared it Jim Craig Day in Georgia, and he was on the cover of *Sports Illustrated* after he played one game. He and his father filmed a Coke commercial, a $35,000 deal. He was 22. Ten days earlier, almost nobody outside of North Easton knew his name, and now everybody did, and everybody wanted a piece of him. Fame was fun and lucrative for a while, and Craig didn't flee from it. His white Lexus still has an Olympic license plate, complete with the five rings and his uniform number, USA 30. The extension at his office is also 30. After years as a sales and marketing executive, he has made a successful switch to corporate and motivational speaking. In the spotless third-floor office in his house—Craig is as fastidious about his work space as he was about his goalie equipment, and he may have the tidiest briefcase in America—dozens of hockey photos and Olympic keepsakes can be found, including the famous flag he wore after the final Olympic game, folded into a triangular wooden case behind his desk. But fame could also be overwhelming, a roiling tidal wave that was going to go whatever way it wanted, that could just as easily drown you as carry you in triumphantly on its crest. Four games into his NHL career, Craig, physically and emotionally spent after what amounted to two straight years of competition, left the Flames and took a mental-health break in Florida.

"After the plateau he was on, nothing he did was ever going to be good enough," Sharlene Craig said.

"It was like going from being a tavern singer to playing Carnegie Hall, overnight," Jim Craig said. "That kind of change doesn't come with an instruction manual." He has big, strong hands, and they were on the table before him as he rode an Amtrak train from New York to Providence after a memorabilia signing in the city. His voice is deep and thick with a Massachusetts accent. His shaggy Olympic mane of dark brown hair has given way to a shorter style, flecked with gray. The long hair in the family is now worn by his son J.D., short for James Donald, a rangy 15-year-old who likes to play center (don't even try to talk him into playing goal) but who has seen enough photographs of his father from Lake Placid that he wants to grow out his hair. "I like it when you get that little flip in the back," J.D. Craig said.

J.D.'s middle name is in honor of his grandfather. He was born in 1988, the same year Don Craig was suddenly stricken with a brain aneurysm. Don Craig had been teasing his son and Sharlene about giving him a grandchild. Before Don Craig went in for surgery, Sharlene spoke to him as he lay on the gurney: "Dad, don't worry, I'm going to have your grandson." She didn't know it at the time, but she was pregnant with J.D.

Sharlene Craig is a Mormon. One of the beliefs of the Church of Jesus Christ of Latter-day Saints is that babies are gifts from heaven, sent to earth to replace people who are dying. Before the babies come down, they get to know the person who is about to pass away.

"No matter what your beliefs are, it's still a nice thing to think about, don't you think?" Jim Craig said.

After the 1979–1980 NHL season, the Flames relocated to Calgary, where the promotional value of having an American icon on the roster was considerably less than it was in Atlanta. The team traded Craig to Boston, a deal that seemingly scripted another fairy tale—the professional homecoming for an Olympic hero. Craig beat the Canadiens in his Bruins debut and had a solid first year in Boston, but he found out soon enough that playing Carnegie Hall was much more complicated than seeing his name on the marquee. It was hard to hit all the right notes, harder still to perform up to people's expectations and to control what the reviewers would say. Everything was magnified because he was playing for his hometown franchise. Before the 1981–1982 season, Craig suffered a broken finger, required shoulder surgery, and then ripped up his ankle when he fell through a ladder. The same day he fell through the ladder, his dog was run over by a car. He struggled to find his game, and things weren't much better in the locker room, where some veteran teammates found him aloof and didn't necessarily appreciate the adulation and attention being accorded an as-yet-unproven pro goalie. The Bruins have long been a lunch-pail organization, and Craig and his sudden celebrity were not a good fit. He did himself no favors by letting himself get overbooked with appearances, a distraction no rookie needs, especially one who came bundled with the expectations that Craig did. "I think he was very isolated during his time with the Bruins," LeBlond said. When Bruins general manager Harry Sinden wanted to send him to the minors to get some work in, Craig refused and effectively wrote his own ticket out of town.

"I think he could've developed into a pretty good goaltender, but he had an aversion to going down to the minors and it kind of deteriorated from there," Sinden said. "He had problems dealing with his success. He just couldn't accept that he'd won the gold medal but couldn't make our team."

Craig felt lost and confused and then, twenty-seven months after Lake Placid, close to midnight on a wet and treacherous stretch of Route 6 in Mattapoisett, Massachusetts, he hit a much deeper bottom, his BMW colliding with a Toyota, a young woman dying, the newspaper headlines blaring. He had just purchased the BMW from a friend of Fila's, and Fila is convinced the sturdiness of the car saved his life. Craig was charged with vehicular homicide. The media coverage of him being acquitted was much more restrained than the coverage of the crash.

"If it had been me in the accident, it would have been nothing. But because it was him, it was big news," Fila said. Fame turned on Craig as fast as it had arrived. Some were quick to cast him as an NHL washout, a poster boy for the perils of instant stardom. "All of a sudden people are saying harsh things, making harsh judgment—people who have no idea," Craig said. "You just want to be you, left alone, and there's never, ever a chance. What I learned is that I spent so much time trying to make everyone else happy and trying to be what they wanted me to be that I didn't know who I was." For someone who loved to be in control of his world, it was also hard to have so little. There was no stopping people from taking shots at him, connecting dots that weren't there, and no stopping reporters from asking him to replay the accident, either, even after more than two decades. Do you know what it's like to be regularly reminded about one of the worst moments of your whole life? Craig has never wanted to hide, or lie, but the experience made him wary, and careful about who he puts his trust in.

"To me it's a terrible tragedy, something I wish had never happened," he said. "You can't explain an accident. You can't change it now. You just try to live your life and be a better person every day."

Craig was let go by the Bruins, and he returned to play for Team USA under coach Lou Vairo in 1983, helping the United States qualify for the 1984 Games, then got picked up by Lou Nanne, general manager of the Minnesota North Stars. Nanne had seen Craig dozens of times before and during the Olympics and was convinced he could be a capable NHL goaltender. "I don't know if anyone can imagine the kind of pressure that kid was under after the Olympic Games," Nanne said. "I thought if we got him out here, away from his hometown and where there weren't such high expectations, he could get on solid footing." This time Craig willingly went down to the minors, where he played well and met Sharlene. He worked hard and fit in well, according to Nanne.

Craig was recalled to the North Stars in 1983–1984. He played in three games, one of them against the Washington

Capitals in Minneapolis. The Capitals' goaltending coach was Warren Strelow. Before the game Craig saw Strelow in the hallway and hurried over to talk to him, asking if he could take a look at him, offer any insight into his game.

"Jimmy, I'm not your goaltending coach anymore," Strelow said. Strelow felt awkward saying it, but it was the truth. Strelow told the Caps to shoot low on the stick side on Craig. The Capitals scored six times.

Not long after, Craig was in goal against Detroit. Nanne had told Craig he was going to trade Don Beaupre to the Los Angeles Kings and make Craig the No. 1 goaltender. Up 5–2, withstanding a furious Red Wings charge in the third period, Craig made a sprawling save, reached back to snare the puck as it rolled down his back, and ripped up his hamstring muscle, a significant injury that would require extensive rehabilitation. He decided he'd had enough. He was 27 years old. The body of Jim Craig's NHL work consisted of thirty games. He never played in the league again.

"My goal was to prove that I was good enough to play, and I did that," Craig said. "I didn't play for the adulation. I never sit on a bar stool or go to a party and say, 'I could've done this,' or 'I could've done that.' I never look at it that way. It's over. I'm comfortable with what I did, and that's important. I wasn't very good as a pro. So what? I made a choice. Ask how I'm doing as a father or husband. That's what's important."

Jim and Sharlene Craig still lead a hockey-centered life, except that now the players are J.D. and his 12-year-old sister, Taylor, a top player in her age group in Massachusetts. The family has a vacation home in Mattapoisett—a retreat on 15 acres of land overlooking Buzzards Bay, a place with marshes and tidal pools and osprey and cranes and salt air that Jim Craig could breathe forever. You can walk out of the house and jump in a kayak and paddle away. The Craigs want to live there full-time, as soon as they can work it out with the kids' school and hockey schedules.

Relaxation doesn't come much more easily to Jim Craig than it did to Herb Brooks. He's spent most of his life being on the move, a goalie in a hurry to get good, to go places, to be in the net, always. If he put off some people with his chatter and his swagger, there are many others like Billy LeBlond and Andy Fila who value his honesty and kindness and think he is as misunderstood as anyone they've ever known. As Craig edges toward 50, his view is getting longer, and clearer. It was a Friday night game against the Russians that made him famous, but that isn't how he defines himself. Herb Brooks constantly prodded him and goaded him and made him feel uncomfortable. Craig didn't always like it, but it made him better in the long run, as a goalie and as a person. It taught him to take risks and dream big. Life is all about change, and you have to embrace it. You can't devour yourself with regret, get consumed with second-guessing, worry about people who think they know you but don't. You deal with what is, strap your pads back on, and get ready for what's next. You remember what really matters. He has the same tender relationship with his kids that his own parents had with him.

"Life is a marathon," Craig said. "It doesn't matter if you're in front in the first five meters or the first five miles. It's where you get to. It's how you're doing, and where you are when you cross the finish line. That's how I look at it."

THE
THIRD PERIOD

Chapter Seven

SHORT END
OF THE SHIFT

A few minutes before the game, Herb Brooks made a re-cruiting trip. He didn't have to go far. He found Dr. George Nagobads and called him into his office and handed him a stopwatch. Nagobads had known Brooks since 1958, when Nagobads, an immigrant from Latvia, was the new team physician for the University of Minnesota in Minneapolis and Brooks, a fleet forward, was an import from across the Mississippi in St. Paul. The friendship spanned three decades, hundreds of players, and three national championships, and if Nagobads had learned anything, it was to expect the unexpected from Herb Brooks.

"Doc, we have to have our legs," Brooks said. "We need short shifts. It's the only way we can beat them. No shift can go more than thirty-five seconds [at least ten seconds shorter than a typical shift]. If somebody is on the ice for longer than that, I want you to tug on my sleeve." Nagobads, a short, balding man in a brown blazer and glasses, stood behind the bench and followed orders. "I didn't even get to see the game," Nagobads said. "I was too busy looking at the watch."

Not that he minded helping the cause. He had a history with the Russians, and it wasn't pleasant. Nagobads lost his home, his education, and very nearly his life when Joseph Stalin's troops invaded Latvia in June 1940. He was forced to withdraw from the University of Riga and get a job loading wood at a freight station. A year later, there was a mass deportation of Latvian dissidents to Siberia; the Nagobadses were on the list because Nagobads's father was a leader of the resistance. If George hadn't been off playing a basketball game on the other side of Riga, the capital, he might have gone to Siberia and never come back.

The family fled to Germany, moved to the States in 1951, and now all these years later, the Russians were coming again, in Lake Placid. "After we were ahead at the end of the second period, we were already celebrating," Valery Vasiliev told Nagobads later. "Nobody can skate with us in the third period." That had long been accepted as hockey gospel. With Nagobads on the watch, the American players went all-out for their 35 seconds, sometimes 40, then hopped off. On one comparatively long Russian shift, center Vladimir Petrov had a face-off with Johnson, another with Broten, and a third with Pavelich. He knew Nagobads from various international competitions. He caught the doctor's eye and asked in Russian, *"Shto ta koy?"* What is going on?

"Sprashike washe treneru," Nagobads replied. Ask your coach.

In the opening minutes of the period, Ken Morrow made a rare end-to-end rush, carrying the puck to the right of Vladimir Myshkin, but could find nobody in front to connect with. The Soviets broke out but couldn't build a threat either, and soon defenseman Dave Christian was controlling the puck directly behind Jim Craig, starting up ice, a sure-handed breakout up the middle. Of all the personnel decisions Brooks made, none was more inspired than switching Dave Christian from forward to defense. Brooks initially made the move in December, after Bobby Suter broke his ankle and they needed another defenseman. Christian had played some defense in high school, when he would go back to the blue line to take a break, then would play 40 or 42 minutes of a 45-minute game. He had never played defense at this level—and never would again. He was probably the only player on the team capable of making such a switch, and he did it with no perceptible angst. If it was good for the team, it was a no-brainer as far as Dave Christian was concerned. "I would've thought it would be totally scary," said Neal Broten, his roommate and best friend on the team and fellow northwestern Minnesotan. "But he never said a word about it. Dave was the ultimate team player."

Suter was the same way. The only Wisconsin Badger on the team other than Mark Johnson, Suter eventually made it back from his injury, but wasn't near full strength. A pugnacious defender who played beneath a thatch of wayward, straw-colored hair, Suter had fast skates and a feisty temperament and, at five feet ten inches and 170 pounds, relished taking on bigger guys. He specialized in mayhem, which explains how he came to leave Wisconsin as the school's all-time leader in penalty minutes. Suter would whack you when the officials weren't looking, kick your skates out, yap nonstop. His little brother, Gary, followed him to Wisconsin and became an NHL All-Star, and his son, Ryan, is a rookie millionaire, having left Wisconsin after his freshman year and signing with the Nashville Predators, the club that made him the top defenseman selected in the 2003 NHL draft. Bob had his own modus operandi, a guy who was equal parts red-faced puck rusher and blue-line troublemaker. "He was an abrasive little son of a bitch," Gary Suter said. "He always had people chasing him around the ice. He was the sort of guy you hated playing against and loved having him on your team."

Suter played a solid game in the rout of the Czechs, but his gimpy ankle curtailed his mobility enough that Brooks did not use him against the Russians. Suter spent the game at the end of the bench, in a snit, but kept it to himself for the good of the team. Toughing things out was nothing new to him. Once, after a morning skate during his Badger career, Peter Johnson accidentally sliced Suter's toe with his skate blade amid some locker-room hijinks. The toe was partly detached. Suter told the team doctor to stitch it up. He did. Suter didn't miss a game. "No big deal," Suter said, before getting on a Zamboni to resurface Capitol Ice Arena, the rink he owns just outside Madison, Wisconsin. In the arena lobby is a store called Gold Medal Sports. For some two decades Suter has coached youth teams with the Madison Capitols, a program started by his father. The mayhem has stopped, but Suter still lives a rink-centered life.

———

Lou Vairo likened Christian to a "Picasso on ice," and it was a widely shared opinion. Christian didn't just have speed. He had the ability to accelerate, to create space, to read the flow of a game before almost anyone else. He was a defenseman with a centerman's psyche, a playmaker whose offensive skills put enormous pressure on defenses. In the upset of the Czechs, he saved a goal by clearing a puck that had trickled through Jim Craig's pads. Then he set the tone for the third period with an early rush, splitting two defenders, going in on goal, getting off a shot even as he got hooked and slammed into the goaltender. Phil Verchota knocked in the rebound, and the rout was on.

If anybody on the U.S. team had an Olympic pedigree, it was Christian, of Warroad, Minnesota, in the state's northwest corner, six miles of forest and field from the Manitoba border. When one of his uncles was giving directions to a visitor, he said, "Come down from Canada and make your first left."

Christian was born on May 12, 1959, which made him nine months old when his father, Bill, scored two goals, including the game-winner, the last time the Americans beat the Soviets in the Olympics, in another semifinal in Squaw Valley, California, in 1960. Bill's linemate and brother, Roger, took it from there, scoring four goals against the Czechs the following morning. Another brother, Gordon, competed for the 1956 U.S. team that won the silver medal in Italy.

Bill and Roger Christian were Olympians again in 1964 in Innsbruck, where they teamed with Herb Brooks in a tournament that wasn't so inspired; the United States went 2–5 and lost to the Russians and Czechs by an aggregate score of 12–2. When they returned to Warroad and their lives as carpenters, Roger's brother-in-law, Hal Bakke, suggested the idea of a company selling "hockey sticks by hockey players." And so Christian Brothers, Inc., was born. Dave Christian played fifteen solid years in the NHL—he scored seven seconds into his first shift with the Winnipeg Jets—and was the only player in the game that whole time with his own brand of stick. "I get pretty good service," Christian liked to say. At their peak in the mid-1980s, Christian Brothers was turning out 500,000 sticks a year. The company fell on hard times when mega-manufacturers such as Easton began marketing graphite and composite sticks, and it closed shop briefly in 2003 before getting bought out and reopening. Even now when you call their 800 number, you don't hear the Captain and Tennille when you're on hold; you hear a piece of the audiotape from the 1960 gold-medal game. Marvin Windows is the big employer in town, but in a place that calls itself Hockeytown, U.S.A. (and is the proud home of the Warroad Lakers, a well-known senior amateur team), Christian Brothers is the business that speaks the language of the locals.

Warroad (pop. 1,722) is 358 miles from the Twin Cities but only 88 miles from Thief River Falls. Sited on the shore of Lake of the Woods, a wannabe Great Lake with 65,000 miles of shoreline, 14,000 islands, and a width that stretches to 55 miles at one point, Warroad is a place with seven police officers (offering twenty-four-hour service, according to the Chamber of Commerce), terrific fishing, and sufficient ornithological interest to warrant a weekly birder update on the area website. If birds don't do it for you, maybe the aurora borealis (northern lights) will. Originally a Chippewa Indian settlement, Warroad for years was subject to attack from the nearby Sioux, who coveted the Chippewa's rice fields and invaded by canoe on the Red and Roseau rivers so often that their route (and the village) became known as the war road.

Dave Christian learned to skate on a frozen river, and

learned well. He starred on the high school team, regularly dueling with his buddy, Neal Broten, the star of Roseau High School, down Highway 11. The two parted ways in college, Christian going off to North Dakota, after Brooks offered him only three-quarters of a scholarship. By his sophomore year, he was good enough to get drafted in the second round by Winnipeg, and to score two goals to push North Dakota past Brooks's Gophers in the WCHA final. The second goal was an open-netter. Christian came down one-on-nobody, stopped in front of the goal, and wound up and blasted a slap shot into the empty goal. It was at least partly for Herb Brooks's benefit.

Some of Christian's Olympic teammates kiddingly nick-named him Koho, after the rival Finnish stick company. Christian was quiet, but he played along. Before the Czech game, he arrived in Locker Room 5 early and made wings for his helmet using cardboard, tape, and a clothes hanger. Then he went out and flew around the ice. On another game day a few years earlier, in Houghton, Michigan, North Dakota coach Gino Gasparini was out for a walk when he saw a couple of police cars with lights flashing in front of the team's hotel. A few stories above, Christian and a couple of teammates were leaning out the window firing snowballs, provoking a call to the law.

Christian seemed most content hanging around Broten, his northwest connection, two prodigious talents with under-sized egos. They roomed together in the Olympic Village, played video games together, and made runs to McDonald's together. Christian isn't in Warroad anymore, having moved to Moorhead, near the North Dakota border, but he's still a Warroad kid at heart and still spends his summers at the family cabin, amid the pines and birches of northern Minnesota, on Upper Bottle Lake.

Bill Christian was in Lake Placid with a stock of extra sticks, never knowing if there might be some business to drum up. "It was as good as anything there is in my life," he said once in describing the thrill of seeing his son carry on the Christian Olympic torch. "I just don't have the words to explain it."

Dave Christian used to read his father's scrapbook as a kid and dream about being in the Olympics himself. He doesn't really have words for it, either. "To have that come true, to be in that position, playing against Russia, with my father and my uncle in the stands . . . for me it was as impossible and far-fetched a dream as you could have."

———

Christian came up ice smoothly, into the neutral zone, where he saw Pavelich darting toward the Soviet blue line on his left. Christian put the puck on his stick and Pavelich slipped through two Russians and skated in deep, momentarily losing control when Sergei Makarov took a whack at his stick and the puck skipped ahead into the endboards. Pavelich got it back and hit Harrington behind the net, but neither a shot nor a real threat came of it and soon Vladimir Golikov was carrying it out.

The pace of the game seemed to be slowing, the action disjointed. With just over four minutes gone, robust forechecking by the United States had throttled the Russian attack, and O'Callahan took the puck behind the U.S. net. He slipped a pass by Valery Kharlamov to Strobel on the right side. Out the Americans came, Strobel centering to Wells, who pushed it over to Verchota on the left. Verchota, a former state discus champion at Duluth East High School, was a powerful physical presence, broad-faced and broad-shouldered, a six-foot two-inch, 195-pound winger who could pound opponents and the books with equal facility. At the U, he was a decorated student who was twice the recipient of the John Mayasich Award, presented to the team's top student-athlete. He'd grow a bushy beard as soon as hockey season was over and take on a mountain man look, Grizzly Adams with a bandana, and was regularly mistaken for being the team's goon, which he definitely was not. During the Herbies-in-the-dark game in Norway, Brooks sent Verchota out to get physical with a Norwegian player who the coach thought was cheap-shotting people. Verchota fought the guy but forgot to drop his gloves.

"Way to dust his clock, Phil," the guys teased.

Strobel went hard to the net and Verchota slid a cross-ice pass in front. Sergei Starikov, a thick-bodied defenseman, skated back with the swift Strobel and was able to get his stick on the puck and break up the play. The Soviets controlled and Petrov, the 32-year-old center, carried up ice, Wells hounding him and prodding him with the stick the whole way, rarely more than the width of a puck away. If Herb Brooks wanted him to check, Wells was going to check, with vigor.

Bow-legged and thick-chested, Mark Wells looked a little like a barrel on skates when he headed down ice, low to the ground, accelerating fast, his stride a muscular, stick-swinging roll. At five feet eight inches and 175 pounds, he was sturdy in body and stout in disposition, a kid with Chippewa ancestry who played with no reservation and was almost impossible to knock off his skates. Wells was a good enough scorer to pile up 83 points in 45 games in his senior year at Bowling Green, but Brooks already had Mark Johnson, Neal Broten, and Mark Pavelich playing center, each of them a mite-sized maestro. Brooks put Wells on the fourth line of the Olympic team, and as much as Wells wanted to prove to Brooks that he could be as dynamic as the others, he knew this wasn't the time to engage him in debate. "I don't care if you don't score one goal," Brooks told Wells. "I need you to be my defensive center man. I need you to shut people down."

Wells, in truth, was very nearly not on the team at all. Four months before Lake Placid, he suffered a hairline fracture in his ankle after stepping in a hole at the end of a training run in Norway with Craig Patrick. Brooks doubted that Wells could make it back and that he was the ideal fit for the team, besides. Wells had his headstrong moments and could get easily frustrated. On a train ride during the autumn swing through Europe, he got into a spirited wrestling match with roommates Jim Craig and Ken Morrow, because Wells insisted on having the bottom bunk. He was a kid who seemed to have an answer for most everything, clinging to a sometimes unbending conviction that his hockey ideas were right. His stubbornness served him well in his year with the Junior Red Wings in 1975, a season spent fending off derision, and worse, from Canadian teams and fans. One night two opponents mugged Wells—then five feet six and about 140 pounds—and beat him up so badly he wound up in the hospital and had to wear a face shield for weeks afterward. Brooks loved Wells's grit and there was no question that his squatty bursts of acceleration made him perfectly suited for the coach's system, but was it worth the maintenance, dealing

with Wells's retorts and overzealous desire to prove he belonged? "He wasn't the easiest guy to coach," said Ron
Mason, Wells's coach at Bowling Green. "He had his own
way of doing things. He was hard to get through to sometimes." There were other forwards—Ralph Cox of the University of New Hampshire and Dave Delich of Colorado
College were two of them—who were more natural goal
scorers. During one game on the tour, Brooks tapped Wells's
shoulder and told him to play right wing. Wells informed the
coach he was a center, not a wing. Brooks shot him a cold
stare and was of a mind to ship him out right there. "Mark
Wells was a super-duper hockey player and one of the nicest
kids you could ever meet, but sometimes he was his own
worst enemy," said Gale Cronk, the co-founder, along with
Don (father of Ken) Morrow, of the Eastern Michigan
Hockey Association and a longtime mentor for Wells. "He
could've been in the NHL for a long time, he was that good.
He just had a knack for ticking people off. When you played
on a Herbie Brooks team, you played what position he told
you. Mark thought he was right, but I told him, 'Mark, that
don't mean nothing, because you are not the coach.' "

Wells was raised in St. Claire Shores, Michigan, thirty-five
miles northeast of Detroit, in a 900-square-foot home that
was scarcely different from all the other 900-square-foot
homes in town, boxy and brick. It was a working-class town
and the Wellses were working-class folk. His paternal grand-
mother worked as a riveter at the bomber plant in Ypsilanti,
Michigan, during World War II, one of the few women
around to take on such an occupation. After the war she
worked on the line for General Motors, making sideboards
and earning $41 a week. Mark's father, Ron, would make $6

for a few hours of dusting off seats at Detroit Tiger games in Briggs Stadium, and couldn't understand how his mother could work so long and hard for so little.

Like a lot of undersized athletes, Wells felt that he was habitually underestimated, that every coach he met was another coach he had to prove himself to. It happened in squirts and peewees and bantams, and even at Bowling Green, Wells beginning his freshman year without a full scholarship and finishing it as the team's rookie of the year. As a 10-year-old Little Leaguer, Wells entered a national Pitch, Hit, and Run competition. Other kids snickered at the sight of him, chest-high to his rivals. He wound up second in the nation, making it to the final round in Yankee Stadium, finishing right behind a kid from southern New Jersey—future Los Angeles Dodger Orel Hershiser.

So Wells could already feel his defiance building when Brooks asked him to meet him for an early-morning skate at the Met Center, the team's training base in Bloomington, Minnesota, not long after the team returned to the States from Europe in late September. Wells left the apartment he was sharing with John Harrington and Mark Pavelich. The arena was cold and empty. Wells's ankle hurt, but he laced up the skates and met Brooks on the ice, anyway. There were going to be six more cuts, taking the touring roster of twenty-six down to the twenty that would be allowed in Lake Placid. The selection process was anxiety provoking enough without giving people cause to doubt your durability. Brooks and Wells met near center ice. Brooks told Wells that he didn't think he could make the team, and said he was going to send Wells down to the International Hockey League—effectively the coach's taxi squad, a place to park players he may or may not ultimately want. Wells felt as though his heart were being sliced into pieces with every word Brooks spoke. He had dreamed of being in the Olympics ever since he watched Mark Spitz win seven gold medals in Munich in 1972. He had turned down the Canadiens after they drafted him in the twelfth round in 1977, so he could preserve his amateur status. He thought of the words his brother, John, had told him: "Don't let one person destroy your dream." When the coach was done, Wells circled around him. His mind was racing, his defiance deepening. He searched for the right words and looked at Brooks and skated a little more. Then Mark Wells stopped and spit at Brooks's skates. "I don't play games, Herb," he said. "I am going to be back on this team. I am going to be back." And then he skated off.

Wells was indeed sent down, but he wasn't wrong. He spent the rest of the fall playing for the Flint Generals in the IHL, living in Cronk's basement, and then he went to Halifax of the American Hockey League. When the Olympians came to Flint to play the Generals, Wells was called back from Halifax, and Brooks gave him his Olympic sweater and put him on a line with Phil Verchota on his left and Dave Silk on his right. Wells scored several goals and had a couple of assists. The Olympians won, 15–0. After the game, Brooks dispatched Craig Patrick to talk to Wells. "Do you like it here?" Patrick asked him.

"I'm doing good," Wells replied.

"OK, you're staying here," Patrick said. Wells was confused and angry, a state that Brooks left a lot of players in. What else did he have to do? Why did the coach always have to be so cryptic? Wells kept asking Brooks when he would rejoin the team. He got no answer. Before the team left town,

Brooks took him out on the ice and drilled him, down and back, down and back, no pucks, just lots of hard work and intense skating. Near the end, bent over and beating back exhaustion, Wells said, "Herb, I'm going to puke."

"If you do, that will be good for you," the coach said.

Wells was beginning to think more and more of turning pro. His brother urged him not to be hasty. Wells's agent, Art Kaminsky, told Brooks that Wells was getting close to signing with Montreal. In mid-January, Wells's phone rang in Halifax. He was told to meet the Olympic team in Oklahoma City, and he did. A week later, the team was in Detroit. The Olympians played the Canadian Olympic team in newly opened Joe Louis Arena, then stayed in town for the NHL All-Star game. Wells was sitting in the upper level with his father, still unsure of his status. "If I don't make this team, I'm done with hockey," he told his father. Between periods Brooks came and found him.

"You're going to Lake Placid," Brooks said. The team was leaving the following morning. Wells was the final player named to the roster. He didn't even have a change of clothes, but his wardrobe was the last thing on this mind. He got some new things to wear from one of the Olympic sponsors in Lake Placid. Wells still gets goose bumps when he watches footage of the game against the Soviets, or the finale against Finland.

He had no idea there wouldn't be another highlight in his life for more than twenty years.

"I've seen the best of life, and I've seen no life," Wells said. "I like the best of life better."

Wells's travails began not long after the Olympics, when the Canadiens wanted to trade his rights to the Red Wings.

The Wings were his local team, except that Mark Wells always saw himself as a Canadien. He told them he wouldn't go. It wasn't about being a prima donna, just his stubbornness again. "To me I had won the biggest prize I could ever win," Wells said. "It was above and beyond winning the Stanley Cup. I couldn't do anything that could be better. I wanted to be with Montreal. I didn't want to go play for just anyone." Craig Patrick, who had gone on to be the general manager of the New York Rangers after the Olympics, signed him to a $23,000 minor-league contract. Wells played the 1980–1981 season for the Rangers' American Hockey League affiliate in New Haven, but his heart wasn't in it. Like Mike Eruzione, he wanted his enduring hockey memory to be from Lake Placid. Soon, the memory was about all he had to hold on to.

———

Crippled is not a nice-sounding word. It is jarring and indelicate, and Mark Wells uses it without hesitation. "Not too many of my teammates know what I went through—that I was crippled," he said in a slightly nasal voice with a smoker's rasp. Words come from Wells at full throttle, the way he used to skate, his mind tumbling from topic to topic, his pauses all but nonexistent. He has plans at last and can't wait to tell you about them. Wells wants to quit cigarettes and knows he will. He wants to get his body down from the 210 pounds he has ballooned to. He is back in school, at Walsh Business College in Detroit, getting the degree that he never got twenty-five years ago. So what if he's a 46-year-old undergrad? "The studies are great. School for me is rehab. I'm finishing something I never finished. Knowledge is my dream now—becoming as knowledgeable as possible. I will get back into the mainstream. To me where I am is a blessing, because I could be sitting in a group home in a wheelchair."

The tortuous trail that took Mark Wells from Olympic glory to near incapacitation began in a walk-in refrigerator, in 1989. He was in the restaurant business in Michigan, unloading forty-pound crates of cooked turkeys. As he bent down to lift one of the crates, he twisted to his right and heard a snap in his back, the knifing pain sending him to the floor. Wells had cracked a vertebra in his lower back. Even worse, the X-rays revealed he was also suffering from a degenerative disk disease that left bone rubbing against bone. Doctors told him that he was fortunate it hadn't been a problem before, that his strength had delayed its onset.

Wells was back at work after two weeks, but then he started having numbness in his foot. He was told it wouldn't heal on its own. Wells underwent an eleven-hour back operation in which screws and brackets were attached to stabilize his spine. His expectation was that he'd walk out a day later and get on with his life.

When his mother and brother came in to see him in post-op, his head was bloated with fluid, his body slumped. His mother began to cry, and doctors told them that he'd never have a day without pain. Wells couldn't get out of bed for seven days. He needed to use a walker for nearly a year. In physical therapy, they asked him to get up and reach for the two bars a few feet away. He couldn't do it. The room was spinning, his equilibrium a mess. His mind raced in all kinds of directions, all of them taking him straight into an emotional pileup. He thought, *I'm like one of those United Way kids. How am I going to exist? Where do I go from here? How can I put this on my family?*

Unable to work, barely able to walk ten feet, Wells moved in with his mother. He required a bedpan. He fought a long, debilitating battle with the workers' compensation board to get some benefits. He became addicted to Vicodin, his pain-killing medication, and it didn't even take away his pain. It was hard not to think about how he'd gone from an Olympic hero who was honored with parades and celebrations and invited to lunch by the governor to an invalid who couldn't even get to the bathroom. He withdrew from everything. He moved up north to Hale, Michigan, where his family had a cabin by a lake. His closest friends were the geese. He fed them. The mother would make noise outside and wake him up. "The geese were what got me to the back door," Wells said.

Wells had a second operation in 1993 but came out of it pretty much the way he came in—with limited mobility and lots of pain. His mood darkened. He wondered if he'd ever have a life again. Thoughts of suicide began to cross his mind. He tried returning to school but couldn't sit in class very long before his back acted up. He finally got a workers' compensation settlement and Social Security benefits but saw solvency end when a landscaping business he'd started folded, leaving him $40,000 in the hole. Soon he'd graduated to morphine for his pain, taking 80 milligrams every 12 hours before he got disgusted with his reliance on it and took himself off it, cold turkey.

He heard about a new laser surgery technique being used for back pain and contacted a surgeon at Madison Hospital in Madison Heights, Michigan. They scheduled a meeting. It was short. Wells didn't want to see his X-rays or discuss spinal anatomy or have an expansive conversation about his options.

He was a desperate man in desperate pain, and the suicidal thoughts were getting to be less and less a novelty. "I can't live this way anymore," he told the doctor. In truth, maybe the only reason he'd made it this far was an IRS compliance officer named Tom Krozak.

"He was a gift sent from somewhere," Wells said.

Wells and Krozak met by chance one night in Chesterfield Township, in a roadside diner called C.J.'s. Krozak was stopping off on his way home from work. Wells was stopping off after another bleak day inside the four walls of his mother's house. Krozak saw this stocky man by the counter digging for enough change to buy a cup of coffee. Krozak had seen Wells in C.J.'s a few times before and asked him if he could buy him the cup. Wells thanked him and said sure. Over coffee and an act of charity, friendship took hold. "He'd have tears in his eyes, he was in so much pain, but you never heard him let on," Krozak said. When Wells's brother and father, Ron, a retired chemical-company executive, would ask how he was, they'd get the same dodge: "I'm okay." There was no reason to elaborate, on anything. For two years Wells didn't even tell Krozak about his involvement in the 1980 Olympics. Krozak found out by accident as he absently leafed through an Olympic magazine that Wells had brought with him for a talk at a local middle school.

"Look, here's a guy with your name in this magazine," Krozak said. "He even looks a little like you."

"It *is* me," Wells replied.

The friendship deepened. Wells and Krozak met regularly for coffee and pizza and conversation. The more Krozak got to know Wells, the more he could see how beaten up by life he'd been. Once Wells lent his Jeep to a fellow he met from

Detroit. The guy turned out to be a drug dealer, who not only didn't return the car but sold it. When Wells lived in Hale, he met a woman who was behind on her mobile-home payments. Wells loaned her money and never got it back. "Mark's problem is that he's too nice a guy," Krozak said.

When the 1980 team was selected to light the cauldron to open the Salt Lake City Olympics in 2002, every player was allowed to bring a guest. Wells's guest was Tom Krozak. The IRS man had four of the best days of his life, and even had an impromptu meeting in their hotel with one of his heroes, former Polish president Lech Walesa. Krozak keeps telling Wells that he doesn't owe him anything, but Wells, unyielding as ever, will never forget that Tom Krozak bought him a cup of coffee and offered him friendship when he had nothing.

In August 2001 Wells had his third surgery, this one a laser procedure that aimed to lessen the pain by burning the nerves in the lower back. The results were immediate. Even in post-op he could feel relief. When he said to his mother, "Mom, let's go get a pizza," she started to cry. His back is still stiff and Wells walks with a cautious, erect gait, but the acute pain is gone. For the first time in years he began to make plans, set goals. Early in 2002, the 1980 team met for a reunion game that was part of the NHL All-Star weekend in Los Angeles. Mark told his brother, "I'm going to go buy a pair of skates. I've got the itch. I want to get out on the ice, even if it's for one shift." Wells hadn't skated for fifteen years. John Wells tried to talk his brother out of it. Mark refused to listen. He wasn't going to talk to his doctors, get their opinion. He was going to get back on the ice with his teammates, and that was the end of it. He had felt separate and different for so long, a soloist in the grip of pain, out of harmony with the guys, with the world. "He led a very lonely life for ten years," Krozak said. Even in the Olympics there were times he felt apart, underappreciated for the good work he'd done as Brooks's designated checking center. Maybe it was that he played only fourteen games of the pre-Olympic tour. Maybe it was that the acclaim always went to the goal scorers, the marquee names. Wells knew he'd never be a Mike Eruzione, a less skilled player than he but a guy with man-in-the-street magnetism and volubility to spare. Wells never expected that sort of visibility or recognition. He just wanted to matter, to belong. To be on the ice. "I could skate better than I could walk my whole life," Wells said. "This was going to be my lift. In my mind if I could get back out there I could get back in school, get my degree, get back in the mainstream."

With Herb Brooks standing behind him, Mark Wells sat on the bench in the Forum that night, in his new skates and his old No. 15 USA jersey and with a heart that raced with excitement. He skated one shift, had a shot on goal, and skated back to the bench. That was it. He had done it. It felt good to have the cold wind in his face and the warmth of old teammates all around him. He thought, *This is the last time I'm going to put on skates. I can retire. This is how I want my hockey life to end.*

Mark Wells is scheduled to have one more operation. He's on the dean's list at Walsh, and his plan is to graduate in 2006. He's thinking of getting into financial planning, helping people prepare for the future. There are so many options, and now he *does* want to think about them, get excited by them. Mark Wells is out of hiding and full of optimism.

"Every day I wake up now and find out what's on the agenda," Wells said. "It's a beautiful thing."

———

Wells had effectively tied up Petrov, but with about five minutes gone, the Americans had a more acute problem. With his back turned, Rob McClanahan tried to shoot the puck down ice from near the U.S. blue line, but the puck caromed off the boards right to Zhluktov. The Soviet picked it off and backhanded the puck to a surging Sergei Makarov, who ramped up to full speed in a hurry. Makarov blew around Mike Ramsey, then knifed inside Ken Morrow, and swept in front. He was alone on Craig, ready to fire, when the puck rolled off his stick as he skidded toward the corner. It was frightening how fast the threat had developed, and how easily the score could've been 4–2.

The 21-year-old Makarov had been creating mayhem from the beginning of the game, and indeed, from the beginning of the Olympics. If his teammates weren't playing with urgency, he sure was. On the Soviets' next rush, he came bursting through the defense again, splitting Ramsey and Morrow and heading toward goal before the puck spilled ahead and he lost his balance and went sliding into Craig by the right post, the two of them in a pile that was soon joined by Ramsey. Craig and Makarov, Centipede competitors the night before, were both slow to get to their feet. From his knees, Craig patted Makarov on his backside with his stick, a goalie's salute to a forward on the rise. Makarov reciprocated with a stick tap on Craig's right pad, then skated off to the bench. The game was three-quarters over, the score stuck at 3–2. A "U-S-A, U-S-A" chant went up. Time was getting short.

Chapter Eight

LEADING MEN

There were just over 13 minutes to play, and the Americans had been able to mount almost no sustained offense. Myshkin had been in the net 27 minutes and seen just two shots—and none in the third period. From the left point, Krutov shot the puck diagonally across the ice, and Neal Broten chased it down along the boards and veered behind the U.S. net, building speed, ready to carry out and try to create something. Krutov bumped with Morrow and then slid over and took a swipe at Broten with his stick. Kaisla blew his whistle, raised his arm. Krutov was sent off for high-sticking. He sat down in the penalty box, his youthful face a study in bemused annoyance. The United States had its first power play since the opening minutes of the game. It was a borderline call, and the crowd fired up immediately. Broten won the draw and got the puck to Christian, who hit Christoff, who carried it in the U.S. zone. The Soviets cleared, but Ramsey carried down the right side and shot it in around the boards, and Christian controlled and fired cross-ice to Broten. Broten steered the puck to Ramsey, who fired from the point, a low blistering drive that Myshkin stopped. In front, Eruzione tried to stuff the rebound in traffic but got sandwiched by Bilyaletdinov and Pervukhin, the Russian defensemen, and the puck bounced wide. Bilyaletdinov shot it out along the left boards and Vladimir Golikov raced across the U.S. blue line and wound up, a typically swift Soviet counterattack. Ramsey fell to the ice and got a piece of Golikov's shot, deflecting it wide. The U.S. defensemen had been blocking shots effectively for six games, at no small cost. "You should've seen what they looked like—black and blue all over, especially Kenny Morrow," Nagobads said.

Broten carried the puck inside the Russian blue line and couldn't find anyone to pass to, so he backed into the corner and backhanded a pass to Baker along the boards. Baker threaded the puck back to Broten, near the left of the crease, but the Soviet defense converged and knocked it away, and then Christian lost the puck to Petrov. The power play was disjointed, the positioning out of sync, the two minutes almost over. Baker, behind his own net, passed to Silk on the left side. Silk carried along the flank and edged toward center as he crossed into the Soviet zone. Valery Vasiliev, the man whose clean, hard check had injured Jack O'Callahan's knee in Madison Square Garden, moved with Silk and went low to body him off the puck, and it worked. Silk started to sprawl to the ice but didn't give up the play, sliding the puck toward the goal as he fell, toward Mark Johnson, who was stationed in front. Silk was one of those guys who had been on Brooks's bubble for months, a player who heard constantly that he wasn't skilled enough, wasn't fast enough. He worked the door at a Boston rock club called the Paradise when he wasn't beating goaltenders, but nothing prepared him for the drum-beat of criticism he got from Brooks.

"Start skating, Silk," the coach would bark. *I am skating,* Silk would think. Silk was among the most diligent weight lifters on the team. There was a signup sheet where you were supposed to write down what you'd lifted, but the guys who signed up usually were the ones who came by once a week and wanted to get credit. Silk lifted conscientiously but never signed. "Hey, how about the weights? They're there for a purpose," Brooks said to him one day. Silk did a slow, silent burn, wondering, *What does this guy want from me? Is this how he is trying to motivate me, or does he just hate me?*

Dave Silk lost his father when he was eight years old. The coaches who meant the most to him—people like BU coach Jack Parker—were usually those who became surrogate fathers, men who were strong and kind and present. "I wonder if coaches' careers shouldn't be measured by wins and losses as much by the number of weddings and christenings they're invited to," Silk said. In time he came to appreciate how much Brooks's demands and incessant prodding had helped build both his character and his game, but the coach's harshness and aloofness were difficult to get accustomed to. Compliments from Brooks came around only a little more often than Halley's Comet.

"The greatest compliment I can give you is a sweater," the coach said.

A few months before Brooks's death, Silk sipped black coffee early one morning in a Boston office building, sunlight streaming through a wall of glass, commuters streaming in from the T station across the street. He has a rugged, handsome face and a sturdy, five-foot-eleven physique.

"Herb didn't have much of a bedside manner," Silk said. "He had no bedside manner. He had a decision early on whether to be a doctor or a veterinarian. He chose to be a veterinarian."

Silk came to BU from Thayer Academy in Braintree, Massachusetts, and the town of Scituate, Massachusetts, an old seacoast port on Cape Cod Bay between Boston and Plymouth. The town is known for fishing and its historic lighthouse, the eleventh oldest in the nation, and for two of the youngest heroines in early American history, Rebecca and Abigail Bates, teenage daughters of lighthouse keeper Simeon Bates and his wife, Rachel. During the War of 1812, the girls were on watch at the lighthouse one night while the rest of the family was away. Looking out to sea, they saw rowboats full of British soldiers making their way to shore. With no time to alert others, Rebecca and Abigail grabbed their fife and drum and played as loudly as they could. Believing that the music heralded the approach of the town militia, the British turned around and rowed back to their ship.

Dave Silk had his own technique for commanding attention: he scored goals. He had 35 of them in 34 games in his freshman year at BU, 1976–1977, getting named New England's Rookie of the Year, and he had 27 more in the national championship season a year later. His hands were strong, his shot hard, his touch soft. He said once that after graduating college his goal was "to own my own island." That hasn't happened yet, but much else has. Silk played parts of seven seasons in the NHL, starting with the Rangers and finishing with the Jets, and then played five more years in Germany, where he watched the Berlin Wall come down even as his own life was being rebuilt. The man who Dave Silk thought hated him turned out to be one of the great influences on his life. A year before Brooks died, Silk told him so. "It was not a problem at all, Silkie," Brooks said.

The BU teams Silk was on were talented and combative and hard-driving on the ice, and hard-partying off it. Their regular hangout was the Dugout, a bar near campus where they'd head for the back room and decompress after practices and games. The night the Beanpot Tournament was postponed because of the blizzard of '78, a bunch of the guys were in the Dugout until dawn. Silk didn't miss any of the rounds, and by the time he got to the pros, his drinking had gotten out of control. Being a strong, young pro athlete lends to feelings of invulnerability by itself; throw in Olympic glory and it is heightened that much more. When he was with the Rangers organization, more than a few people were worried about his alcohol consumption.

"It was a hard time for me," Silk told a reporter once. "It took me some time to get my head screwed back on straight. I had trouble after the Olympics and most of those troubles were due to use and abuse of alcohol. I thought I could control it. I didn't know it was something I couldn't control until years later." When he had to confront his problem, he did it with a courage and intensity that didn't surprise people who knew him. "He's had to fight a few demons, and he's won," BU coach Jack Parker said.

Parker had told Brooks long before the Olympic roster had been set that the sum of Silk's game was so much more than its parts. Silk had a competitive edginess hard-wired into him. His grandfather, Hal Janvrin, played seven years for the Red Sox and was the first high school player to go right from the schoolyard to Fenway Park. His cousin, Mike

Milbury, had a solid NHL career with the Bruins and is now general manager of the New York Islanders.

"He doesn't get around the rink like some of the other guys, but he's so smart, and he's as much a competitor at both ends of the rink as anyone I've ever had," Parker told Brooks. "I guarantee that if you have a one-goal lead and there are thirty seconds left in the game, he's one of the guys you're going to have on the ice."

Parker was right. Brooks knew that now. Silk started the Olympics on the fourth line, but he put in the first U.S. goal of the Olympics to get them going against Sweden, and found himself playing with Johnson and McClanahan on the first line.

Now Silk's pass skittered toward the net at the end of an almost completely ineffective American power play. Soviet defenseman Sergei Starikov, in front, couldn't control it, the puck caroming into his skates, squirting free. Right behind Starikov stood Mark Johnson, who picked it up and shot it right through Myshkin's splaying pads.

Three to three.

Starikov slammed his stick on the ice. Myshkin stayed frozen for a moment, his legs still split. On the bench, Tikhonov leaned forward and spoke sharply to the players in front of him. The arena shook from the noise. You could feel the tremor at the Woodshed, a restaurant across the street. Brooks thrust both arms overhead, fists clenched. Johnson's first goal had come from nowhere, in the final tick of the first-period clock. This was even more from nowhere, born not of a harmonious and artistic buildup but of a bounce, a blade, and a Badger, who more than anyone else on the team knew exactly what to do in such a circumstance. Upstairs in the standing-room-only press box, officials from Tass, the Soviet news agency, closed the door to their office and locked it. They were tired of the Scandinavian press coming over to taunt them about how the Americans might win. The din in the building would not let up for the rest of the game.

Not even thirty seconds later, Vladimir Petrov got the puck as he was stationed at the red line with an open captain, Mikhailov, skating hard on the other side of the rink. Petrov pivoted and passed wildly ahead of Mikhailov, and an icing call resulted. Another icing call brought the face-off to the right of Myshkin, and Pavelich outdueled Zhluktov and got the puck back to Bill Baker at the left point. Baker flipped it in and defenseman Bilyaletdinov controlled it behind his net and swung it along the left boards to Helmut Balderis. He centered to Zhluktov, who found Makarov, whom a tinkering Tikhonov had just switched off his regular line with the brothers Golikov, trying to get something going. Makarov flew down the right wing and rifled a hard wrist shot toward the lower right corner, Craig making a fine save with his left pad. Pavelich, back to help, knocked away the rebound. The Soviets pushed forward again, Balderis sweeping behind the goal, centering a dangerous pass in front that Christian got to before Zhluktov could.

Forty seconds were up, and the United States needed a line change. Christian passed to Schneider on the left side, who carried it out of the U.S. zone. Just across the red line, Schneider launched a slap shot on goal and turned for the bench as the puck traced toward the boards. Eruzione hopped on. If overachievement were an Olympic sport, Eruzione would've won the gold. His name is the Italian word for "eruption," and that was how he played, with a spirit and energy as hot as lava. He knew when to erupt. His breakaway goal helped launch the rout of the Czechs in the second game of the Olympics, and two days later he knocked in an unassisted goal to awaken the team from its lethargic start against Norway. Six years earlier, in his senior year at Winthrop High School, he was in the middle of a three-goals-in-a-minute rally to carry the team to the Massachusetts state title. Eruzione was about five feet six inches and 145 pounds at the time, but his teammates will tell you a disproportionate amount of the weight was heart.

"He never shied away from anything," said Eddie Rossi, who was a year ahead of Eruzione at Winthrop, before going on to play at Harvard. "You could always count on him in the clutch."

Said Jack Parker, Eruzione's coach at BU, "If you woke him up at three in the morning and told him you were going to have a little pickup game at the Boston Skating Club in Brighton, he'd be out there backchecking and forechecking like crazy."

Close to forty years ago, Rossi and Eruzione were pint-sized hockey pioneers in Winthrop, an old seaside town on a jutting piece of land a little east of Boston, bounded on the east by Massachusetts Bay and on the west by Logan Airport and the harbor, a compact place where 20,000 people live in just over one square mile, rows of clapboard and shingled homes wedged together like Monopoly houses, on lots not much bigger than a penalty box. The Boston skyline rises across the harbor but feels much farther away. You can walk along the well-worn cement seawall and see the surf hit red rocks at sunrise, then look at the Boston cityscape against an orange-pink sky at sunset. Gentrification has nibbled at some of its soul, but mostly Winthrop still feels like Winthrop.

The winter sport of choice in town during Mike Eruzione's childhood was basketball. The town had no more hockey tradition than Albuquerque. There were no youth hockey programs and few rinks, and not even a high school hockey team to root for. Rossi and Eruzione had to head to Revere, the next town up the coast, to have the privilege of playing in a game. When nothing official was happening, they'd play on lakes or flooded tennis courts, inspired by Mike's cousin, Anthony Fusillo, a teacher and football coach at Winthrop High School and the only person they knew who actually owned a pair of skates.

Fusillo lived in the same three-decker building as Eruzione, a family compound partitioned into apartments, the doors always open, aunts and uncles and cousins forever coming and going, the air thick with the smell of pasta and sauce. They spoke Italian and stuck together, the way many immigrant families stick together. Eruzione is a second-generation American, the son of Eugene Eruzione, whom everyone knows as Jeep and who worked as a maintenance man in a sewage treatment plant and as a waiter in Santarpio's pizzeria in East Boston, right by the Sumner Tunnel. Mike Eruzione spent his summers painting houses and watching planes come and go, and if his collar color has changed from blue to white, not much else has. He could live in much leafier Boston suburbs but has stayed put on a sloping street not more than 100 yards from Winthrop Golf Club and not even a mile from Winthrop High School, walking distance from the houses he and his wife, Donna, grew up in. He still goes to his aunt's for dinner on Christmas Eve and still plays hockey at Larsen Rink, an aging brick building with a gabled metal roof, across from Scott's Auto Repair. The rink has blue cinder-block walls, except at the ends, where the colors are a blue-and-gold checkerboard, in honor of the Winthrop High Vikings. On the far wall, there is a big American flag by the refrigeration coils, and a collection of championship banners and another banner honoring Eruzione, the 1980 Olympic captain. Just up Pauline Street is the main town square and a stately nineteenth-century town hall, a building with weathered brown bricks and arched windows, and monuments honoring the veterans of every war the nation has ever fought, along with a row of miniature flags. There are flags all over town, including the one outside Mike and Donna Eruzione's gray colonial. Winthrop is a very patriotic place. Eruzione is an officer of the Winthrop Youth Hockey Association. His boys, Michael and Paul, came through the program, and his sister, Nettie, is the secretary. Eruzione's roots are as deep as the Atlantic, though they were shaken early in 2004, when Winthrop voters turned down a budget increase that effectively shut down the entire sports program at Winthrop High.

"I'm not moving," he told the *Boston Globe* once. "I live here nice and easy. When I cross the bridge, it's like a gate closes behind me and says, 'I'm home.' "

Twenty-five years old in Lake Placid, Eruzione came to the Olympics from Toledo and the International Hockey League with a wide face that made him look older than his years and a skill level that did not compare to that of most of his teammates'. Eruzione was a football and baseball star growing up, but he wasn't the most fluid skater and dazzled nobody with his puck-handling. He didn't even have a Division I hockey scholarship until the summer after he finished high school. The University of New Hampshire was his first choice, but the school's interest in him was as a football player, not a hockey player. Parker, who had just taken over at BU, was scrambling for players. He had seen Eruzione play before and hadn't been overly impressed, but while refereeing a summer league game he saw Eruzione—four inches taller and 40 pounds heavier—and was starting to become intrigued.

"Where are you going to school?" Parker asked him.

"I think I'm going to Merrimack," Eruzione replied, referring to a Division II school.

"Why not a D-I school?"

"Because no D-I school has talked to me."

"I'm talking to you right now," said Parker, who offered him a partial scholarship. Eruzione accepted, enrolled in the fall of 1973, two years ahead of O'Callahan and three years ahead of Silk and Craig. Eruzione would go on to become BU's all-time leading scorer, with 208 points, a fact of absolutely no consequence to Brooks, who was on the verge of cutting Eruzione more than once in the weeks before the Olympics, railing at team doctor George Nagobads, who had pushed Brooks to make him captain. Nagobads had been the Team USA physician at the 1975 worlds, where the U.S. team went winless and where Eruzione kept up his spirit and intensity better than anyone else on the team. Brooks didn't know if Eruzione's intangibles were enough to cover up his tangibles. His skating had never been his selling point, and now he was in a terrible scoring slump as well.

"Now I'm going to have to cut my captain, and it's all because of you," Brooks told Nagobads. Right before

Christmas, Brooks reached out to University of Vermont star Craig Homola, Pavelich's friend and former teammate from Eveleth, asking if he'd like to join the team. Homola was given a USA jersey with his name on the back right above No. 21, the number Mike Eruzione wore. The implication was clear: you impress us, and the number, and the spot on the team, are yours. Homola, however, wasn't eager to bail out on his Vermont team midway through the season or to forfeit the semester he'd almost completed. He also didn't want to be a pawn in one of Brooks's motivational gambits. Homola wound up declining. Brooks kept searching, and when Eruzione hit his drought, he found a willing pair of freshman forwards: Tim Harrer and Aaron Broten from the U. Brooks had recruited both of them, and both were players with speed and skill and explosive scoring ability. Brooks's plan was to tell the press that Eruzione had injured his back, then make his erstwhile captain an assistant coach; that way he could still be in Lake Placid and contribute to the team. When the coach laid out this scenario to Eruzione, the captain was aghast. Making the Olympic team meant everything to him. In the fall, he had fractured his wrist one day in a collision with Eric Strobel, then fainted in the van as trainer Gary Smith drove him to the hospital for X-rays, not so much from the pain of the fracture as from the prospect of it costing him his roster spot. Now he was on the brink again, and for once this was no Brooksian mind game. In a hotel lobby in St. Paul, before a team dinner in late January, Brooks had a private conversation with Gus Hendrickson, his friend and the coach of Minnesota-Duluth.

"I'm going to cut Eruzione. He's just not very good," Brooks said. "I think I'm going to go with Tim Harrer."

"But Eruzione's your leader. You need a leader," Hendrickson said. "Herbie, don't start screwing things up now." It was exactly the sentiment of the team. They'd been through Brooks's boot-camp grind for six months. Eruzione had become a widely admired captain, an emotional linchpin.

"If he cuts Eruzione, we're not going to go," John Harrington told Hendrickson, his former coach.

The players on the team were furious when Harrer and Broten arrived—even the Gopher guys who knew and liked them. "Great to see you, Tim," Janaszak said to Harrer. "When's your flight back?" Not even three weeks before Opening Ceremonies, the team confronted Brooks about his revolving door and had a four-letter suggestion for him: stop. It wasn't fair to bring in guys so late, to send guys packing who had been making sacrifices for months. Of course the imports might stand out during their audition; they hadn't spent months getting beaten up by Central Hockey League thugs looking to make a name for themselves by working over an Olympic kid. Led by Eruzione and O'Callahan, the players told Brooks that they were a family and that the team needed to come from the guys in the room right there. Brooks for once backed off. The final cuts were Jack Hughes, a defenseman from Harvard, and Ralph Cox, a forward from the University of New Hampshire. Cox had broken an ankle in the summer and struggled to catch up ever since. He was another guy whose skating wasn't what Brooks wanted, but he had a goal-scoring gift that was the equal of anyone on the team. Hughes was a smart, strong player who set a school record for points for a blueliner and had the sturdy disposition to make everyone on the ice better. They were brutal cuts for Brooks; it was impossible not to go back to the way he had felt twenty years before, when he heard the same news from *his* Olympic coach Jack Riley. A bunch of the players were together in an apartment in Minnesota when Brooks called and spoke to Hughes and Cox.

"I can't even imagine what that must've been like," Dave Silk said.

Eruzione ultimately survived because of his heart and leadership and his ability to get along with almost everybody. But he sweated it out to the end. He talked to Rossi after the 10–3 game in the Garden, and his angst was deep. "He thought he was gone," Rossi said.

Eruzione's day job is director of athletic development for Boston University, but mostly he is Keeper of the 1980 Flame, a role he fills with a pronounced Boston accent and a natural storyteller's flair. He comes into a room with his brisk, short-legged stride and takes control of it like a traffic cop on Commonwealth Avenue. Mike Eruzione has never seen a hand he wouldn't shake or a speech he wouldn't make. Listening to him is like listening to a guy on the next barstool. Rossi went with him to Hawaii for one of his first corporate appearances, at an IBM sales conference later in 1980. What Eruzione may have lacked in polish and slickness he more than made up for with his wise-cracking sincerity and regular-guy demeanor. At the team's induction into the U.S. Hockey Hall of Fame in the fall of 2003, Eruzione was asked about the honor and said, "I thought we were already in, to be honest with you."

Said Rossi, "He made people comfortable because he was very comfortable with himself."

Years went by, and Eruzione kept expecting his bookings to drop off and the miracle's legs to give out. They never did. The calls kept coming, and so did the checks. His father used to ask him, "When are you going to get a real job?" The answer is probably never. When the 1980 team was selected to light the Olympic cauldron at the opening of the Salt Lake City Games in 2002, the first time the Winter Games had been back in the United States since Lake Placid, Eruzione did the honors. He took the usual grief from his teammates. "There are four billion people watching. Don't drop it," Mark Johnson told him.

Eruzione knows better than anyone how improbable it is that a former Toledo Goaldigger has morphed into America's Guest, one of the more sought-after sports celebrity speakers around. He has made a handsome living out of his captaincy, providing inspiration for hire, showing a rare ability to improvise and personalize and not just make his boilerplate speech, eat his chicken, and be on his way. "Michael's just a natural leader, and it's what got him to the Olympics and got him to where he is today," Mark Wells said. Wells once was at a memorabilia signing with Eruzione in New York. Eruzione had gotten hit in the face with a puck in one of his adult hockey games at Larsen Rink and had two black eyes, but what really wowed Wells was how Eruzione cranked out his signature as if he were a one-man assembly line. "I've never seen a guy sign autographs so fast in my life," Wells said. "He must've written his name thirty-five hundred times in six hours."

Fifty years old, a quarter-century beyond Lake Placid, Mike Eruzione, the captain who was almost cut, travels all over the country talking about his team, his dream, about what happened after he hopped over the boards of the Olympic Field House midway through the third period against the Russians.

"If that's how people want to remember me, that's fine," Eruzione said once. "I have no problem being remembered for one thing. Some people never even have that."

———

With just over ten minutes left in the game, Harrington dug along the boards for the puck Buzz Schneider had shot in as he ended his shift. It squirted to Pavelich a few feet up, toward the blue line. Falling down, back to center, Pavelich did a half-pivot and flicked the puck in the middle. Eruzione, who had just come on, skated after it and caught up to it. His linemates, Neal Broten and Steve Christoff, hadn't even made it on the ice yet. Eruzione moved right. He pulled up. He had room. He let fly with a twenty-five-foot wrist shot off the wrong foot. Vasily Pervukhin, No. 5 in red, went down to block it. He didn't get it. Myshkin hunched low in goal. The puck was coming. He didn't get a good look because Pervukhin was screening him. The puck was getting closer. Myshkin tried desperately to pick up its flight. Then the puck was on him, flying between his right arm and his body, into the left side of the net.

Goal.

United States of America 4, Soviet Union 3.

Eruzione threw up his arms and ran along the boards, a joyous, leg-pumping jig, and the crowd erupted right along with him, even louder. Behind the ABC microphone, Al Michaels said, "Now we have bedlam!" For the entire

Olympics, the whole U.S. team had been racing on the ice when the Americans scored. They were not going to start holding back now. Brooks half-coiled his body and again thrust both arms overhead, this time even more emphatically. A tight-lipped smile began to form until he suppressed it. The coach hitched up his plaid pants. He exhaled. The United States had its first lead of the night, its first lead against the Russians in an Olympic game in twenty years. There were exactly ten minutes to play. The building throbbed. Ken Morrow, a defensive stalwart the whole night, readied for the face-off and the onslaught he knew was coming. *These are going to be the longest ten minutes of my life,* he thought.

Chapter Nine

DREAM WEAVERS

Before Eruzione was even done with his dance, Jim Craig was looking at the scoreboard, doing math that required no computation. *They've got to get two to win,* he thought. There were two five-minute periods left to play. His job was to keep the puck out of his net. On the bench, as the head rubbing and merriment subsided, Eruzione had a minor panic attack: *What if my stick has too big a curve on it? What if the referee checks it and disallows the goal? What if it costs us the victory?* There was no reason to think the stick was illegal. Kaisla, the referee, had made a visual inspection of the players' sticks on both teams before the game and detected nothing objectionable. It still made Eruzione uneasy. He called over general manager Ralph Jasinski, a 225-pound man in a pen at the corner of the bench, told him about his concern, and handed him the stick. The general manager did the only thing he could think of: he laid the stick out flat and stood on the blade, trying to flatten it.

"It probably bounced right back, but it's a good story," Jasinski said.

Behind for the first time, the Soviets began to play with an urgency they hadn't shown all night. Twenty-two seconds after Eruzione's goal, Lebedev centered to Krutov, who redirected the puck beautifully to Maltsev, who swept in on goal from the right, hitting the outside of the right post with a flick of a shot, then leaping across the goal-mouth to avoid Craig. The goaltender immediately looked over his left shoulder to make sure the puck wasn't in the net. Craig was fiercely territorial and sometimes nasty when an opponent got anywhere near his crease. In the game against Sweden, he whacked forward Per Lundqvist in the face with his stick. In the game against the Soviets at the Garden, Kharlamov's face also got in the way of Craig's stick, resulting in a gash that required stitches. "If you were in the neighborhood, you were going to feel Jimmy's stick around your ankles," said Gerard Linehan, his high school coach at Oliver Ames. And sometimes well above the ankles. Craig didn't have time to administer frontier justice this time. The Americans were scrambling in their zone and Krutov found Maltsev again, alone by the left post, a half-open net in front of him. Maltsev, the man who scored the most astonishing goal the U.S. players had ever seen in Madison Square Garden, shot wide. Maltsev looked to center the puck but as Krutov cruised in front, Ramsey tackled him as if he were a linebacker taking down a ballcarrier.

Finally, the Americans cleared the zone, but the respite was brief. Vladimir Golikov raced in on the left and backhanded a shot to the near side. Craig blocked it. Alexander Golikov fought for his brother's rebound and crunched Buzz Schneider into the boards. They got tangled in the corner and Schneider ended up with Golikov's stick, the puck frozen, play whistled dead. The Russian held out his hand to get his stick back. The normally good-natured Schneider tossed it on the ice and skated away.

"That was my Kodak moment," Schneider said. "Maybe all those years of getting pounded by those guys finally took its toll."

Just under eight minutes remained. The U.S. defensemen were dropping to the ice at every chance to stop the puck from even getting to Craig. Ramsey met Kharlamov along the boards and flattened him, the Russian's red helmet slamming into the ice, maybe the hardest hit of the night. Fetisov teed up from the left point, but Morrow went down and smothered the shot. Alexander Golikov sped in on the left side and fired from the top of the left circle, way wide. Kasatonov launched another shot from the point, and Craig gloved it. Petrov came down, saw a lineup of four white shirts at the blue line, and cranked a slap shot from sixty-five feet. Craig kicked it away with his right skate.

"Play your game. Play your game," Brooks kept telling his players as he paced behind them on the bench. He said the words from the side of his mouth. For all his demands on the players for all those months, he was a different person when he managed a game behind the bench, a thin-lipped general who exuded confidence and control and rarely lost his cool. The Finns and especially the Canadians had gone up on the Russians, then retreated into a defensive shell and gotten pummeled for their trouble. The Soviets scored four times in fifteen minutes in the third period against the Canadians, Mikhailov and Vladimir Golikov getting two goals apiece. The Russians won, 6–4. Letting them break out, conceding center ice, was a recipe for disaster. "Play your game," Brooks said. The "U-S-A, U-S-A" chants filled the Field House, over and over. Nagobads kept close track of the stopwatch and the Americans kept to their short shifts. Kaisla was struck by the results. "The U.S. team skated the whole time, the same speed from the beginning to the end," he said. "They never slowed down."

Five minutes remained.

Heeding Eruzione's caution, Schneider switched to a straighter stick and took his shift. "You don't want to take any chances," he said. He carried the puck through center, Krutov hounding him. Schneider shot it into the Soviet zone. Lebedev controlled the puck, but his cross-ice pass bounced off the boards and Pavelich picked it up, skated in a tight circle as if he were back on Ely Lake, and snapped a pass to Schneider in front. It didn't connect, but the United States was doing what Brooks had urged them to do. They were not sitting back. After Harrington scrambled with Vasiliev along the boards and the puck popped over the glass, Vladimir Golikov won the draw and Makarov came down the right side and backhanded it right through the crease. At the U.S. blue line, Harrington settled a bouncing puck with his left hand, squeezed between two red sweaters, swept down the left side into the middle, and wristed a shot on goal, Pavelich and Schneider circling behind him, Cone-heads in motion, just as their coach had taught them. Myshkin juggled it but held on. The U.S. players tried to heed Brooks's words and think only about playing, not the clock, but at times it felt almost impossible. This wasn't base-ball, a competition beyond the boundaries of time. Every tick was their ally. Eruzione had seen enough of the Russians to know they were completely capable of a three- or four-goal binge. *Let's get this game over with,* he thought. In goal Craig was yapping more than ever. For most of the game, he was catching the puck, covering up, stopping play to give his defense time to get settled, get a breather. Now he was catching and releasing like a fisherman, holding on to nothing, shouting to the defense to keep the puck alive, keep the clock ticking, keep the Russians from having a chance to regroup. Like a quarterback or a point-guard, he was managing the clock from his crease. Three minutes, 23 seconds remained.

Petrov and Kharlamov worked a give-and-go in the U.S. zone, but Petrov lost the puck off his skate. As Mikhailov tried to center it, Baker stole the puck and skated away from him, up ice. The Soviets themselves were scattered now, and time was getting short. Tikhonov stayed with his No. 1 line for 60 seconds, 75—the shift from hell. The U.S. bench started to keep an eye on Myshkin, wondering when he would vacate the cage to give the Soviets six skaters.

The clock moved under two minutes. The Soviets iced the puck twice, trying to hit Makarov and Golikov as they circled in center ice. Petrov flipped the puck harmlessly in on Craig with 80 seconds to play, but the Soviets couldn't keep it in the U.S. zone. The symphonic passing game was nowhere to be seen. There was no buildup, no tic-tac-toe attack. The Russians were taking wild home-run swings. "We were panicking. We were stiff," Starikov said. On a face-off just outside the U.S. blue line, Johnson beat Petrov and got the puck to Ramsey, who shot it in the Soviet zone. The noise was deafening.

One minute remained. In the U.S. goal, Craig kept talking, imploring his defense: "Push the puck. Don't freeze it up. Keep the clock moving."

Breaking out of his zone, Petrov backhanded a pass along the boards to a streaking Kharlamov, who lost control as he crossed center ice, the puck skidding ahead. Ramsey tried to clear but Mikhailov recovered and carried behind the net, Silk diving headlong to try to block his passing lane, and Ramsey doing likewise not even ten feet away. No effort was being spared. Mikhailov found a clear lane amid the sprawling bodies and centered to Petrov, but his backhand was wide.

Myshkin was still in his net. The American players were shocked. You have to go with the extra skater. The tactic was why the Americans were even in this position; when Baker scored to tie Sweden, there were six U.S. skaters and no goaltender.

"We never did six-on-five. We never even had that situation in practice," Starikov said. "Tikhonov just didn't believe in it." Mikhailov dug the puck out of the corner and pushed it to Bilyaletdinov at the point. He shot it back down, and Morrow and Silk nudged it along the boards, out of the zone. With 33 seconds left, a stride outside the blue line, Petrov drove another slap shot, Craig kicking it out with his right skate, stumbling a bit as he went. It came out, and Kharlamov flipped the puck back in with 19 seconds remaining. Johnson got to it by the end line. He passed it behind the net toward Ramsey, who crashed into Bilyaletdinov, who had charged in from the point. McClanahan hustled into the corner, beat Kharlamov to the puck, backhanded it along the endboards to Johnson, who beat Mikhailov to it and slid it behind the net to Morrow.

When the Soviets needed the puck more than they had ever needed it, they couldn't get it. There was no question which team had the freshest legs. With under 10 seconds to play, Morrow lofted the puck along the sideboards to clear it. It hit Silk in the arm about fifteen feet up ice.

The countdown began. "Five . . . four . . . three." Silk, who was out there just as Jack Parker had predicted, took a swipe at clearing the puck and then Johnson dug in and pushed it out of the U.S. zone. In the ABC booth, Ken Dryden said, "It's over," just a second before Al Michaels was shouting, "Do you believe in miracles? Yes!"

The horn sounded.

Pandemonium followed, the entire bench running, dancing, jumping, an almost comical conga line of jubilation, the destination Jim Craig. Dave Christian with his Christian Brothers stick held aloft was near the head of the line, and Buzz Schneider, arms and legs spread as if he were in mid–jumping jack, was right behind. In an instant Craig disappeared beneath a patriotic scrum of teammates, about five feet from the left post. Flags were waving everywhere and the roar wouldn't stop. People in the building said it was the loudest and most joyful sports sound they had ever heard. Jack O'Callahan sat atop a prone Mike Ramsey, arms overhead and a toothless grin for the world to see, even as Ramsey flailed deliriously at his stomach and chest. The four BU players on the team—Craig, Eruzione, O'Callahan, and Silk—had an unscripted reunion near the bench, a Terrier group hug. The players kept looking for teammates they hadn't embraced yet, the configurations of ecstasy shifting over and over. Assistant coach Craig Patrick was out there in the middle of it, and so were Doc Nagobads and general manager Ralph Jasinski. The head coach was not. He was gone within seconds of the sounding of the horn. After throwing both arms overhead and doing a tiny pirouette and punching the air with an emphatic left fist, Brooks walked straight off the bench, turned right into the runway, got patted on the back by weepy state troopers, and went back into Locker Room 5. Ten feet from where he had stood two and a half hours earlier and told his team they were meant to be there, Herb Brooks locked himself inside an orange toilet stall and cried.

On their own blue line, a cluster of Russians stood and took in the spectacle at the other end of the ice, a mixture of amusement and disbelief on their faces. Alexander Golikov was smiling. His brother Vladimir, chin propped on his stick, wasn't. Viacheslav Fetisov, future NHL star, looked as stone-faced as a Kremlin guard. "I just watched how they were, young guys, smiling over what they do on the ice," Makarov, another future NHLer, said. "We won lots of tournaments all over the world, and we never do that. It was more than hockey for those guys. We were happy for them." In his own way, Makarov's reaction brought to mind the actions of Soviet captain Nikolai Sologubov twenty years earlier in Squaw Valley. After losing to the United States in the semifinals, Sologubov made an impromptu visit to the U.S. team between the second and third periods of the gold-medal game against the Czechs and broke into a locker-room pantomime, telling the Americans they needed to take oxygen. It was a sporting gesture and dovetailed nicely with the Soviets' own agenda, since any result was preferable to a victory by their bitter rivals from Czechoslovakia. Six third-period goals later, the Americans had their first hockey gold medal. And now they were one victory away from their second.

———

The teams lined up and shook hands. For ten days, Jim Craig had made a point of studying Tretiak whenever he saw him in the Village or after practice. He looked intently at his face. "I'd heard so much about him. I wanted to get a feel for who this person was. I think you can always tell a little something about a person when you look at their face," Craig said. On the handshake line, there was Tretiak's face again, except now it looked blank and distant. When the last Russian hand had been shaken, Craig did a hop and a little spin, a huge smile on his unshaven face.

Mikhailov went to the referees' dressing room and sought out Kaisla. Mikhailov shook his hand. "Thank you," the Russian captain said. "Everything was correct. You did good job." He returned to the Soviet locker room, where an irate Tikhonov jabbed a finger in the face of four of the biggest stars in the hockey world—Tretiak, Kharlamov, Petrov, and Mikhailov—and told them one by one, "This is your loss!" "This is your loss!" Later, in his room in the Olympic Village, Tretiak spent a long time by himself, head in his hands. He had come to hate the room and the whole Village. It felt as if it were dropped in the middle of the woods, with no pulse to it, no Olympic energy or sense of place.

Vasiliev went shopping for moon boots with some teammates and actually pulled out a champagne bottle and said, "Let's drink to the Americans." Zhluktov joked, "Yes, we can drink to the Americans. If it's the Czechs who win, then we jump in Lake Placid." Helmut Balderis made it a point to find Brooks and congratulate him, doing it within view of Tikhonov. Nagobads, Balderis's fellow Latvian, urged him not to do this in front of his coach. "He can go shit in his pants," Balderis said of Tikhonov, his long-running tormentor.

Vladimir Lutchenko, the previously exiled star, watched the U.S. game at home in his Moscow apartment, staring vacantly at a small black-and-white television until the very end, which came about 2:30 in the morning Moscow time. It was hard to know what felt worse: that his teammates lost or that he was unable to do a thing about it. If he were a more vindictive sort, Lutchenko probably would've found some pleasure in the defeat. But these were Lutchenko's teammates, his comrades, the guys he grew up with and played with all over the world. How could he take joy from their hurt? Years later, Lutchenko would move to the United States with his wife and daughters, settling in Massachusetts, where he started a hockey clinic and coached kids alongside Jim Craig. They would became friends, and they would both laugh when Craig would tell Lutchenko that he had made it possible for him to be an Olympic hero—by not being there. But there was no joking about it in the winter of 1980.

"It was heartbreaking," Lutchenko said. Several weeks after departing Lake Placid, Tikhonov brought Lutchenko back to the team, and the Soviets won a major international tournament in Sweden.

"It was too late. The Olympics were over," Lutchenko said.

In the locker room, a couple of Communist party bureaucrats came up to Starikov and shook their heads. "You guys just made one of the biggest mistakes of your lives," one of them said. "Ten years from now, twenty years, everyone will still remember this game."

"They were right," Starikov said.

Mark Johnson had worn his knockoff Soviet sweaters for years and had his first exposure to the real Russians in the 1975 world championships in Düsseldorf, Germany. He was awestruck at their skating and creativity. He took special note of the guys whose jerseys he wore. Now, five years later, Johnson was randomly selected to be drug-tested after the United States beat the Russians. He walked into a little room off a corridor beneath the Field House stands, and sitting there waiting were Kharlamov and Mikhailov, the Russian designees. The language barrier might as well have been an Iron Curtain, but the Russians didn't need English to be gracious. Johnson thought about all those private screenings of the Summit Series, all the Sundays when he wore their jerseys, a boy impersonating world-class hockey players. His mind flickered happily with reminiscences of his life in the sport and where it had already taken him at age 22. There was one game left in his amateur career. It would be his last drug test as an amateur, and his favorite one.

In the locker room, the team broke into a spontaneous chorus of "God Bless America," filling in the words they couldn't remember with hums and whistles. President Carter called and Jack O'Callahan joked that Brooks probably put him on hold. Mike Moran, U.S. press officer, dispatched three attachés to the locker room to try to get Craig, Eruzione, Johnson—someone—to meet with the world's press, per Olympic requirements. All three attachés were summarily rebuffed by Brooks, who wasn't about to veer off his no-interview course now. "The sports moment of the century, and we couldn't get a single player to the interview room," Moran said. Main Street in Lake Placid had turned into Miracle Boulevard, thick with revelers, the "U-S-A, U-S-A" chant cascading from one end of town to the other. Craig and Eruzione and their fathers walked through the snow and the mayhem, ABC's Jim Lampley in tow. A bunch of players and their families went up the hill—the same hill Brooks had them run in full gear—to the Holiday Inn. In the hotel bar they watched ABC's taped delay broadcast. The United States won again. People put down $10 apiece and closed down the bar. A few hundred yards down Main Street, Mirror Lake Liquors sold out of champagne and had to bolt the doors to stop any more customers from coming in.

"It was a retailer's dream," said Jim Shea, a 1964 Olympian who was working in the store that night and would later own it.

Amid the iron mines of Virginia, Minnesota, Mary Harrington, mother of Bah, listened on the radio in the family room. Her husband, Charles, caught all the action he could on a scratchy transistor radio in the cab of his locomotive as he hauled iron ore from the mines. Neighbors descended on the Harringtons' new colonial for a Friday night party, whether the Harringtons wanted them or not (they did). In Winthrop, Massachusetts, the lawn in front of the Eruzione home on Pleasant Street was as crowded as a Cape Cod beach on the Fourth of July. Before long, Eruzione's picture would be on the cover of the Winthrop phone book and Eruzione would be the recipient of two marriage proposals and for the first time in his life people were actually pronouncing his name right.

On the Iron Range, from Babbitt to Grand Rapids and

even in Embarrass—"The Nation's Cold Spot"—people ran outside and hollered and shot off guns. In the Mediterranean Sea, the U.S.S. *Nimitz,* an aircraft carrier, flashed the score to a Soviet intelligence ship that was nearby.

Chris Ortloff, the director of ceremonies and awards for the Games, had to leave the Field House with 10 minutes to go, an ill-timed medal ceremony requiring his presence. The ceremony—held on Mirror Lake—wound up being delayed because the only thing people were paying attention to was the hockey game. Ortloff was listening on the radio as he sat in an Econoline van when he spotted Sergei Pavlov, the chief of mission for the Soviet Union. Ortloff invited Pavlov to warm up in the van and listen to the end of the game with him. As time got short, Pavlov clasped his hands together.

"Are you praying?" Ortloff asked.

"Don't tell Brezhnev," Pavlov replied. They both smiled. When the game ended, they shook hands.

"Congratulations," Pavlov said.

Two days after the loss to the United States, the Soviet Union scored nine times in the first thirty-five minutes and crushed the Swedes, 9–2. The Soviets would not lose another official international game for five years. They would not lose to the Americans again for eleven years, and would beat the U.S. teams by a total score of 38–9 in their next five meetings in world championship play. But the future domination came with no rewind mechanism, no clause that could undo what happened on Friday night, February 22, 1980. It was the thirtieth anniversary of the film debut of Walt Disney's *Cinderella.* Maybe it figured.

No unbiased observer could credibly claim that the United States was the better team in Lake Placid, or even that it played the stronger game, a difficult argument to support when you are outshot, 39–16. What the Americans did do, however, was to score more goals, 4–3, and that is enough to be called the winner. They didn't concern themselves with the skill and experience and international pedigree they were giving up. They simply skated and hit and never relented, and they got sixty minutes of stubborn brilliance from Jim Craig. "It was the greatest game he ever played, before or since," said Harry Sinden, general manager of the Boston Bruins, who would trade for Craig before 1980 was over. Rob McClanahan put it well in a newspaper interview for the tenth anniversary of the victory. "We were just naïve college punks," he said. The naïveté spawned a boldness to shoot for a completely far-fetched goal. You never know if you never try. They put aside their regional issues and fed off their unanimous abhorrence of how they were treated and became a whole that was something to behold. Or as Sergei Makarov said, "Their eyes were burning. They were team."

George F. Kennan, Russian scholar and Cold War expert, once said, "Heroism is endurance for one moment more." And indeed, it was ultimately the U.S. players' endurance that made them so endearing, and so heroic. They endured their coach and his ceaseless demands and mind games. They endured his Herbies. They endured their own doubts and insecurities and youthfulness and the almost universal conviction that they would be doing swell to get the bronze. They kept falling behind. They kept coming back. Each time they did, each time they lined up before leaving the ice and raised their sticks in salute to the crowd, on one side of the rink and then the other, thanking their fast-growing legion of fans for their support, they were more and more becoming poster boys for the American dream, homegrown proof of what's possible if you work hard and stay together. You watched them play and you were struck by the power of a simple, single thought: *Hey, we really can still do it.* In a profoundly pessimistic time, they brought hope. In a time of malaise, they brought spunk and spirit. The hostages and gas lines and the rolling Russian tanks were fairly flogging the American psyche, until Phil Verchota and Mark Pavelich and Mike Ramsey and the rest of them started flogging back. And the best part was they didn't even know they were doing it. They thought they were just trying to win hockey games.

The most storied U.S. Olympic hockey victory in history also turned out to be the most serendipitous. The winning goal of the Russia game was scored by a captain who had almost been cut, on a broken play, off the wrong foot. Two of the three goals that preceded it were the work of hard work and hustle but also of bounces that bordered on the karmic. The opponent was arguably as great a hockey team as has ever been assembled. The coach was not the first choice for the job, and maybe not even the second. But he was a man as daring as he was detached, and it's hard to say which was bolder: reprogramming his players to learn an entirely different style of hockey in seven months or uniting a team rife with geographical factions by making himself the common enemy.

A little bit of the miracle of Lake Placid died with Herbert Paul Brooks on the hot, hard asphalt of Interstate 35 in Forest Lake, Minnesota, on August 11, 2003. He was, after all, the architect of it. But even amid the tears and the sorrow as the team gathered for its last reunion in the Cathedral of Saint Paul five days later, there somehow remained the same sense of possibility that the team had so powerfully come to symbolize twenty-five years before. To see the honorary pall-bearers raising their sticks as his body was carried down the steps, the salute this time for the coach, was to celebrate Herb Brooks's passion for the game and his quietly held conviction that in one game on one night, his team of overmatched and underaged kids could beat the best team in the world. It was to believe again in the nation's capacity for greatness, in the collective power of a true team, foibles and frailties notwith-standing. For the cover of the program that was handed out before the service, the Brooks family chose not a formal por-trait or an image of Brooks as 66-year-old grandfather or family man but a close-up photo of a 42-year-old coach on the ice in Lake Placid, USA warm-up suit in place, whistle around his neck, an uncharacteristic softness to his smiling face. The miracle was still before him. Hope was high.

Six months after the funeral service, the NHL All-Star game was played in Herb Brooks's hometown. A statue of Brooks was unveiled outside the Xcel Center, and many of the 1980 team members were on hand for the occasion, among them Jim Craig. The day before the game, Dan Brooks, Herb's son, met Jim Craig at his hotel and they drove together to the cemetery where Herb Brooks was laid to rest. Dan Brooks brought an extra pair of boots and the two of them, the coach's son and the coach's goalie, tromped through knee-high snow and quiet and unspoiled whiteness. They shoveled snow off the graves in the family plot, and when they finally found Herb's gravestone (the headstone hadn't been completed), Jim Craig stood at the foot of it with Dan Brooks, and then he had a conversation with his coach. Jim Craig thanked Herb Brooks for being hard on him and for making him a better goaltender and a better person and for preparing him for the greatest three periods of his hockey life. He thanked him for believing in him. Mostly he thanked Herb Brooks for a night in the Adirondack Mountains in upstate New York when snow fell and the Olympic Field House throbbed and whether you were in the goal or on the ice or in the seats or at home, you came away feeling that greatness wasn't a realm strictly for the superhuman, remote and unattainable, but rather something much closer, real, and reachable, something within every one of us.

FINNS AND FAREWELLS

Outside the U.S. locker room in the Olympic Field House, a cinder-block wall was disappearing beneath a pasted-up patchwork of yellow congratulatory telegrams that had come in from all over the world, faster than a Buzz Schneider slap shot. As soon as they arrived, Sheldon Burns would tape them to the wall. Burns, a young physician, was relocating his practice in Minnesota and had a little free time that winter and had contacted Ralph Jasinski, the team general manager, asking if he could volunteer to help. Burns has since gone on to be a prominent sports physician for several U.S. Olympic hockey teams as well as the Minnesota North Stars, Timberwolves, and Vikings, but then he was just a well-educated go-fer who wanted to be part of the team. The messages inspired the Americans, and annoyed others, specifically Jorma Valtonen, the Finnish goaltender who had stoned the United States in the world championships the year before.

"Who's playing?" Warren Strelow, the U.S. goaltending

coach, inquired of Valtonen upon meeting him in the hallway before the U.S.-Finland final.

"Who the hell do you think is playing? I am, and you are not going to be getting any more of those," Valtonen said, pointing to the yellow wall.

Brooks needed no reminders whatever that his team's business wasn't finished with the victory over the Russians. The morning after the miracle, he ripped into his team after seeing them signing autographs and schmoozing with fans and, to his way of thinking, acting as if they had no further challenges ahead of them.

Brooks, always wound tight, was even antsier than usual Sunday morning, February 24. He shared a trailer in the Village with Craig Patrick, equipment manager Buddy Kessel, and Jasinski. He got in the shower, medal permutations bubbling in his brain. The order of the final standings would be determined by all the games between the final four teams— even games in the preliminary round. You got two points for a victory, one for a tie, none for a loss. If teams had the same point total, goal differential would decide the order. Here's how the hockey standings looked heading into the final day of the XIII Winter Games:

TEAM	W	L	T	POINTS	GOALS FOR	GOALS AGAINST
U.S.	1	0	1	3	6	5
U.S.S.R.	1	1	0	2	7	7
Sweden	0	0	2	2	5	5
Finland	0	1	1	1	5	7

If the United States beat Finland, the gold medal was assured for the Americans. But if the Americans lost to Finland

and the Soviets beat Sweden, the Soviets would win the gold, the United States the bronze. If Finland beat the United States by two goals and the Swedes managed to tie the Soviets, the gold would go to the Soviets—and the United States would actually slip out of the medals altogether, since all four teams would have three points and the United States would have the worst goal differential. Brooks kept lathering, and got himself into more and more of a lather. "Herb, you're wasting your time," Jasinski told him. "Don't go through all this folderol about how we could end up with nothing. Let's go out and play the game."

The game started shortly after eleven a.m. On the ride over to the arena, Neal Broten and Dave Christian held out their usual hope that figure skater Tai Babilonia, their favorite Olympic athlete, would be in their shuttle van. She wasn't. Brooks told trainer Gary Smith, "You better get your kit ready, because if we lose, a lot of people are going to get hurt jumping off our bandwagon." The coach's message to the players wasn't much more long-winded than it was in the Soviet game. "If you lose this game, you'll take it to your bleeping grave," Brooks said.

"He didn't have to say much more than that. We knew he was right," Mark Johnson said. Steve Janaszak was struck by the utter contrast from the Friday night speech. In thirty-six hours, Brooks had gone from mystical and uplifting to pragmatic and threatening. "His speech before the Finland game was negative, but the impact was positive," Janaszak said. "You wanted to avoid that scenario at all costs." Janaszak sat in the locker room and envisioned a 40-year-old guy sitting at a bar and saying, "We were that close. We could've had it all." "It was the classic rip-your-heart-out kind of picture," Janaszak said.

Finland had never won a medal in Olympic hockey and had never beaten the Americans, but this was no team of pushovers. They had a gold lion on their chests and a lot of guys who could get up and down the ice and, in the 33-year-old Valtonen, a confident veteran of a decade of international competition. The Finns were a strange team to peg, though. They opened their Games by losing to Poland, 5–4, right after Baker's slap shot tied the Swedes on the first day of hockey competition. They lost despite outshooting the Poles, 49–25. A week later, they were tied with the Russians with five minutes to play, before they were done in by a trademark Russian rampage, three goals in 79 seconds.

Jukka Porvari, the Finn captain, wanted to keep the crowd out of the game as much as possible, and did his part just over nine minutes into the final game, one-timing a slap shot that flew over Craig's glove from fifty feet to give Finland a 1–0 lead. It was the sixth time in seven games the United States had fallen behind. Valtonen turned away fourteen U.S. shots in the first period, the Finns content to play most of the game in their zone and pick their spots for a counterattack. Mike Ramsey was sent off for roughing early in the second period, but the Americans did a superb job of killing the penalty, and as Ramsey was coming out, Neal Broten checked Finnish forward Ismo Villa, who coughed up the puck to Steve Christoff in the right circle. Before the game Brooks had laced into both Broten and Christoff for their spotty play over the fortnight, not knowing he'd get such an immediate return. With a little under five minutes gone, Christoff moved in on goal. Valtonen had robbed him in the first period, making a stop on his knees, then reaching up and plucking the puck out of the air before it could go in.

With Finland's Marku Hakulinen trying to ride him off, Christoff kept moving, got off a soft backhand shot—and was as surprised as anyone to see it slip through Valtonen's pads. The score didn't stay tied even two minutes. Schneider uncharacteristically missed a perfect pass that would've given him a dead-on shot in front, and even more uncharacteristically swung his stick like an ax on Finn defenseman Olli Saarinen about five seconds later. It took thirty seconds for Finland to score on a power play and the United States again found itself down a goal going into the third period.

Just over two minutes in, Christian started in his own end, weaved up ice, split the defense. He held on long enough to draw the defense toward him, then shoveled a pass on the left wing to Verchota, who ripped a wrist shot inside the right post. The game was tied, 2–2. In the stands, Bill Christian, Dave's father, scorer of two goals to beat the Russians in 1960, and Roger Christian, Dave's uncle, scorer of three goals against the Czechs in the final, stood and cheered.

The fans started a new chant: "We want a goal!" Johnson stickhandled away from two defenders behind the Finland goal and slid the puck to McClanahan, who waited for Valtonen to go down, saw him split his legs, and shot it right through the gap. The next gap you saw was the one in a beaming McClanahan's mouth, where a tooth used to be.

United States 3, Finland 2.

Broten pulled down Villa and got two minutes for hooking. The United States killed the penalty. Six seconds after Broten got out, Christian got whistled for tripping. Brooks took a deep breath. "Gotta do it, gotta do it. Let's be positive now," Brooks said calmly as he walked up and down the bench. The only permutation he was thinking about now was winning. It was still a one-goal game when Verchota got called for roughing with 4:15 to play. Broten and Christoff forechecked like madmen, locking the Finns in their own zone. The puck shot out toward the blue line. Johnson picked it up, skated in, and backhanded a shot that a diving Valtonen stopped. Johnson got the rebound and popped a forehand over the goalie's right skate, into the net, and in an instant he was buried in blue shirts and the arena was erupting, as loud now as it had been Friday night.

United States 4, Finland 2.

Buddy Kessel wrapped his arms around Brooks and bounced him against the Plexiglas behind the bench. "Attaboy, Magic!" the coach shouted. Now there was yet another chant: "We're No. 1." Craig made one last sparkling save, kicking out a slap shot with his left skate. The noise kept building, and the Americans kept coming, pressuring, the bench standing, players smacking their sticks against the boards, even as Schneider blasted a slap shot that hit both posts, and a rebound that hit the crossbar. No goal. No matter. The clock went to 10 seconds and 5 and then 0:00, and the conga line, this time in blue, was on for one last engagement, the whole bench spilling onto the ice, heading for Jim Craig. Dave Christian flung his stick into the stands. Broten saw him do it, so he flung his over the glass, too. Brooks took off for the locker room again. Eric Strobel took a swig from a champagne bottle and he and John Harrington doused each other. Leslie Schorr, Mark Johnson's fiancée, jumped on the ice in her red-and-white Badger cheerleading top, because she always jumped on the ice after games in Dane County Coliseum and why should the Olympics be any different? The first player she got to was Dave Silk, so she leaped into his arms. One of Mark Johnson's wedding presents later that summer was a blown-up photo of his bride wrapped around Dave Silk in Lake Placid. A handful of other fans got on the ice and handed players flags and gave them hugs. It was madness. It was beautiful. The players lined up and shook hands with the Finns. When the last hand had been shaken, Craig, mop-haired and delirious, skated over to the edge of the ice and searched the stands. He clutched a flag someone had given him. "Where's my father?" he said. He counted the rows. He kept looking. Dave Silk came over and hugged him. "Where is he?" Craig said. Finally, Jim Craig found him. He skated toward the gate and held up a single finger. The noise would not let up. There was one event left in the 1980 Winter Olympics—the Soviet Union–Sweden hockey game. It would have no impact on the gold medal. That belonged to the United States of America.

There was more delirium in the locker room, and a goaltender with a message. Still in his pads and his No. 30 sweater, Craig revisited Brooks's stinging mind game of a month earlier when he called the goalie in his office and told him he was going with Steve Janaszak. He playfully jabbed a finger in Brooks's chest.

"I showed you," the goalie said.

"You showed me all right, Jimmy," the coach replied.

The medal ceremony was moved from Mirror Lake to the Field House, at the urging of ABC. Mats Waltin, captain of the bronze-winning Swedish team, got on the lower step of the podium, and then Boris Mikhailov, captain of the Soviet team, made his way to the second step. On the top step was Michael Eruzione of Winthrop, Massachusetts, representing the United States. "The Star Spangled Banner" began, the

American flag went up, and twenty U.S. hockey players sang, loudly and proudly. Once they all got their individual medals, Eruzione beckoned the whole team to join him on the top step, and the dash was on, the ice full of kids in blue warm-up suits trying to squeeze into a space meant to hold one person.

After the Soviets were awarded their silver medals, they never turned them back in to have their names inscribed on them—the customary procedure. "I don't have mine," Makarov said. "I think it is in garbage in Lake Placid jail."

As a team and a culture, the Soviets did all they could to expunge the memory of February 22, 1980. In the next day's edition of *Pravda*, the Communist party newspaper, there was no mention of the game with the United States—nor in an Olympic wrapup article on February 25. Not far from the Moscow River, the offices of the Russian Ice Hockey Federation are bisected by a corridor that runs for fifty meters or more, the length of it covered with historic photos of hockey glory from all over the world. Conspicuously absent are all images from Lake Placid. After the Russians cleared out of their rooms in the Lake Placid Olympic Village, cleanup workers found 121 empty vodka bottles in the dropped ceiling of their units, the detritus of despondence.

On the team's flight home, Tikhonov continued to rail about the poor play of his No. 1 line—Vladimir Petrov, Boris Mikhailov, and Valery Kharlamov, along with Vladislav Tretiak. Defenseman Valery Vasiliev had heard enough. He got up and went over to Tikhonov's seat and grabbed him around the neck. "I will kill you right now!" he shouted, before being pulled off.

When the Soviets landed in Moscow, there were crowds

gathered to greet such athletes as skier Nikolai Zimyatov, a big hero of the Games. "We were demonstratively shoved aside, and rightly so," Tretiak wrote in his autobiography. The response from party officials was not so indifferent. "The politicians almost wanted to kill us," Makarov said. "The relations with the U.S. were not good. We had invaded Afghanistan. They gave a very hard talk to coaching staff and older players."

Bill Schneider, Buzz's father, had to leave Lake Placid before the hockey medal ceremony Sunday afternoon to catch his flight home from the Albany airport. In the car were his wife, Ann, Buzz's sister Amy, and Dave Brooks, Herb's younger brother. They stopped at a little roadside tavern about forty miles out of Lake Placid to watch the medals being handed out. When the bartender found out who they were, he bought them a round of beers. Everyone cheered. Ann Schneider cried when she heard the national anthem and when she saw Mike Eruzione calling everybody up to join him on the platform. The Schneiders got home to Babbitt, Minnesota, on the eastern edge of the Iron Range, at midnight. Bill Schneider, an industrial engineer, was at work at seven a.m. It was about the time that Buzz and his teammates were boarding Air Force One and flying to the White House to meet President Carter, most of them not having had the benefit of sleep and thankful no Breathalyzer tests would be administered. Somewhere over upstate New York, Neal Broten phoned home and reached his father. "Guess what, Dad? I'm calling from the president's plane." By early that afternoon, the players on the U.S. Olympic hockey team were hugging and saying goodbye, their time as a team complete. The parting felt sudden and wrong. Soon the Midwestern guys were flying in one direction, the Eastern guys in another. On the flight back to Logan Airport in Boston, Eruzione, Dave Silk, and Jack O'Callahan got one more rousing cheer after the captain announced their presence. As the plane descended and Winthrop and Charlestown and the city of Boston came into view, Eruzione looked over at Silk. Silk had tears in his eyes. "It's over," he said.

Years passed, and the impact of what happened in Lake Placid seemed only to grow. On the twentieth anniversary of the Soviet game, Makarov was in San Jose when Eruzione was introduced before a Sharks' game and got a prolonged standing ovation. "I played twenty-four years of professional hockey and I never hear noise like he hears twenty years after one game," Makarov said, more in wonder than resentment.

The legacy of the game went far beyond clapping hands. In the seventeen years of the NHL draft to that point, there had been 1,780 players selected and not one was an American high school player. Two years later, 47 of 252—nearly one in five—was an American high schooler. Just like that, the old Canadian guard in the NHL, a group that tended to change its thinking every lunar eclipse or so, started to realize there were some players south of the border who might be worth looking at. "Those U.S. players really changed the view that NHL people had of U.S. players," Michael Smith, general manager of the Chicago Blackhawks, said.

A whole generation of young American players suddenly had heroes and role models, and new heights to aspire to. Pat LaFontaine celebrated his fifteenth birthday the night the United States beat the Russians. Four years later, he'd emerge as the brightest young U.S. star in the 1984 Games in Sarajevo, beginning a career that culminated with his enshrinement in the U.S. Hockey Hall of Fame—on the same day the 1980 team went in.

"They blew the doors wide open and made it possible for guys like me to get a chance to play in the NHL," LaFontaine said.

Thirteen players from the U.S. team—Ken Morrow, Neal Broten, Mike Ramsey, Dave Christian, Mark Johnson, Mark Pavelich, Rob McClanahan, Jack O'Callahan, Steve Christoff, Dave Silk, Bill Baker, Jim Craig, Steve Janaszak—went on to play in the NHL. One of them was not Eruzione, whose last competitive goal was the wrong-footed wrist shot that beat the Russians. Eruzione retired a week after the Games, having no notion that he'd still be talking about them twenty-five years later.

In time, almost all the players came to appreciate that all Herb Brooks wanted was their best, and he simply had his own way of getting it. He was 42 in Lake Placid. He was a week past his sixty-sixth birthday when he died; friends said that he seemed to be lightening up a little, a bit less inclined to do the windmill-tilting, more inclined to enjoy himself. "I'm just a guy from the East Side," he'd always say, and those who knew him best agreed with the simple self-assessment of a complex man.

"He led a far greater life, with far greater impact, than one Friday night in Lake Placid," said David Conti, the director of scouting for the New Jersey Devils. "That may have been his defining moment, but that was just one game. He coached a lot of games—and meant so much to so many people."

Four months after the Friday night in Lake Placid, Herb

Brooks wrote every player on the team a personal, eight-paragraph letter. It read:

> Under separate cover, you will be receiving a laminated team picture from Craig and myself. This reflects our complete respect we have for you as an athlete and as a person.
>
> I feel respect is the greatest reward in the world of sport. You have earned that from the coaching staff.
>
> Personally, this year was not only my most enjoyable year in coaching, but also my toughest. Toughest because it involved making so many difficult decisions regarding the makeup of our final team.
>
> Because of that, and because I wanted to be as objective as possible, I stayed away from close personal contacts with you. I did not want the U.S. Hockey Community to say that regionalism and/or favoritism entered into my final selections.
>
> This year was a challenge for all of us.
>
> A challenge to:
>
> > Live and work as a unit.
> >
> > Play a positive game—a creative way.
> >
> > Make the most out of our dreams.
>
> You met those challenges and conquered them.
>
> If there was any team I ever wanted to identify with on a personal basis, this was the team. Hopefully that day will come.
>
> Respectfully,
>
> Herb Brooks

BOX SCORE

U.S.A. VS. SOVIET UNION,
February 22, 1980, Olympic Field House

U.S.A.	2	0	2—4
Soviet Union	2	1	0—3

FIRST PERIOD
U.S.S.R.—Vladimir Krutov (Alexei Kasatonov), 9:12
U.S.A.—Buzz Schneider (Mark Pavelich), 14:03
U.S.S.R.—Sergei Makarov (Alexander Golikov), 17:34
U.S.A.—Mark Johnson (Dave Christian, Dave Silk), 19:59

SECOND PERIOD
U.S.S.R.—Alexander Maltsev (Krutov), 2:18

THIRD PERIOD
U.S.A.—Mark Johnson (Silk), 8:39
U.S.A.—Mike Eruzione (Pavelich, John Harrington), 10:00

SHOTS ON GOAL

U.S.A.	8	2	6—16
U.S.S.R.	18	12	9—39

GOALTENDERS: Jim Craig, Vladislav Tretiak, Vladimir Myshkin (1)

PENALTIES

First period:	U.S.S.R., Boris Mikhailov, 3:25, hooking.
Second period:	U.S.A., John Harrington, 0:58, holding;
	U.S.A., Jim Craig, 9:50, delay;
	U.S.S.R., Yuri Lebedev, 17:08, unsportsmanlike conduct;
	U.S.A., Ken Morrow, 17:08, unsportsmanlike conduct.
Third period:	U.S.S.R., Vladimir Krutov, 6:47, high sticking.

AFTERWORD

At exactly twenty-six minutes after seven on the evening of February 22, 2005, on the shores of Mirror Lake, history repeated itself. It was 20 degrees and snowing in Lake Placid. The flakes were the size of quarters. On a makeshift Jumbotron by the lake, a few rink lengths from the Olympic Field House, several hundred people were watching a replay of the closing minutes of the game between the United States and the Soviet Union. The tape was cued up so it would end at the precise time the original game did, an idea that came from Sandy Caligiore, an official with the Olympic Regional Development Authority.

"Why not celebrate the twenty-fifth anniversary at the moment it happened?" Caligiore asked.

When the clock reached the one-minute mark you could feel a surge of excitement go through the crowd. On the screen, Mark Johnson was digging the puck out along the boards, nudging it into center ice. The clock hit ten seconds and then five and then one and then came the horn and delirium, and the people who had gathered on the Mirror Lake ice began to chant, "U-S-A! U-S-A!," a robust re-creation of the chant made famous a quarter century before. Behind the people, near the center of the lake, fireworks shot up into the snowy sky. On a stage erected for the occasion, six members of the 1980 U.S. Olympic hockey team watched themselves and thirteen team-mates dive into a pile on top of Jim Craig, and then skate around and try to find a way to express the greatest feeling they had ever had. The players were Steve Christoff, Neal Broten, Mike Eruzione, Mike Ramsey, Dave Christian, and Dave Silk, and they were standing in the very spot where all the Olympic medal ceremonies but one were held in 1980. The only excep-tion was the sport of hockey, which had its medals distributed in the field house, for good reason.

"There was no way you were going to fit ten thousand people down on the lake," as one official put it.

The replay of the U.S.-Soviet game was part of an eleven-day commemoration of the Lake Placid Olympics. It began on February 12, when Jim Craig relit the Olympic torch, and culminated on the night of February 23 with a gala and the renaming of the Olympic Field House in honor of Herbert Paul Brooks.

"It was his vision, it was his commitment that helped lead the way for the Miracle on Ice to occur," New York governor George Pataki said. Brooks's wife, Patti, was there, and so were his son, Dan, and daughter, Kelly Paradise. Eighteen months after Herb's death, Patti Brooks was overcome with emotion during the ceremony. In a quiet moment afterward, she smiled and said, "Herbie would've hated this. He never wanted any fuss made over him. It just wasn't the way he was," and Mark Johnson, the team's star center, agreed.

"He never enjoyed those types of banquets and festivals and whatnot. He was a hockey coach," Johnson said.

The newly christened Herb Brooks Arena is a North Country mecca for people who visit Lake Placid, whether they are peewee hockey players or senior-citizen tourists. You walk along Main Street and it's almost as if you are at the end of a ski-tow, getting tugged toward the top of the hill and the white, flat-topped building that sits just beyond it. For most of us the tug is constructed not just of the history that went on there, but of an appreciation of the faith and commitment and love that underpinned the history. It's perilously easy to look back on the final result of those Games and to sanitize the process that got the players there. To do that, though, is to rob them of the full measure of their triumph. This was a team that had to overcome doubts and fears and defeats, along with a deep distaste for a coach who seemed impossibly hard at times. It was a team that could have emotionally crumbled after the 10–3 drubbing in Madison Square Garden four days before the Games began, that could easily have taken the ice on February 22 not with the burning eyes that Sergei Makarov so eloquently spoke of, but with eyes that were cold and cowering.

These players had a staggering run of good fortune in the Olympics, but they had an even greater run of resilience, a capacity to overcome pain and uncertainty. Three years after I started working on this book, amid unsettling thoughts that people might think they know all they need to know about the game, my favorite moments along the way remain the times when I felt I'd gotten insight into the sources of this resilience. I see Neal Broten skating on a flooded rink that his father got up at 2 a.m. to make in 25-degrees-below-zero weather. I see a young Steve Janaszak making saves by the lights of his father's Rambler, and hear Mary Harrington telling her son, John, who was constantly trying to prove he was good enough, that perseverance is everything in life. I see Mary's late husband, Charles, skipping overtime at work to watch his kids' games, because his overtime would always be there but the games would not, and see him listening to John skate against the Russians from the cab of his locomotive. I envision Margaret Craig running her goaltender son and all her other kids all over southeastern Massachusetts, a devotion that was absolutely unstinting, until her cigarette habit caught up to her and cancer arrived. Behind every player there were stories of love and sacrifice and struggle, of human beings being human, be it Mark Wells rebuilding a life that was once reduced to painkiller addiction and goose feeding, or Mark Pavelich finding his way after a tragic death in the woods.

Life is hard, and Olympic gold medals provide no exemption. You push on, do your best, and if you are really brave, you dream big, doubts and fears be damned. This is the stuff that miracles are made of, and the proof was there to see, on February 22, 1980.

AFTERWORD FOR THE FORTIETH ANNIVERSARY OF THE MIRACLE ON ICE

By Ken Morrow

When people commemorated the tenth anniversary of our victory over the Soviets at the 1980 Olympics in Lake Placid, I was a little surprised and thought it was very nice that everybody remembered. When they commemorated the twentieth anniversary, I was that much more surprised. Now here we are at 40 years of a never-ending miracle, and my surprise has gone the way of eight-track tapes.

For years I kept waiting for people's memories of February 22, 1980, to fade away, and the outpouring to slow to a trickle. It has never happened, and that's almost a miracle in itself. I haven't kept precise count, but I'd guess I've gotten thousands of letters/notes/cards in the mail over the years. (I do my best to answer every one, because I believe that if someone takes the time and trouble to reach out to me, the least I can do is respond.) Usually people begin by telling me their story of that night—where they were, who they were with, what they did when Al Michaels started his famous countdown. Then they often ask for an autograph, a signed photo, some kind of keepsake, which I am happy to oblige. Most of the writers, for a long while, were people who were old enough to remember the game, but the film *Miracle* has brought it to life for younger generations. I actually got a letter from a kid who told me he'd never seen his father cry before until they watched the game together. It really is almost beyond belief.

Of course, it was only one hockey game—and not even a gold-medal hockey game—but it remains a moment in time that has become embedded in people's minds. Everybody who was old enough to watch seems to have complete recall of it. There are a lot of theories about why this is so, about everything that was going on in the world then and the difficult period our country was going through, but for me it comes down to the fact that we were a huge underdog and an easy team to like. We were mostly college kids, up against as great a collection of hockey players as had ever been assembled. On every 35-second shift, we skated as hard as we could, played as hard as we could, just as our legendary coach, Herb Brooks, told us to. We knew who we were up against, of course, but Herb taught us to never think about that. "Play your game. Play your game," he kept saying as he walked behind us on the bench. When your focus is not on the outcome but on putting everything you have into every moment, it changes everything. Shift by shift, we started to believe.

Not long ago, I was in Dallas for my work as director of pro scouting for the New York Islanders. I was eating dinner by myself at a bar. The guy next to me, a fellow probably in his early 40s, saw the Islanders logo on my laptop and struck up a conversation. He said he wasn't a big hockey fan but had some friends in New England who used to play and were. He asked me my name.

"Ken Morrow," I said.

It didn't mean anything to him. He texted his friends. One texted right back.

"Holy crap. You are sitting next to a 1980 Olympic gold medalist and four-time Stanley Cup winner."

I wound up talking to one of the guy's friends for a while, about hockey and the Soviets and the Islanders. It was a nice conversation. His friend at the bar insisted on buying my dinner. Almost four decades later, at a tavern in Dallas, Texas, the night became all about the miracle. As I said, I've stopped being surprised.

I am a 63-year-old grandfather of six, and don't play hockey anymore, and probably won't. I go back to Lake Placid every year now for a fantasy camp our team has, and it's still one of my favorite places anywhere. Very little has changed in town over the years. The arena is now named for Herb, but it still has the same red seats and the same black grid on the ceiling. It looks and feels very much like the way it was in 1980. I walk in that building and I can almost hear 10,000 fans chanting "U-S-A, U-S-A."

Up and down Main Street, Lake Placid is the same picturesque Adirondack village it has always been. How many places can you say that about, with all the change going on in the world? Next door to the arena is the hilltop hotel where we stayed—and where Herb would make us run up a driveway as steep as a ski slope. Across the street is the old wooden toboggan chute where kids climb up to the top and make a run halfway out onto Mirror Lake. Main Street hugs the shore of the lake, dotted with gift shops and restaurants and a movie theater and an Olympic-themed store where you can load up on USA Hockey gear. Time hasn't stood still in Lake

Placid, but it's come close, and somehow I think that's perfect. It's an authentic village where an authentic miracle happened on February 22, 1980. I have a big pile of notes and cards to prove it.

Ken Morrow

ACKNOWLEDGMENTS

I spent the night of February 22, 1980, in the basement of a friend's house, alone with the images of a taped-delay hockey game, the voices of Al Michaels and Ken Dryden and an old dog named Fang. I was allergic to Fang, so I sneezed a lot. Otherwise I was as mesmerized as most every other American at the game between the United States and the Soviet Union.

Fang has passed on, and so have my allergies. The marvel of what happened in Lake Placid has not. Two years of work have gone into this book, and it's no reach to say there is someone to thank for every single day. Liz DeFazio, Steve Vassar, and Sean Ayers, the staff of the Winter Olympic Museum in Lake Placid, housed a slap shot away from where the miracle occurred, threw open their files and archives and had the courtesy not to laugh when I asked if they could help me find the guy who drove the Olympic Zamboni. Ted Blazer, head of the Olympic Regional Development Authority in Lake Placid, was a staunch ally, as was Sandy Caligiore, his aide-de-camp and PR man extraordinaire. Jim McKenna of the Essex County Visitors and Convention Bureau and his staff provided valuable information. Virtually everyone who was involved in the organization of the Lake Placid

Olympics who is still around was a big help, too, especially Bob Allen, Phil Wolff, Jim Rogers, Jim Shea, Ray Pratt, Chris Ortloff, Ed Lewi, and Ed Stransenbach. Thanks, too, to Tom Sersha, executive director of the U.S. Hockey Hall of Fame.

A trip to Moscow was a highlight of the research, for reasons far beyond the exposure it gave me to new flavors of vodka and one of the world's great subway systems. Robert Edelman, Russian scholar and professor at the University of California–San Diego, pointed me in the right direction, read the manuscript, and had dozens of suggestions, all of them valuable. Steve Warshaw of Universal Sports Marketing has done a great deal of business in Russia, and it shows. Igor Rabiner, a widely respected columnist for *Sport Express*, a Russian sports newspaper, was tour guide, translator, interview facilitator, and colleague. Venerable journalist Seva Kukushkin, who knows Russian sports as well as anyone, was a key conduit and cordial company besides. Special thanks to Sergei Makarov, Vladimir Lutchenko, Zinetula Bilyaletdinov, Sergei Starikov, and Viktor Tikhonov. John Sanful, seasoned hockey journalist, was a valuable eleventh-hour sounding board, and Igor Kuperman of the Phoenix Coyotes, expert on all things pertaining to Russian hockey, shared his knowledge generously.

Frank Brown, a former *Daily News* colleague and renowned hockey writer who has since gone on to become an NHL VP, covered the U.S.-Soviet game in Lake Placid and offered the expertise anyone who ever read him would expect. John Dellapina, a current *Daily News* colleague, was always an e-mail or a phone call away, even when he had to write about the latest tumult in the Rangers' front office and roster. If I were going to be a full-time hockey writer, John is who I would want to be. Brian Walker of the NHL, Jim DeMaria of the Chicago Blackhawks, Chris Botta of the New York Islanders, Kurt Kehl of the Washington Capitals, Keith Wehnert of the Pittsburgh Penguins, and Chuck

Menke, formerly of USA Hockey and now of the St. Louis Blues, are pros who provided information and helped arrange interviews. Szymon Szemberg of the International Ice Hockey Federation had answers and contacts all over the globe. Mike Moran and Darryl Seibel, the man who replaced him at the U.S. Olympic Committee press office, are superb at what they do, and have been for years.

My editors in the sports department at New York's *Daily News*—Leon Carter, Adam Berkowitz, Teri Thompson, and Jim Rich—keep raking in awards from the Associated Press Sports Editors, and are terrific people to work for besides. Scott Browne of the *Daily News* library is a crackerjack researcher who throws in acerbic commentary for no extra charge. Thanks to head librarian Faigi Rosenthal and her whole *Daily News* staff: Shirley Wong, Peter Edelman, Ellen Locker, Jimmy Converso, Scott Widener, and Dawn Jackson.

Lou Vairo, a longtime fixture at USA Hockey, was one of the first men in this country to appreciate the genius of the Soviet system and to teach it actively, and was an enormously valuable resource from beginning to end. Robert O'Connor, go-to archivist, let me borrow his entire collection of 1980 Olympic hockey videotapes—surprisingly scarce commodities. Bob Fleming, Hal Trumble, Walter Bush—all former AHAUS and USA Hockey leaders—were generous with their time and their recollections, and so were team USA's general managers, Ken Johannson and Ralph Jasinski. Jack Parker, Bill Cleary, and Tim Taylor are all renowned college coaches who have devoted much of their lives to amateur hockey, and were kind to share their knowledge. Lou Nanne and Glen Sonmor were immensely helpful sources of information about Minnesota hockey, Herb Brooks, and so much else. A first-rate sports information director is a vital ally for anyone writing about college athletes, and I had the good fortune to be helped by four of them: Ed Carpenter of Boston University, Steve Malchow of the University of Wisconsin, Michael Hemmesch of St. John's University, and J. D. Campbell of Bowling Green. Thanks, too, to Jessica Burda of the Wisconsin sports-information staff, and to the wonderful Rosenthal family—Vic, Chris, Ben, and Aaron—for providing a base of operations in St. Paul.

Warren Strelow, the goaltending coach; Gary Smith, the trainer; and Dr. V. George Nagobads were with the 1980 Olympic hockey team from start to finish. They've never gotten full credit for their contributions, but people on the inside know how much they gave and how good they were at what they did. I know how much they gave me, and it was gold medal material all the way.

Pete Fornatale came up with the idea for the book and came through with his customary sharp insight, even after leaving to hang out his own editing/writing shingle. Andrew Stuart, my literary agent, ably handled the commerce and provided reassurance and big-picture wisdom. Hugh Gorman III has been Jim Craig's attorney and confidant for a long time, and you find out quickly how capable he is when you deal with him. Charlie Euchner, a dear friend, was a beacon of clarity and encouragement and had the brainstorm for the book's structure. I had the good sense just to get out of the way. The book got started in a yellow cottage in Round Pond, Maine, the splendor, rocks, and quiet coming courtesy of Ann Swett. It got finished in the library of Union Church of Pocantico Hills, a blessed haven with no telephone and a wonderful rendering of the Sermon on the Mount right over the fireplace. The space was made possible by the kindness of Dr. Rev. F. Paul De Hoff.

This project could not have been completed without the cooperation and patience and support of so many of the players on the team, and of their families and friends, as well. Special thanks to Dan Brooks, Martha Johnson, Peter Johnson, Leslie

Johnson, Bill Schneider, Steve Schneider, Gayle Schneider, Lefty Curran, Ron Castellano, Newell Broten, Sally Broten, Aaron Broten, Butsy Erickson, Greg Morrow, Barbara Morrow, Loretta Morrow, Bill Torrey, Gord Lane, Bob Hallstrom, Craig Homola, John Rothstein, Gus Hendrickson, Dave Hendrickson, Keith Hendrickson, Chris Howe, Mike Sertich, Ron Wells, Mary Harrington, Tom Harrington, Chris Harrington, Sharlene Craig, Andy Fila, Bill LeBlond, Gerard Linehan, Eddie Rossi, Joe Micheletti, Don Micheletti, Larry Hendrickson, Don Lecy, Bill Houlihan, Len Lilyholm, Gregg Wong, Kevin Pates, and Chris Miller. Pete Giacomini lent wonderful insights about his friend Mark Johnson, as well as about narrative and goodness and the right way to do things, and embraced the project almost as if it were his own.

Shana Wingert Drehs, my editor at Crown, got married and added a name as we were getting started, and added so much more than that to the entire writing/editing process, both with her astute eye and sunny disposition. This project went as smoothly as any I have ever been a part of. It's a wonderful thing for a writer to trust his editor implicitly. Shana earned every bit of it. Thanks, too, to the superb design and production team at Crown, among them Jim Walsh, Jennifer O'Connor, Karen Minster, and Leta Evanthes. Caley Cronin, a late roster addition, did yeoman work in publicizing this book, and so did the estimable Marty Appel.

My bride, Denise Willi, was as loyal and kind and supportive as ever, and even let my files overtake the dining room table for six months. I couldn't have done it without her, and wouldn't have wanted to. Alexandra, Sean, and Samantha are the home team, and a father absolutely cannot do better than that.

Wayne Coffey
Sleepy Hollow, New York

ABOUT THE AUTHOR

Wayne Coffey is an award-winning sportswriter and twenty-year veteran of the *New York Daily News*. He has been voted one of the premier sports feature writers in the nation by the Associated Press Sports Writers, most recently in 2005. His previous books include *Winning Sounds Like This*, an acclaimed account of a season with the women's basketball team at Gallaudet University, the world's only four-year college for deaf and hard-of-hearing students. He lives with his wife, three children, and two kittens in New York's Hudson Valley. For more information on *The Boys of Winter*, please visit www.boysofwinter.net.